Radio's Captain Midnight

RADIO'S CAPTAIN MIDNIGHT

The Wartime Biography

by STEPHEN A. KALLIS, JR.

McFarland & Company, Inc., Publishers
Jefferson, North Carolina, and London

The present work is a reprint of the illustrated case bound edition of Radio's Captain Midnight: The Wartime Biography, *first published in 2000 by McFarland.*

LIBRARY OF CONGRESS CATALOGUING-IN-PUBLICATION DATA

Kallis, Stephen A., Jr.
    Radio's Captain Midnight : the wartime biography / by Stephen A. Kallis, Jr.
      p.   cm.
    Includes index.

    ISBN 0-7864-2176-2 (softcover : 50# alkaline paper)

    1. Captain Midnight (Radio program)   I. Title.
PN1991.77.C29 K35   2004
791.44'72 — dc21   99-54976

British Library cataloguing data are available

©2000 Stephen A. Kallis, Jr. All rights reserved

No part of this book may be reproduced or transmitted in any form or by any means, electronic or mechanical, including photocopying or recording, or by any information storage and retrieval system, without permission in writing from the publisher.

Front cover: Artwork from 1946 Secret Squadron manual; back cover: Code-O-Graph issued just before the beginning of 1945 *(photograph by Stephen A. Kallis, Jr.)*

Manufactured in the United States of America

McFarland & Company, Inc., Publishers
  Box 611, Jefferson, North Carolina 28640
    www.mcfarlandpub.com

To my wife, Carmen,
and to fellow Secret Squadron members, past and present

Contents

Preface	1
1. Genesis	7
2. The Hidden Years	13
3. The Call	21
4. The Early Secret Squadron	27
5. Ivan Shark and Early Skirmishing	31
6. Pre-War Operations	35
7. War Clouds Thicken	73
8. The War: Moves	91
9. The War: Countermoves	123
10. The War: Resolution	205
Appendix 1: Secret Squadron Equipment	241
Appendix 2: Captain Midnight in the Media	246
Appendix 3: A Quick Overview of Cryptology	249
Appendix 4: The Radio Show	253
Appendix 5: Rocket Planes	256
Index	259

Preface

In the 1930s the dominant entertainment media were motion pictures and broadcast radio. Of the two, broadcast radio was an almost constant companion. Prior to television, radio was the basic "home entertainment" medium.

In many homes a console radio was a prominent feature of a living room, and in the evenings families would gather in the living room to hear what was being broadcast. And a lot was. Programs included adventures, dramas, comedies, mysteries, quiz shows, and even news commentaries. Some types of shows transitioned and translated into television; others didn't. But radio was very influential in its heyday.

In one sense, radio helped truly unite the United States. More than newspapers, books, film, or any other medium, radio broadcasts provided a common experience throughout the nation. The great shows, including *The Jack Benny Show, Theater Guild on the Air, Fibber McGee and Molly, The Shadow,* and *Amos and Andy*, were shared by listeners from Maine to California. Though they were entertainment, they formed a common thread throughout the society. Shows like *Mr. District Attorney* voiced ideals of society. Programs like *Gang Busters* helped focus the public's attention on criminal activities, in a semiadventure format. Many shows of the period reinforced a feeling of national identity.

In the afternoon, between the hours of 5:00 and 6:00 P.M., there were shows mostly aimed at schoolchildren. These were usually in the form of 15-minute "cliffhanger" serials. Each of these was structured so the listener had to tune in to the following broadcast to find out how the show's characters extricated themselves from whatever dilemma they faced at the close of the show. There were shows for many venues, including *Jack Armstrong, the All-American Boy; Tom Mix Ralston Straight Shooters; The Adventures of Superman;* and *Buck Rogers in the Twenty-Fifth Century.* These shows were sponsored by products usually favored by children, such as cereals.

In 1938 a syndicated show made its debut in this time slot, but while it had similarities to the other serials, it had a couple of differences. One was that it was sponsored by Skelly Oil; its service stations sold tires, gasoline, and other products aimed at adults rather than their offspring. The other was that the vocabulary used by both narrator and characters was adult: that is, the script used vocabulary and sentences children wouldn't use. This show was *Captain Midnight.*

The show featured the adventures of a daring aviator and his ward. The aviator, Charles Albright, was known (and usually referred to) as "Captain Midnight" for reasons that were explained later.

The show's creators were Robert Burtt and Wilfred Moore, and the series was very aviation oriented. In the 1930s through 1950s, aviators were among the most glamorous figures in the public's mind. Burtt was a former World War I pilot, and the aviation aspect of the show was extremely accurate.

Aviation was being established, with commercial airlines enabling the more daring citizens to participate in the adventure. An aviator was considered rather heroic just by his or her profession; one who would also go on exotic adventures—fighting wrongdoers in the process—would be considered especially heroic.

Although the time placement and format of the show meant that the majority of the audience was composed of children, from the first, the show had a sizable "minority" audience of adults. A cast of "regulars" was developed. Besides his ward, Chuck Ramsay, Captain Midnight had several other associates, including a girl about Chuck's age, Patsy Donovan, and a mechanic, Ichabod Mudd. There was also a villain, Ivan Shark, who was considered one of the finest of the breed by listeners and students of old-time radio.

After two years' successful run in syndication, *Captain Midnight* went national, also with a change of sponsors. Several things led to this move. To explain this, it's useful to understand the historical context.

By 1939 Europe was at war. International tensions were rising, and though the United States was officially neutral, its neutrality was leaning in favor of Britain. Many people within the United States believed that the country would become embroiled in the conflict. Some of the nation's industries were developing and manufacturing weapons of war, including aircraft. Because of the United States' immense manufacturing capability, whether or not the country became a combatant, it was clear that the country would become an important factor in the conflict.

Up until 1939, Ovaltine Foods, manufacturer of a milk supplement, had sponsored a children's show, *Little Orphan Annie*, based on the famous newspaper comic strip of the same name by Harold Gray. The show made its first appearance in 1931, and the central character was supposed to be less than ten years old. Although the show was popular, it was dropped in favor of *Captain Midnight*. Possibly the war tensions had something to do with it; Captain Midnight was a vigorous, mature figure who could easily be identified with the defense of the United States. Orphan Annie, no matter how clever a youngster, was hardly such a figure. (*Orphan Annie* was picked up by another sponsor and ran another two years.)

One concept carried over from *Orphan Annie* to the Ovaltine-sponsored version of *Captain Midnight*. On the earlier show, Ovaltine had developed the "Radio Orphan Annie Secret Society." A feature of this "society" was that listeners could join it by sending in an inner seal from an Ovaltine container. In return, they would get an item that would identify them as belonging to the organization. The second year of the "society" saw the member receive a "pin" (actually a badge) that had an alphabet-number combination on it to "decode" secret messages. With this premium, listeners could decipher messages broadcast from time to time at the end of an episode.

Such a "decoder" *and* secret organization fit perfectly with the concept of an aviator who might have to deal with enemy agents as the winds of war started to pick up. Thus were born the Secret Squadron and its secret-communication device, the Code-O-Graph.

To set the stage for this, Ovaltine had the origin story of the name Captain Midnight and also the formation of the Secret Squadron written for its first show, broadcast in 1940. During the fall season, the Code-O-Graph was introduced as a premium.

The shows were scripted by Burtt and Moore, and most of the characters carried over from the Skelly-sponsored episodes. One exception was the girl sidekick, Patsy Donovan (who left the action, according to the show, to attend a school in order to become an airline stewardess). In time, she was replaced by Joyce Ryan. Joyce would be shown to be an atypical girl companion; she was brave, resourceful, and heroic, not just someone to be rescued.

Although Skelly Oil was no longer a sponsor, there were still plenty of adult listeners to the show. During World War II it was the favorite of many U.S. Army Air Corps flight crews when stationed in the United States.*

---

*Enola Gay, *by Gordon Thomas and Max Morgan Witts, Stein and Day, 1977, p.111.*

There were even some unsubstantiated reports that a small number of servicemen overseas used Code-O-Graphs as unofficial field cipher devices.

Captain Midnight was broadcast throughout the war years and for four years more in the 15-minute serial format. Throughout all those Ovaltine years, the title character was played by Ed Prentiss. His arch-foe, Ivan Shark, was played by Boris Alpon. Agent Kelly, aka SS-11, was played by Olan Soule. Gardo was played by Earl George. Various actors played Ichabod Mudd (Art Hern, Sherman Marks), Chuck Ramsay (Bill Rose, Jack Bivens), Joyce Ryan (Angeline Orr, Marilou Neumayer), and Fury Shark, Ivan's daughter (Rene Rodier, Sharon Grainger).

The last year of the radio show, *Captain Midnight* changed format to a half-hour complete show. This was in response to other shows adopting the new format. After one season, *Captain Midnight* left the air. (To students of the show, the last year and the later *Captain Midnight* television show were not "canonical," meaning that they did not jibe with what had been established and run for a decade before. Besides a simplified plotting and writing level, Ed Prentiss was replaced by another actor, Paul Barnes, reportedly without consulting the sponsor. To fans of the show, the voice of Ed Prentiss represented the "real" Captain Midnight.)

The book that follows is a "biography" of the radio character. The story is derived primarily from the radio scripts of the show. More than a decade ago, Ovaltine Foods, located in Villa Park, Illinois, provided the author with access to these scripts in its central files. The necessary data were recorded; and over many years, in spare time, the "biography" was developed. To bring the story as close to actual historical events as possible, it was necessary to research available technology of the time, particularly the aircraft and electronics.

World War II was a period of rapid technological advances. Aircraft evolved from the likes of the Brewster Buffalo and the Bell Airacobra to the beginnings of jet aircraft. "Superweapons" like the V-2 rocket and the nuclear bomb were developed. Radar and electronic countermeasures were developed. And more important, the intelligence activities behind the scenes evolved their own technologies.

Burtt and Moore scripted with skill; however, they were not privy to anyone's military secrets. Where the episodes were close to historic fact, it was because the scripters paid attention to historic and technical developments and extrapolated well.

Where there were gaps in the scripts' history (the show was seasonal, and they didn't have summer reruns), the current author interpolated a couple of adventures. These are consistent with both the other adventures and the developments of the times.

A "biography" of a fictional character is not new. In 1962 William S.

Preface

Baring-Gould wrote *Sherlock Holmes of Baker Street*, subtitled "A Life of the World's First Consulting Detective" (Clarkson N. Potter, publisher). In one modest volume he covered the professional life and retirement of Sherlock Holmes. A few years later he did an equivalent "biography" of Nero Wolfe. The science-fiction author, Philip José Farmer, wrote two: *Tarzan Alive* and *Doc Savage: His Apocalyptic Life*. Thus, this modest effort is following a well established literary tradition.

The following "biography" follows the story of Captain Midnight from his beginnings to the time around the close of World War II. Where technical corrections are at variance with what was originally broadcast, the difference is noted, with an "explanation" of why what was broadcast was aired. Outside of corrections in the main text, it is understood that the "real" Captain Midnight, as noted, is the character as presented in the Skelly Oil and Ovaltine 15-minute serial broadcasts.

To many people, Sherlock Holmes, Perry Mason, Nero Wolfe, Sam Spade, and even Tarzan are old friends, as "real" as any celebrity. The following work illustrates that Captain Midnight, aka Charles J. Albright, is another member of this distinguished group.

In closing, I would like to express my special thanks to Lyle Bergmann of Ovaltine Foods for providing access to the original radio scripts, and to Gregory Jackson, Jr., and Frank Coghlan, Jr., for their encouragement and advice.

Finally, a note about the Captain Midnight name and trademark: The Captain Midnight trademark was first owned by original sponsor Skelly Oil, which used it for premiums such as badges and newsletters. In 1940 the Wander Company picked up sponsorship for the show for its Ovaltine product, and used the name for its premiums. "Captain Midnight" was associated with Ovaltine from the time the sponsorship began until 1990. After the successful radio decade, *Captain Midnight* was broadcast for a few years as an Ovaltine-sponsored television program. During this period (in 1984) the Sandoz corporation acquired Wander and its trademarks. Well after the show left the air, Ovaltine offered a few Captain Midnight premiums via print advertising; the last of these was in 1989. In 1990 Sandoz discontinued its association with "Captain Midnight" by officially canceling the Captain Midnight trademark. Currently, Ovaltine is distributed by Himuel Nutrition.

—Stephen A. Kallis, Jr.
Tampa, Florida, 1999

1

Genesis

The proper place to begin the biography of a legend is where the legend originated. The man who came to be known as Captain Midnight received that code name because of an exploit during the closing days of World War I. The official report of the incident is brief, and it appears to have been deliberately vague.

Paraphrased, the official report tells the following: After the United States entered the war, a "moment of crisis" was reached. The Allied armies were in danger of being subjected to what was officially termed "terrible destruction." An American general, from a secret headquarters in France, dispatched a young American pilot, a captain in the Air Corps, on a highly secret mission. Indeed, the mission was so secret that its details were known only to the pilot, the general, and one of his superiors in Washington. The odds against the young pilot's success on this mission were estimated as 100 to one. His assignment: to defeat an international criminal, Ivan Shark. Failure could only mean the complete defeat of the Allied armies.

When the general asked how he would learn of his success, the pilot replied that if he hadn't returned by the stroke of twelve that night, his mission would have failed. He then went off on his mission.

He did return, arriving dramatically just at the stroke of twelve. The general was so moved that he immediately gave the young pilot the code name of "Captain Midnight."

As can be seen, the report leaves a lot of questions unanswered. First, by the time the United States entered the war (in conventional military terms), the war had either been won or, at worst, been forced into a stalemate. It had

Nieuport XVII*bis* was the aircraft that Captain Charles J. Albright used for much of his active duty in World War I France. One of these aircraft was used in his one-man mission against Ivan Shark; this mission earned him the code name of Captain Midnight. (Photograph: *National Air and Space Museum, Smithsonian Institution*, SI Neg. No. A 48745.)

become a war of attrition; in the long run, a war of attrition was one the Germans could not win. The fresh infusion of United States troops could only hasten an Allied victory.

Further, it is intriguing to note that the threat to the Allied forces was from a single man, and one classified as an international criminal. Also, there is the question of what power a single individual could possess that would threaten the Allied armies — and the question of how a lone man could cope with that power.

Viewed in the light of today's knowledge, some suggestions take form. Any threat that could endanger *all* of the Allied forces had to be some new form of mass weapon, one that could be controlled by a single individual or a small group of highly trained agents.

World War I saw the introduction of new and fearsome weapons. These ranged from the Big Bertha long-range guns to gas warfare. In particular, gas warfare was a weapon of mass destruction, yet while it killed thousands, it was not a decisive weapon.

The logical conclusion is that the weapon held by the international criminal was something that could be developed by a single individual of genius, someone who could develop the weapon without the vast financial support of a government.

What fits this picture is a biological weapon. Statistics indicate that at about the same period, an influenza epidemic killed more than half a million Americans and millions more elsewhere. The conditions of warfare in those days encouraged the spread of illness. Thus, a properly released biological agent could have devastated the Allied armies as nothing else could have. Countermeasures would have been difficult.

There are hints that more people than Ivan Shark had been engaged in unorthodox biological research before and during the World War I period. Hints dropped in reports of the unequaled detective Sherlock Holmes (notably in the adventure of the Creeping Man, plus certain inexplicable allusions found in the opening narrative of his Thor Bridge adventure) even suggest that some areas of research met with success.

If the weapon Ivan Shark possessed was biological, it's understandable why reports of its existence were suppressed. That sort of biological research was too easy to establish. A twisted genius with limited facilities could manage to develop some deadly form of disease. Public knowledge might encourage others to do so.

The actual oral order given to the pilot was to "exterminate Ivan Shark" utterly, according to the official report of the incident. It may be that the young pilot, having previously read his sealed orders, found a double meaning in those instructions.

We can surmise that Ivan Shark's base of operations was well guarded from ground or air attacks. Possibly there were previous attempts to infiltrate Shark's base on land; this necessitated an attempt from the sky. Naturally, and particularly at night, the mission was extremely hazardous.

We can assume that a high-flying aircraft had managed to take photographs of Shark's installation, so the pilot had knowledge of the layout. Perhaps the pilot had taken the pictures himself without realizing their significance. The reconstruction of what the pilot did that night follows.

Though isolated, Shark's base required supplies. Thus, a reasonably well-traveled road led through the protected area. The aircraft that the young pilot flew was a high-lift biplane with a gentle glide slope, a Nieuport XVII*bis*. The plane has a service ceiling of more than 18,000 feet, and the pilot brought it close to that value.

When he approached the stronghold, the pilot cut his engine totally for a glide-in "deadstick" landing. This enabled him to infiltrate the base of operations in relative silence.

The landing was dangerous because the night was dim. After landing, the pilot prepared the aircraft for a quick takeoff, aligning it with the road. Once the plane was rigged, he hurried off to the enemy base.

As to what weapon that lone pilot carried to counter Shark's threat, there seems only one obvious answer, if indeed the menace was biological. At that time, as is true today, one sure way of eradicating disease from an area is by fire. Because of the weight limitation of his aircraft, it is certain that the pilot carried some type of a triggering device rather than something that could destroy the whole base by itself.

We know that the pilot was successful. He either dealt with or avoided the guards. To destroy the menace, he had to penetrate the headquarters, avoid any traps, and find a store of flammables sufficient to do the job.

The device(s) he left behind must have been controlled by timing fuzes; otherwise, the pilot couldn't have made it back to his airplane. As the device triggered, he was able to start the engine and take off into the night. Doubtless the glare of the base burning behind him helped light the road he used as a runway.

The mission was a success in its main objective. Whatever foul weapon Shark had was destroyed utterly. But Ivan Shark escaped.

But who was Captain Midnight? He was a superlative pilot (and was still flight qualified well into his seventies), but his name doesn't appear on the list of World War I aces.

Charles Albright doesn't talk much about his boyhood, but this much has been determined. He was born in North Carolina around the turn of the century. From the time he was old enough to read, his main interest seems to have been flying.

Before the United States' official entry into World War I, Albright heard of Americans who were serving in French and English units already in the thick of the fight — and that some of them were serving in air units.

Filled with the spirit of adventure common to boys of the era, Albright managed to work his way to Europe somehow. There he joined the French forces and was taught to fly. He was a natural pilot.

Rather than being permitted to join the more illustrious flying groups such as the Escadrille Americane (later known as the Lafayette Escadrille), Albright was given scouting missions in an unarmed Nieuport. (In one of the 1940 radio episodes, he refers to World War I photoreconniassance and implies that his missions involved such activities).

The Nieuport was an aircraft with a great deal of aerobatic characteristics, but because of its design, the wrong type of dive could tear the fabric from the upper wing, converting the biplane into a dangerously overloaded monoplane. In an unarmed observation plane, Albright needed to develop superlative flying skills, or perish. He survived.

Though young, the information he gathered for the Allied forces earned him promotions, and he eventually rose to the rank of Captain. With the entry of America into the war, U.S. citizens in the armed forces of Allied countries were placed under American command. Charles Albright was one of these, and he retained his French rank.

He did little combat flying. His observation work was so good, so necessary, that, save for the extreme dedication he showed and the nature of his mission against Ivan Shark, he might have spent the remainder of his days during the war as an observation pilot.

The loss would have been great, for in Charles Albright lay the seeds of fame.

2

The Hidden Years

Between the time of Captain Midnight's daring one-man mission and the rekindling of the flames of war in Europe, not too much has been recorded about him. Neither "Albright" nor "Midnight" appear in the list of Allied aces; therefore, we know that the pilot's actions throughout the rest of the war were not connected with air combat. As will be seen, his flying skills were so superlative that his prowess as a combat pilot would have earned him fame equaling or surpassing that of the "Balloon Buster," Frank Luke.

What has been publicly known is that shortly before the United States entered World War II, Albright was "called out of retirement" to head the organization known as the Secret Squadron. We also know, as dramatized in the first and second radio programs under the sponsorship of Ovaltine, that along the way, he had become the guardian of a youngster, Chuck Ramsay, who was the son of Albright's best friend. The elder Ramsay asked Albright to look after the boy as he lay dying.

Also, we are told in the pre–Ovaltine radio dramas sponsored by Skelly Oil that Albright, usually known by his code name, had been helping people in trouble throughout the world. Since he seems to have spent most of his time involved in such altruistic activities, it's easy to deduce that he was independently wealthy. The rest of the story, the "lost years," has until now been shrouded in mystery.

Although Albright/Midnight is a modest, nontalkative man in regards to his activities, the fundamental story has been reconstructed. Besides accessing previously confidential memoranda and private files, by tracing the career of his ward's father, an accurate picture was developed.

After World War I, the pilots who returned to the United States were considerably more air-minded than the average American. Prior to the war, advances in aviation had been concentrated in Europe, despite the fact that the first heavier-than-air flight occurred in the United States. The returning pilots had been galvanized by the equipment and maneuvers that they'd employed in the war.

The pilots, who wanted aeronautics to grow, organized air shows to help "sell" aviation. Aviation activity encompassed air shows, air mail, and barnstorming.

In this environment, Albright returned to the United States with a special gift. The top-secret nature of his mission precluded him receiving the Congressional Medal he otherwise would almost certainly have received. However, the general who had given him the mission was able to present him with the Nieuport XVII*bis* he flew. This reward Albright would treasure above all others.

With the Nieuport, Albright was able to earn a modest living, participating at times in such activities as experimental air messenger services. While he was not a barnstormer, he occasionally participated in air shows, particularly those featuring mock dogfights.

It was at an air show that Albright met Sean Ramsay. Both pilots shared a deep love of aviation, but otherwise they contrasted significantly. Ramsay was impulsive, extroverted, and enthusiastic. He was a good stunt pilot and had spent most of his postwar time barnstorming. Albright, though highly skilled, was restrained. He was not willing to "stunt" unless absolutely necessary for the success of a mission. Yet each saw things in the other that he admired, and they became fast friends.

During the years of shared adventures, the impulsive Ramsay had fallen in love "at first sight" and had wooed and won a pretty but quiet girl, Mary Wainwright, who was thrilled by the dashing young aviator. The resulting three-way association altered the pilots' lifestyle.

In due course, Charles A. Ramsay was born. Albright was the godfather. This further restricted the range of the pilots' activities. They settled in southern California for a while.

The work begun by air shows, barnstormers, and the like started to have an impact. Aviation began to capture the imagination of the average American.

Hollywood responded to the demand. Studios began to produce wartime epics — pictures that were supposed to show the heroism of the American aviator during, and sometimes after, the war. As a result, there was a demand for veteran pilots to fly the aircraft shown in the films.

At this time, a tragedy struck the Ramsays. Mary Ramsay was stricken by an illness that only worsened over time. The illness was obscure.

2. The Hidden Years

Specialists, laboratory tests, and other measures became a severe drain on the family finances. Albright helped out, both with gifts of cash and by actual assistance managing the household.

As the expenses mounted, Ramsay hired out as a stunt pilot for films, flying the most hazardous stunts because the extra money would help defray medical expenses. Albright did stunt work, too, under the stage name of Bill ("Red") Roberts, to earn money for his friends.

The medicine of the time was inadequate. Mary died quietly in her sleep.

Sean Ramsay was stricken. His beloved wife had become the keystone of his happiness, eclipsing even his love of flying. With her presence gone, he drove himself to even more reckless stunts, earning even more money — all earmarked for the care of his son. Sean Ramsay loved young Charles in his own right, but he represented to the grief-stricken pilot the last physical manifestation of his love for his wife.

Albright suggested more than once that Ramsay was taking unnecessary chances in some of his stunting. However, Ramsay didn't change his flying style, even though he'd amassed sufficient funds to care for his son, no matter what happened.

The inevitable happened. During filming of an epic war film, one of Ramsay's maneuvers was too violent. The aircraft suffered structural damage that rendered it almost unflyable. By incredibly skillful flying, Ramsay nearly managed to land the plane safely, but he crashed.

Albright was the first to the wreckage. Though hurt and dying, Ramsay was conscious. His last request to Albright was that he take care of young Charles. After Albright promised he would, Ramsay died, a smile on his lips. It was only then that Albright realized that his friend had subconsciously driven himself past the breaking point so that he could be with his wife once more.

The movie studio made an additional payment, far above Ramsay's salary. This, together with the money from the Ramsay estate, was more than enough to take care of the needs of young Charles. Albright, who became his guardian, took money he'd been accumulating to help defray the Ramsay expenses and invested it.

Albright was incredibly lucky. He'd never tried any heavy investment before, yet the results were such that he was virtually guaranteed a lifetime income. His degree of luck is illustrated by the fact he got out of the market about six months before the 1929 crash. With his own income assured, he could devote himself to looking after young Ramsay.

Being financially independent, Albright spent much of his time learning more about different aspects of aviation. He put in a lot of flying time during the school years of young Charles. During the summer months, he took the youngster to various places in the country, via air, to broaden his education.

Albright became aware that young Charles was becoming extremely air-minded and that he seemed to have all the instincts of a natural aviator. Considering the way Charles' father had met his death, Albright didn't initially encourage the youngster's interest. However, it soon became evident that the boy had inherited more of his mother's quiet ways than his father's runaway enthusiasms. Since Albright loved the air himself, he relented and began to teach the youngster the rudiments of flight.

For many years life was idyllic. Young Ramsay accepted Albright as a surrogate parent, but the youngster never forgot his mother or father.

Albright also became aware that as a high-school dropout, there were certain gaps in his education. During much of the time when Chuck was in school, Albright set himself a program of study. Over time, he gave himself the rough equivalent of a college education, though his choice of subjects was rather eclectic.

Albright picked up a little mathematics, some "practical engineering," and a wealth of cultural information. In addition to learning a great deal of history, some biology, and some languages, he studied a little paleontology. As will be noted later, this curiosity in prehistoric life forms proved more useful than Albright could have dreamed.

Each year, as young Ramsay grew older, the range of Albright's "summer trips" grew greater. By the time Chuck reached his early teens, the two of them had explored large areas of the American southwest, as well as some areas of Canada. He also took the boy on many visits to Washington, D.C.

It was on one of the trips to the Nation's Capitol that Albright ran into his old commanding officer, Major Barry Steele, U.S. Army, Retired. They met in the Smithsonian, where he'd brought Chuck to show him some early machines. He ran into Steele at one of the exhibits; the major had decided to visit the museum on a whim.

Initially, Steele didn't recognize Albright. Once he did, the major decided a celebration was in order. The three of them retired to a posh restaurant and had what might be called a late lunch or early dinner.

They retired to Steele's residence, where the two men caught up on each other's doings. During the visit, Steele told young Ramsay about some of his guardian's exploits during the war. Without detailing it, he mentioned that Albright had performed a hazardous mission that gave him the code name Captain Midnight.

The youngster was taken by the name. He'd always been a little uneasy about how he should address his guardian. He couldn't call him by his first name — it was too familiar for those days. "Mr. Albright" was far too formal. Albright himself indicated that he not be referred to as "father" or

2. The Hidden Years

"dad." Chuck had addressed him primarily as "Sir" and, once in a while, jocularly as "Red," Albright's old stage nickname from the film days. "Sir" seemed restrictive. Upon learning of the old code name, the youngster appropriated it and used it from then on, either in full or abbreviated to "Captain."

Albright considered the name a little flamboyant, but since Chuck adopted it with such alacrity, he made no strong objections. The form of address became so ingrained that after a short time, he often found the boy introducing him as Captain Midnight.

After a while, he became rather fatalistic about it. Frequently, if a newcomer asked him if he was Captain Midnight, he would generally reply, "I'm the one who is known by that name." Once, when someone observed that the name sounded a little melodramatic, he snapped, "The name was not of my choosing."

In the meantime, Albright and his ward found adventure in their travels. Albright, who was becoming increasingly known as Captain Midnight, often found himself in situations where he could help deserving people out of difficulties. People in the 1930s were more willing to get involved than now; giving a fellow citizen a hand instead of a handout was a reward in itself.

Into this idyllic life came dark complications. One was the increasing international tensions that foreshadowed a new and more terrible war. The other was the international arch-criminal, Ivan Shark.

Shark has justly been called a criminal mastermind. Although Albright's mission resulted in the destruction of Shark's weapon, the arch-criminal escaped. His criminal network had been temporarily shattered. So he regrouped.

Shark's activities were worldwide. He had plenty of funds available to rebuild his organization. He was determined to discover the identity of the lone pilot who was singlehandedly responsible for the near ruin of his criminal empire. It was not easy.

During the remainder of the war, Albright had acted strictly under the code name of Captain Midnight. Shark and his operatives were unable to determine that Albright and Midnight were the same person. One thing they did learn was that Midnight survived the war and had left the armed forces after the Armistice.

As Shark's criminal empire renewed, he acquired two able assistants known only be their nicknames: Gardo and Fang. Gardo was recruited from the American underworld. Though he was quite loyal, his dullness of wit frequently led Shark to suspect him of being untrustworthy. Yet it was through Gardo that Shark was able to establish several important contacts with American criminal elements.

Fang was in Shark's inner circle. Outside of the master criminal's daughter, Fury, Fang was his most trusted aide. In times of stress, Shark frequently adopted an Oriental-style philosophy of near fatalism. The combination of intellect and philosophy appealed to Fang, who was Oriental, and he became Shark's devoted servant. While other members of Shark's group addressed him as "chief," or in times of stress, "Shark," Fang always addressed him as "Master." This did nothing to lower Shark's good opinion of him.

Shark had married when young; not so much for love, but more from the desire to establish a dynasty. His wife died in childbirth, but the child, a daughter, survived. During the First World War, the daughter, Fury, was being educated in Switzerland. With the near collapse of his empire, Shark decided to defer establishing his dynasty until he'd developed an organization so firmly entrenched that he'd never again be in danger of losing it.

Yet Fury was flesh of his flesh, and he was as devoted to her as to any living thing. As she grew, Shark was delighted to see that she'd inherited an intelligence equal to his own. She shared many of his views of the world, and she could bring an intensity of effort to a problem that Shark himself found hard to equal. Besides being blood kin, Shark realized that she was a valuable addition to his empire-in-the-making.

It's ironic that Chuck Ramsay's adoption of Albright's old code name brought word of the pilot to Ivan Shark. News of a mysterious aviator who helped those in trouble began to circulate. Shark and his minions had been on constant alert to hear of somebody named Captain Midnight; so, after many years, the master criminal rediscovered his old foe.

Although Shark had a widespread international organization to run, he devoted significant resources to combat Albright. For of all the people who had tangled with Shark, only Captain Midnight had succeeded completely, without even sustaining an injury.

Albright found himself in adventures that had to involve a powerful leader. In short order he learned that this enemy was in fact Ivan Shark. The master criminal was able to move his forces rapidly and surely; and Albright found himself under increased pressure.

One adventure dramatized on the radio by Skelly Oil involved a Shark activity that Albright had to counter. Shark's gang had at its disposal several fast and efficient aircraft, all painted black. This "black fleet" was preying on the owners and operators of a mine in the western United States. Albright and a number of his friends and acquaintances opposed the air fleet.

To maintain a certain degree of anonymity, Albright operated as "Red Roberts," an adaption of his stunt-pilot stage name. (This spilled over to his true name: a number of people knew him as "Red" Albright.) Shark's

2. The Hidden Years

forces were foiled, and the master criminal was subsequently captured and imprisoned.

During the adventure, something significant happened. Albright met Ichabod ("Ikky") Mudd, who subsequently became one of his closest friends and associates.

Mudd was a mechanic. Initially, he seemed to be a bit of a braggart. Yet beneath his bluster, he proved to be an excellent mechanic. He would be involved with many adventures that history would show were highly important. But that was some time off.

Prior to that, Albright reached an important milestone in his life, one that would result in high adventure.

3

The Call

It was September 1940. War clouds were gathering, and the dark currents of increasing international tensions washed across the shores of the United States. The Battle of Britain had been building to its incredible climax. Japan mounted an invasion of French Indo-China. The North Atlantic was plagued with German submarines. The United States declared it would maintain neutrality; circumstances were drawing the country closer to war. And a number of factions tried to make certain that the country would not work against their interests. Some did through peaceful assembly; others took more drastic measures.

At a remote building in Virginia, a meeting was held. The Slater Farm, in the Virginia hill country, was far more than it appeared. Albright had just returned from a trip to China when Major Barry Steele contacted him and set up a meeting. Upon approaching the door of the farmhouse, Albright was surprised to see the door open before he could knock or ring a bell.

The next few minutes were almost as melodramatic as Albright's final battlefield orders before the raid on Shark's stronghold. He and the person who greeted him went through a complex ritual of signs and countersigns. Albright was led through a secret entrance to a flight of stairs that ended in an underground chamber.

Albright was just seating himself when a portal opened, and a man dressed in a business suit — but wearing a mask — entered. Before Albright could say anything, the newcomer asked him if he were Captain Midnight.

Albright smiled, a bit wryly, and said, "I'm the one known by that name."

The other nodded and asked Albright to sit. He seated himself as well.

Albright remarked that few people knew his real name. The other indicated that he knew everything of importance about Albright, and demonstrated his claim by detailing certain of his recent adventures.

The masked individual then said, "Since you recently returned from China with your ward, I don't know if you've had a chance to catch up with the news. However, there's been an alarming increase in un-American activities in the last couple of months. Although as far as the public knows, these are random acts. However, I've come to the conclusion that a sizable percentage of these activities are being directed by a secret criminal organization."

"Criminal?" Albright said. "Why would a criminal organization be interested in such things?"

The masked individual smiled wryly. "Some organizations will take money from anyone, provided the pay is sufficient. This group has wreaked more damage than the general public knows. Certain things have been kept quiet."

He went on. "I'm forming a secret squad—" then, remembering Albright's aviation background, he appended so rapidly that there was barely a break, "—ron to combat this criminal force, and I wish you to command it." By this simple modification of a term, the new organization had been named. (This detail was omitted in the radio dramatization of the event. The portrayal had the masked man say "a secret squadron" without the catch between syllables.) Though nominally "secret," the Secret Squadron was to win high fame and international recognition in the next few years.

Albright, flattered, protested that he didn't even know whom he was dealing with, even though the meeting had been arranged by Major Steele. How could he think of accepting an assignment of such magnitude from an anonymous chief?

The masked man nodded. "I understand. You need to have complete trust in me. I will remove the mask. However, beneath the mask my face has been disguised, so you may still not know my identity." He took off the mask. "Do you recognize me?"

"Sorry, I don't."

The masked man reached into his pocket and withdrew a card case. Without a word, he passed a card to Albright.

"You! *You!* I never dreamed it would be you, Mr. ..." Albright began.

"Please, Captain Midnight. Don't go any further. You must never mention my name."

Neither Albright nor Chuck Ramsay who accidentally learned the identity of the mysterious personage, has ever broken that trust. We are left to speculate on the man's identity.

3. The Call

On the radio dramatization, the actor that recreated the part for the first episode of the 1941 season gave this personage voice characteristics similar to then–President Franklin D. Roosevelt; but it was patently obvious that this was done for purposes of misdirection. Other clues within the program do not bear out the F.D.R. identity. The ease with which the person moved about, for instance, suggests a person other than one who was tragically stricken with polio. Further, in the second episode, the actor slipped and gave an entirely different intonation to the personage.

There is little doubt that the orders necessary for the establishment and funding of the Secret Squadron had to have executive sanction. However, it is clear that someone other than the President caused the Squadron to be formed.

Since Albright addressed this person as "Mr.," it is logical to assume that he was not a high military official. One possibility is that the person was a member of the President's Cabinet, perhaps the Secretary of War. It could even have been the Director of the Federal Bureau of Investigation. Whoever he was, he was well known and respected by the majority of Americans.

Knowing who the person was, and by inference what dangers the United States was facing, Albright agreed to head the new organization, swearing a solemn oath to aid his country. And with that oath, the Albright identity was virtually submerged; and from that time to the present, the aviator was known, and thought of, as Captain Midnight.

The stranger explained details of the new organization to Midnight. Across the country a number of hidden bases had been established. From these bases skilled agents could operate under cover against whatever organizations threatened the United States.

Initially, the chain of command was complex, similar to the "cell" technique used effectively by a number of subversive groups. Each Secret Squadron agent would know only a few additional agents, so that in case of capture, the impact on the total organization would be minimized. Rather than knowing the true identity of agents, each would know the others by numerical identifiers. The agent who was the contact to the VIP, Lyle Kelly, would be known as SS-11 (for Secret Squadron agent 11). Captain Midnight, having agreed to lead the Squadron, would be known as SS-1.

As Captain Midnight was being installed as head of the Secret Squadron, Ivan Shark was already becoming aware that something was afoot. Prior to receiving his oath of office, Captain Midnight and his host had discussed the possibility that some of the new sabotage efforts might be the work of Ivan Shark. Midnight had pointed out that though this was an interesting thought, he'd helped capture the master criminal. He added that as far as he knew, Shark was still behind bars in Canada.

Actually, Shark had been at large for weeks. Even Canadian officials were not then aware he was free. The instrument of his freedom was his daughter, Fury.

Ivan Shark, Fury, Fang, and Gardo were captured in Canada as a result of their kidnapping of Chuck Ramsay. Since Shark's criminal activities were international, he was imprisoned there. He and his associates minimized Fury Shark's part in the affair. After a few months of her sentence, she was placed on probation through a technicality. Several high-priced barristers helped develop the technicality.

Though a potent and effective member of Shark's organization, she managed to avoid prominence in most of her father's campaigns. With Fury set free, she was able to formulate and execute a plan to free her father.

Utilizing the talents of several chemists and doctors associated with Shark's organization, Fury was able to obtain a certain chemical compound. When ingested, this compound produced symptoms identical to an obscure but contagious disease. She managed to smuggle this into prison.

Shark took the compound several days after it arrived. The delay was necessary for Fury to prepare for the next step. She had to infiltrate certain agents into a target hospital.

When Shark took the compound, the apparent illness alarmed the prison's officials. Concerned at the possibility of an epidemic, they had Shark moved to a private, maximum-security hospital.

A few days after Shark arrived at the hospital, Fury arranged for certain alarms to be neutralized for a brief period of time. During that time the master criminal was spirited away. An agent who was a near double was substituted so that Shark could rebuild his damaged organization before his escape was detected.

Two days before it was known that he was at large, Shark received a report from one of his agents in Washington, D.C. He learned that a certain official seemed to be engaging in a clandestine move, leaving a building in the Nation's Capitol and heading to a relatively remote part of Virginia.

Shark previously had received intelligence that suggested that this official was involved in investigations of his activities. The clandestine trip, coupled with what he'd already learned, convinced him that whatever was going on probably was a move against him. Shark couldn't take the chance of there being any threat to his activities. He observed to Fang that there was a possibility that a new organization might be forming to oppose his activities — and that any such organization had to be destroyed.

Chuck Ramsay, who had been inadvertently instrumental in letting

Ivan Shark learn that Captain Midnight was still active, was also instrumental in alerting his guardian that he might be in peril.

Shark's assistant, Gardo, back in favor with the master criminal, had been instructed to participate in the raid on the farmhouse. At an airport, Chuck Ramsay spotted him.

Chuck had been at the airport to visit with a young pilot, Steve Donovan. Donovan was a friend of both Chuck and Captain Midnight. Along with Albright and his ward, Donovan had been involved in a skirmish with Shark. When Chuck spotted Shark's aide, he and Donovan followed Gardo to the vicinity of the Slater Farm; they were surprised to see a grouping of sinister people surrounding the house.

Captain Midnight previously indicated to Chuck that he was going to a special meeting at a remote location. It didn't take Chuck much thought to guess what was happening when a top aide of Ivan Shark traveled to a remote Virginia location to join a group of others. He decided to act.

Moving deliberately to the farmhouse, Chuck rapped on the door. It took a few minutes, but despite the elaborate security measures that had been set up, Chuck managed to convince those guarding Captain Midnight and his host to let him speak to his guardian. When Captain Midnight verified his ward's identity, the information Chuck brought was taken very seriously.

A plan was drawn up quickly. There was a hidden cave beneath the house which could be used as an emergency way out. It formed a dangerous pathway to a concealed airfield on the other side of the hill from the Slater farmhouse. The official, Captain Midnight, and Chuck would attempt an escape by this route. The guards would stay to hold off the raiders.

The official (whom Captain Midnight had introduced to his ward as "Mr. Jones"), agent SS-11, Chuck, and the newly appointed Secret Squadron leader made their way through the cave passageway, but the way was hazardous. On the way, "Mr. Jones" slipped on a wet spot and fell into an underground river.

Chuck, who was nearest to the official, jumped in after him and was instrumental in his rescue. However, between the action of the water and Chuck's exertions, enough of "Jones'" disguise was removed so that the youngster recognized him.

Chuck was sworn to secrecy. Although more than half a century has passed, neither Midnight nor Chuck Ramsay will reveal who "Mr. Jones" was. When it was pointed out that this promise was made many years ago, and that it shouldn't hurt to reveal the identity, Ramsay shrugged and said, "There was no time limit on our promise. Once you start making exceptions to any of your promises, it's easy to start making exceptions to all your promises. I'd rather not get into that habit."

The party escaped.

And Ivan Shark, who had been stymied, had no idea who might be involved in opposing him. But being brilliant and somewhat intuitive, he developed enough suspicion to keep his guard up. He was confident that in a few months he'd know who or what group would oppose him.

4

The Early Secret Squadron

In future years the Secret Squadron was to become "secret" in name only. Like the Secret Service, the OSS, and the Counterspies, the Secret Squadron was destined to become a household word within a decade.

Although the "squadron" part of the organization's name was spur-of-the-moment, the name was fitting. To maintain a tight, effective force that could cover a lot of territory and respond quickly to emergencies, the new group relied heavily on aircraft located at hidden airfields. To man those aircraft, pilots, some veterans from World War I, had been recruited. All had an intense sense of patriotism and, to a man, were dedicated to the success of the new organization.

Operationally, using a "cell" structure for the organization proved unworkable. To maintain optimum security, a modified hierarchy was established. It relied heavily on radio transmissions. Squadron bases across the continent reported directly to headquarters by radio. Orders were sent by radio. Except for extreme emergencies, approval for all actions came from headquarters. Individual bases didn't have precise locations of other bases; only the central headquarters kept complete files.

The commander of each base and his alternate knew the location of the central headquarters and the security procedures to land there safely; other Squadron base members didn't. The Squadron, being aware of triangulation methods, used an ingenious and elaborate shifting retransmission technique to foil attempts to locate headquarters.

The Squadron's numbering system for agents was modified to accommodate the organization's restructuring. Those attached to central headquarters had simple numbers with the "SS" designator: SS-1 for Captain Midnight, SS-11 for Lyle Kelly, SS-243 for Schyler Brownfield, etc. Since each regional base was numbered — Illinois had Base 1, one of the California bases was Base 7, one in Florida was Base 19, etc. — regional base agents incorporated their base into their Squadron number. Thus, an agent in Illinois might be Agent 17 of Base 1 (or SS-1-17). Protocol forbade any regional base from having an Agent 1; convention caused the numbering system at each base to begin as 12.

In conversation, the difference with, say, SS-119 and SS-1-19 was made by pronunciation. The former agent was "SS one hundred nineteen"; the latter, "SS one nineteen." A subtle distinction, but one immediately recognizable to every Secret Squadron agent.

Because the Secret Squadron had to rely heavily on radio communications, security was established through coded transmissions. The code was taken from an official publication, the *Secret Squadron Code Book*. The book contained real code elements, as opposed to a cipher. Various phrases were organized in four-letter groups. For example, "ZDAA" stood for "criminal activities"; "NPAO" stood for "have encountered"; "AQNW" stood for "clue concerning"; and so forth. Thus, the message "NPAO AQNW ZDAA" would decode to "Have encountered clue concerning criminal activities."

The *Secret Squadron Code Book* was bulky. When not in use, it was stored in a safe in, or immediately adjacent to, the bases' communication rooms. Though security at bases and headquarters was thorough, it was possible that a code book could become compromised — that is, somehow fall into enemy hands. Squadron members were drilled to memorize a simple emergency cipher scheme that could be used as a temporary stopgap until a new code book could be issued.

Although the Secret Squadron was organized as a paramilitary force, initially it had only tenuous connections to the Armed Services. Only base commanders and their immediate subordinates were aware of the Secret Squadron. It was a high military secret.

In the field, agents who didn't know each other used simple countersigns to verify their Squadron affiliation. By today's standards, all these precautions were a bit elaborate, but the Secret Squadron was composed of new members who were establishing an organizational identity with no unique traditions.

Since the organization was secret, funding for facilities, aircraft, expendables, and salaries had to be covert. Initially, this was done through clever bookkeeping; a special file of *correct* books was maintained in a certain Washington office to reflect actual expenditures.

4. The Early Secret Squadron

Because of his financial independence, Captain Midnight refused the salary allocated to him. He became what was then known as a "dollar a year man," for legal reasons. Later, when Chuck Ramsay became a member of the Secret Squadron, he followed his guardian's lead, having more than enough income from his trust fund.

The Secret Squadron, due to its limited funds, didn't have massive training facilities. Save for some extremely specialized subjects, it had no training facilities at all. For most things, it had to develop alternate means to train its agents.

The means the Squadron came up with was audacious. With war pressures building worldwide, some foreign troops were already being trained in various United States military facilities. Squadron agents were palmed off as personnel from friendly countries and added to existing classes.

One incident in early 1941 had a major impact on the organization. A small base, almost an outpost, was established in a western State. To cover its activities, it was disguised as a wildcat mining operation. Squadron agents were obliged to spend some time "prospecting" to satisfy the curiosity of the local folk. As luck would have it, they actually found a high grade of silver ore!

The "cover" mine was worked to help defray Secret Squadron expenses. Specialists with a mining background were recruited to work the mine, since the standard Squadron agents had other duties to perform. The miners, who became Secret Squadron employees (though not agents), recovered enough ore that the Squadron actually met most of its operating expenses.

Reliance on passwords, signs, and countersigns were particularly important, because the Secret Squadron had no official symbol. In those days the Squadron *was* known (in a shadowy sort of way) to certain high government officials and selected members of the Armed Forces and other government agencies. It was covert, however, and a symbol might have uncovered its existence. Those who founded the Squadron wanted to keep knowledge of its very existence from its enemies.

Events were to change that situation.

5

Ivan Shark and Early Skirmishing

Ivan Shark truly was a criminal mastermind. There are and have been criminal organizations, international in scope, powerful enough to affect the destinies of nations. Most of these, developed over many generations, can almost be considered nations by themselves.

Shark had such genius he was able to rebuild his organization after it had been nearly destroyed. Fortunately, his efforts were thwarted repeatedly; but this is not a mark against him. Nature often strikes a balance; the man who became Shark's chief opponent was equally gifted.

Shark had been approached by certain foreign agents. They wanted his organization to help spread sabotage in various American facilities. They wanted to demoralize workers and to convince them that their stake in their current jobs was not worth the risk. They also wanted to prevent militarily dangerous projects from being completed; or, failing that, to obtain details on new military developments. For sabotage and espionage, Shark's organization would be well paid.

Shark had contact with these agents through his daughter, Fury. Within weeks of Shark's escape, she delivered messages to these foreign agents indicating that her father was ready to deal.

Fury Shark was a remarkable woman. As noted, she had sufficient genius and charisma to dominate the remnants of Shark's gang while he was incarcerated. Since she did this in the late 1930s, it is even more remarkable from a modern perspective.

In many ways, Fury was more practical than her father. She realized instinctively that the only good enemy is a dead enemy. Several times throughout her career, when her father had managed to capture a top-level Secret Squadron member, she would urge him to dispose of the prisoner quickly, if not painlessly. Shark would dissuade her by pointing out that he wanted to extract information or use the prisoner as a bargaining chip. Almost always, however, Fury's instincts proved correct. A top operative, given time, would often be able to engineer an escape or hold out long enough to be rescued.

Actually, Shark listened to Fury most of the time. She was highly intelligent, daring, and brave. In many ways, her skills complemented his, making the Shark forces particularly formidable for an apolitical freelance organization.

One puzzling feature about Shark's underlings has bothered some for years: Ivan Shark's relationship with Gardo. From time to time, Shark publicly rebuked him and told others about his apparent lack of reliability. More than once, Shark intimated that after a current operation, Gardo would be dealt with permanently. Yet, despite the very real menace of Shark's distrust, Gardo both remains with the group and takes the verbal abuse.

The apparent anomaly is rectified if we consider Fury Shark. Outside of driving ambition and possibly a mild touch of sadism, she was a functional human being with normal drives. Given that she was frequently partnered with Gardo while operating in the field, it's not inappropriate to assume they were sex partners. He doubtless provided her with a degree of physical satisfaction, and certainly he was easy for her to dominate. There were few males that Fury could admire for their intellects; so Gardo, who obviously was no mental giant, became a satisfying and useful appendage for her. This is why Gardo stayed.

Shark must have learned of the relationship shortly after it was established. He probably retained Gardo at his daughter's insistence. If Gardo was really as untrustworthy as Shark told others, he wouldn't have been paired with Fury as often as he was. Thus, the direct taunts to Gardo, and the various comments to others, was the best safety valve for Shark to express his disapproval of the situation without creating a strong rift with his daughter.

Shark assigned Fury to gather intelligence on the most effective companies to move against. It was while she was doing this that Shark received word of the activities that led to his raid on the Slater farmhouse.

The results of the raid led Shark to believe that a secret organization had been established to counter his activities. This was somewhat egocentric, since the Secret Squadron was formed to counter all un–American activities, not just those masterminded by Shark. However, since the new organization was headed by his old nemesis, this egocentricity maximized his chances of survival.

While busily engaged in sabotage and espionage, Shark's forces tentatively extended feelers to try to obtain information about the new organization. Shark's intuition made him feel that his old nemesis was somehow connected with the new group. He ordered some of his agents to stake out the Donovan house and land. Shark knew of the past association between the Donovans and Captain Midnight.

Chuck Ramsay, while not an official member of the Secret Squadron, was for all practical purposes as involved with the new organization as any agent. Thus, when the youngster noticed a man casing a National Guard armory, he followed the man to a hotel. Using a pay telephone in the lobby, Chuck reported it to his guardian. The youngster gave a good description of the man, and, at Captain Midnight's direction, SS-11 called for backup.

As agents arrived, Captain Midnight considered the position his ward was in. He'd decided that the activities of a Secret Squadron agent were too dangerous; he had no intention of letting Chuck become a member. Once the youngster identified the person who was casing the armory, Captain Midnight ordered the boy to go to a safer area. The safest place the Secret Squadron leader could think of was the Donovan home in Wisconsin.

Captain Midnight's forces prevented the destruction of the National Guard armory, which was more important in 1940 than at present because of the manner in which things were organized in those days. Midnight spent much of his time at Squadron headquarters while his agents fed him information on various suspicious activities. He found himself missing field work.

Chuck Ramsay traveled to the Donovan home accompanied by Steve Donovan. The young pilot, only a bit older than Chuck, took a bit of vacation, enabling him to help the youngster travel, as well as spending some time with his widowed mother.

After they arrived, Chuck and Steve Donovan settled in. In wandering around the property one day, they discovered a number of fresh cigarette butts in a secluded area of the yard. Nobody in the home — nor any of the neighbors — smoked cigarettes.

After poking around a bit, the two of them discovered other evidence. Near one tree, also in a secluded area, they discovered a few footprints that could only be made by what the locals called "city shoes." After a trip to the nearest town for supplies, young Donovan heard some talk among the locals of strangers being in the area. From Chuck's standpoint, it was both mysterious and a little disquieting.

Chuck knew a couple of field ciphers used by agents, and he sent a short message to Captain Midnight outlining what he'd discovered. Captain

Midnight decided he'd better investigate personally. So he informed Chuck he'd come to the Donovan home. Between the deployment of Shark's agents around the Donovan home and the open manner of his arrival, Captain Midnight walked into a situation with all the characteristics of a set trap.

6

Pre-War Operations

The Donovan homestead was located in northern Wisconsin near the edge of a cliff above Ribbon Lake. When Chuck's mother became terminally ill, his father sent the boy to spend a "vacation" with the Donovans, who were friends. The widowed Elaine ("Ma") Donovan had a teenage son and daughter who would be good companions for Chuck. Because the son, Steve, was interested in aviation, and Chuck knew aviators and a great deal about flying already, the two became good friends.

Chuck also became good friends with the daughter, Patsy, who was almost his exact age. There was no budding romance in their friendship; Patsy was one of the few nearby children of Chuck's age, and she was something of a tomboy.

She taught Chuck a great deal about camping out, tracking game, and orienting oneself in the woods. What he'd learned from her helped him identify the unusual features of the mysterious footprints he'd found near the tree.

The few times Steve Donovan went into town by himself, he met people who subtly tried to "pump" him about Chuck and his associates. When he mentioned it to Chuck, the boy became worried. Chuck began an intensive watch of the Donovan homestead area.

Captain Midnight arrived at the Donovan cottage at dusk. He landed his aircraft at a small dirt field some distance away and hitched a ride to the cottage.

Just as he arrived, a summer storm broke. This was a stroke of luck for the Donovans and Chuck, as well as Captain Midnight. The storm was sufficiently intense that Shark's operatives spying on the cottage had to call off their observations for the day.

During the evening, Chuck went over in more detail the various indications he had about surveillance. The youngster had been on the verge of panic when Captain Midnight arrived, because of his lack of resources and consequent relative helplessness. Once his guardian arrived, Chuck's morale began to recover.

The following morning, a still jittery Chuck began scanning the nearby woods from a front window. In a few minutes he noticed a slight movement.

While concerned for the safety of Chuck and the Donovans, Midnight wasn't ready to accept the idea of a spy behind every bush. He opened a window and, while standing back a bit so that his actions wouldn't be observed easily, pointed a pair of binoculars in the direction Chuck indicated.

What he saw was a girl. She was a slim blonde about Chuck's age. She appeared to be in some distress. Her clothing had some tears in it, there was a small bruise on her forehead, and she had some smudges of dirt on her face and clothes.

In a dazed manner, she moved in the general direction of the house. Captain Midnight and Ma Donovan ran out to help her.

As Captain Midnight was aiding the girl, Shark's agents had returned, and one of them recognized him. Shark was notified.

Ivan Shark was pleased to hear that his old foe had been located. His intuition connected the failure of his raid to the Secret Squadron leader and to the new organization.

Shark had recently come to an agreement with a foreign agent, one Herr Borgmann. The agent had promised large sums of money for a series of raids. Shark found it was particularly galling for the armory raid to have been completely thwarted. People like Borgmann were always impressed by efficiency.

Shark's thoughts flashed back to the many times Midnight had managed to thwart his plans — during the War, at a silver mine, at a ranch in Mexico, and in Canada. The constant meddling was becoming intolerable.

He consulted a map of the Donovan property, provided by one of his agents. He saw that the lay of the land made the cottage an almost perfect trap. A clearing surrounded the house on three sides, and the back was almost even with a cliff. The house could be surrounded without the possibility of escape. He could destroy his old enemy at last.

Fury Shark was in the field and geographically close to the Donovan homestead. Knowing the effectiveness of his daughter, Shark sent her a message instructing her to bring forces to bear on the cottage so that Captain Midnight and all those with him would be eliminated by sundown. That

6. Pre-War Operations

innocent people might die as a result didn't bother Shark. In fact, he probably never even thought of it.

While Shark was issuing his orders, Ma Donovan and Captain Midnight were trying to help the girl they'd discovered. Shortly, dressed in some of Patsy Donovan's extra clothes, the girl did her best to explain who she was and what had happened to her.

Some traumatic event caused her to lose much of her memory. She knew her first name, Joyce, and that some of her most recent experiences involved the previous night's storm, but that was about all.

Chuck positioned himself at a window to keep watch. He was able to detect indications that people were gathering in the nearby woods. He let Midnight know what was transpiring.

Captain Midnight borrowed the binoculars and took a quick look. There were enough people so that they didn't remain completely concealed. There was a woman out there; though he got only a glimpse, he recognized her as Fury Shark.

The minute he saw her, he realized the utter seriousness of the situation. The cottage had become a death trap. Except for the side facing the lake—the side with a sheer drop of some 50 feet because of the cliff—the cottage was completely surrounded. The clearing was effectively a no-man's land, since anyone venturing into it would be cut down by gunfire.

Fury Shark initiated some very light skirmishing. The return fire convinced her that her father's order to exterminate his foe wasn't practical; those inside were armed. Captain Midnight routinely traveled armed, and the Donovans had hunting rifles and plenty of ammunition. If someone emerging from the house would make a good target, so would someone emerging from the woods.

Fury Shark was a realist. She knew the men with her were there because of pay, not fanaticism. They wouldn't rush the Donovan cottage in what would be a suicide charge.

Contacting her father, she suggested that an attack after dark would stand a much better chance. He agreed, and suddenly broke out in laughter. Knowing that nobody within the house could emerge without being shot, he ordered that the dwelling be put to the torch, cremating those inside alive. He added that, in honor of his old foe, the torching should be done at midnight.

Captain Midnight was as fully aware of the situation as was Fury Shark. Neither he nor his foes could do anything before dark. He and Chuck searched for something to augment their stockpile of defensive resources.

They found precious little. Outside of a small hatchet and a hammer, the only other things they could uncover were a generous coil of rope and some strings of firecrackers saved for the Fourth of July. Captain Midnight reasoned that if it got to the point where he had to defend himself with a hammer or hatchet, it would all be over.

Although things looked almost hopeless, the Secret Squadron leader was used to facing daunting odds. His mind raced, and he came up with a plan.

Fury Shark realized that the only chance those within the cottage had would be to try to sneak out after dark. To minimize that possibility, she had some small fires lit at the edge of the woods — something that could be done without enough exposure to risk being shot. Unlike a car's headlight, it would be difficult to shoot out a fire. They were bright enough so those in the woods could spot anyone in the clearing trying to leave the cottage.

The minute the fires were lit, Captain Midnight implemented his plan. He sent Chuck and the women to the rear of the cottage. Under his instructions, Chuck and Ma Donovan fixed ropes to solid anchors. At the front of the house, Captain Midnight fired occasional shots in the direction of the woods. He was not trying to hit anyone; he was merely setting the stage for their escape attempt.

Captain Midnight stood back from whichever window he was shooting through. This minimized the chances of an enemy seeing the muzzle flash. He spaced his shots so that some occurred in rapid succession while others came with many minutes in between. He shifted weapons, sometimes firing his pistol and sometimes using one or the other rifle.

Because of the shifting of weapons, positions, and firing intervals, it was difficult for those outside to determine just how many people were manning how many guns.

Captain Midnight had always considered twelve at night lucky. Beginning at about half-past eleven, he and Chuck helped Joyce and Ma Donovan lower themselves down the cliff. One rifle and most of the ammunition were lowered.

The Shark forces were getting ready to strike. They'd located a wagon at a nearby farm and appropriated it. They loaded it with combustibles and brought it through the woods to the edge of the clearing. As the hour of twelve approached, they wheeled it into position so that when released, it would impact the Donovan cottage. At precisely one minute to twelve, the agents ignited the wagon and pushed it on its way.

Captain Midnight realized what was happening as the wagon was being pushed into the clearing. He cracked off a shot, but the range was too great. A match was struck, and in moments the wagon was ablaze. The speed with which the flames spread showed that the material in the wagon had been drenched with some highly flammable liquid. The brightness of the flames masked the Shark men who pushed the wagon toward the cottage.

As the wagon rolled toward the house, Captain Midnight and Chuck went to the window where the ropes were. The Secret Squadron leader took

6. Pre-War Operations

a few moments to light the fuses of a number of firecrackers. He'd unraveled the firecracker strings and had added to the length of some of the fuses so that they would take some time to burn. He figured that the firecrackers would explode over an interval of a couple of minutes.

As he and Chuck swung over the edge of the cliff, he could hear the occasional popping of the fireworks. It sounded for all the world as if people well concealed within the house were still making a stand.

Ironically, Shark's idea of torching the house saved the lives of those within. Burning the building held back the Shark forces, masked the escape, and even burned the ropes so that no immediate trace of their departure remained.

And so it was that while those with Captain Midnight stole away, Fury Shark was able to tell her father triumphantly that his nemesis no longer existed.

In the radio dramatization of the adventure, Ivan Shark was supposed to have led the attack on the Donovan home. Actually, the situation since his raid had been thwarted was so delicate that he was effectively shackled to his Midwest headquarters. Some of the works attributed to him were actually performed by proxy, usually by his daughter. Had Shark been leading the attack, he would have stationed men at the base of the cliff as a precaution against the very sort of long shot gamble that enabled Captain Midnight and companions to escape. While his daughter was extraordinary, she was never the equal of her father.

The escapees found shelter in a cabin on the lakeshore some distance away from the scene of the action. No further problems were encountered from Shark's forces.

Some weeks later, Shark learned that Captain Midnight still lived — one of his agents recognized him. Although angered by the news, he fell back on his Oriental-tinged philosophy of life. He hadn't seen Midnight die, and subordinates, even his own daughter, couldn't be expected to be totally reliable. But knowing Captain Midnight was on the scene warned him to be on his guard.

As mentioned, Shark had recently negotiated with Axis representatives. Part of the agreement involved sabotage.

While the United States was neutral, it was developing a formidable war capacity, especially in aircraft technology and production. Certain items under development could spell the difference between defeat and victory if the United States were to enter the war.

As Ivan Shark was organizing and deploying his forces, Captain Midnight was at a secret base near Chicago. He was conferring with Major

Barry Steele, who had come out of retirement as a special member of Army Intelligence. Steele received reports of increased sabotage to the Aerial Instrument Company's main facility in Grant City. On the basis of the work, the Secret Squadron leader noted that it bore the earmarks of a Shark operation.

While they were conferring, a twin-engine, orange and black aircraft overflew the field. Chuck Ramsay spotted it as it was approaching and raced to where Captain Midnight stood. The two of them studied it, and Midnight agreed with his ward's suggestion that it appeared to be an aircraft Gardo frequently flew.

It was a perfect opportunity to capture one of Shark's top agents. Captain Midnight and Chuck sprinted toward an aircraft and, after a quick preflight, took off after Gardo.

Gardo put up a fight but was outclassed; he landed the damaged aircraft in a field.

By the time Captain Midnight and Chuck landed, the trail was cold. It was traced to the highway, and someone must have picked him up, probably as a hitcher.

As he made his way back, Captain Midnight was far from satisfied. His dogfight with Gardo was certain to alert Shark and his forces that he was in the area.

The cloud had a silver lining. Captain Midnight knew that Gardo's presence at Grant City was no coincidence. He reasoned that Shark might be involved in the sabotage there.

Grant City had become important. Besides the manufacturing facilities of the Aerial Instrument Company, there were other factories, three flying schools, and a thriving airport, Burgess Field. The airline Steve Donovan worked for had a route through Grant City; and when Ma Donovan lost her home, she moved to a small house in the city's suburbs.

After careful evaluation of the reports of sabotage, Captain Midnight decided the work at Aerial Instrument Company would be worth investigating. With Ma Donovan in the area, he could take Chuck and Joyce with him — she could help look after them.

What to do with the youngsters wasn't an easy decision for Captain Midnight. Chuck, seventeen, was almost ready to take care of himself. The last move to avoid danger nearly resulted in death for all of them. The Secret Squadron leader was beginning to believe it would be better if Chuck could work near him.

Joyce was a tougher problem. She'd already experienced some of the hazards of a full-fledged Squadron field agent, and yet, she wasn't even sure of her own identity! Shunting her off to total strangers might further delay the return of her memory. Further, since some of Shark's agents must have

6. Pre-War Operations

seen her during the siege at the Donovan cottage, cutting her loose might put her in real danger.

However, since he already had an official ward, he judged it wouldn't make things more difficult if he had an "unofficial" one as well. Further, since Chuck had proven quite capable, he could help greatly in looking out for her. Therefore, it was up to her.

Joyce was presented with the options. She indicated that she would like to stay with Captain Midnight and Chuck. She didn't take much time to think it over. She was surrounded by friendly people who had already demonstrated that they cared what happened to her. Further, as was to be shown many times, she had a great love of adventure.

Thus it was that a swift aircraft, with Captain Midnight at the controls, and carrying Chuck and Joyce, headed for Grant City's Burgess Field.

As they approached the city, Captain Midnight's flight-trained eyes studied the topography. Not too far from the city he saw a region that could be converted to a Squadron base. Because of its location and its proximity to a heavy manufacturing facility, he decided it would be perfect for establishing a permanent site for Secret Squadron headquarters.

Major Steele agreed with Captain Midnight's idea and promised to set the necessary wheels in motion after they landed. The new base could support an airstrip that the natural contours of the land would hide from ground observers. The proximity to Grant City would aid in transporting equipment to the new base. The major considered it a good move.

Before they could even land, the air travelers had a graphic demonstration of the sabotage they were trying to oppose. Major Steele spotted it first.

An aircraft was in trouble. Pointing to a new-looking plane slightly above and to one side of them, Steele observed that the pilot seemed to be experiencing some kind of difficulty. The wings were rocking and the nose was a bit high. Captain Midnight's experience indicated that the pilot would be unable to regain full control.

And so it turned out. The airplane stalled almost vertically and went into an inverted spin. The pilot bailed out. The plane smashed into a field as the pilot drifted to the ground.

Upon landing, Captain Midnight's party went to where a crowd has gathered around the pilot who had "hit the silk." Major Steele recognized the man as Jack Conway, an old friend who'd left the Army to become a test pilot for the Aerial Instrument Company.

Conway, bitter, told Steele and his friends that this was the last straw. He was quitting Aerial Instrument Company as of then. It was one of the most depressing examples of shattered morale that Midnight and Steele had ever seen.

From the story Conway related, it was evident that the plane had been sabotaged. Captain Midnight realized that his investigations couldn't begin a minute too soon. Yet equally, neither he nor Major Steele wanted too many to know of the Secret Squadron at that time.

While the name of his organization was generally unknown to the public, the name "Captain Midnight" was famous within elite aviation circles. If he conducted the investigation under that name, or even as Charles (or "Red") Albright, enemy agents would pick up his presence fairly quickly.

The only practical option was to work undercover. He would be an aviator. Since Conway and another pilot quit, it would be easy to reach the most important areas of the company by being a new test pilot.

His cover identity was "Mr. Lambert." Major Steele's position as liaison from Washington enabled "Lambert" to get the job with a minimum of red tape. The Secret Squadron created documents that showed that he was flight qualified for the job.

It was arranged that Captain Midnight would act as pilot for a "flying laboratory"—an aircraft used to test experimental instruments and systems. It was being used to conduct a series of tests on an ultra-secret bombsight. The aircraft was a DC-3. These normally carried a crew of two pilots and, for special V.I.P. tours, it occasionally included a hostess.

Steele suggested that Chuck Ramsay be the co-pilot. Although only seventeen, Chuck earned a license to handle multi-engine air transports. He'd already proven himself to be a superior pilot. He'd already been checked out on DC-3s, so Midnight agreed.

If she was willing, Joyce could get the job as hostess for the V.I.P. flights. It would give her a good excuse for spending time at the airport and Aerial Instrument Company. Chuck and Captain Midnight could keep watch over her. Nobody would suspect the pert and outgoing Joyce, suitably disguised, of playing a deeper game. And her very interaction with Captain Midnight and Chuck would help convince others that they were only what they seemed. She might even overhear useful information.

It was arranged for Joyce to take a secret crash course on how to be a stewardess, since she had to play the part to perfection. Her association with Captain Midnight and Chuck Ramsay had made her thoroughly capable of flying an airplane, though she had no license then, but the qualifications for stewardesses were quite different.

As Joyce was undergoing her training, Captain Midnight began his investigation. As "Mr. Lambert," he and Steele were introduced to Lawrence Marshall, the top management representative of Aerial Instrument Company's Grant City operations. After introductions, Major Steele asked how production was going.

Marshall indicated that conditions had deteriorated throughout the

6. Pre-War Operations 43

The Douglas DC-3 was perhaps the single most versatile aircraft in the history of aviation. It was used at the Aerial Instrument Company as a Flying Laboratory for, among other things, checking certain aspects of the bombsight they were developing. (Photograph: *McDonnell Douglas*.)

manufacturing facilities. Automatic-pilot quality had slipped so badly that a government inspector had "red tagged" nearly 100 units for defective parts.

When Steele asked him about the safety of the bombsight plans, Marshall glanced briefly at the new pilot. The major assured him that he could speak in "Mr. Lambert's" presence. It was then that Marshall realized the newcomer was more than just a test pilot.

Even as Captain Midnight and Major Steele were conferring in Marshall's office, Ivan Shark was receiving word that "Mr. Lambert" had arrived; infiltration was that widespread. Although Marshall was confident that the bombsight plans were completely secure, Shark had already set wheels in motion to obtain copies of those plans.

In short order, Chuck and Joyce became familiar figures at both Burgess Field and the Aerial Instrument Company's facilities. At the field and in Grant City they'd seen suspicious activities, but nothing concrete. There seemed to be a growing tension in the air.

Captain Midnight as Lambert tried to take a routine familiarization ride in the Flying Laboratory, and to introduce himself to the facility manager,

Eric Jenkins. Entering the man's office, he was confronted by someone who pointed a pistol at him. The person covering him was John Littman, who accused him of being a spy.

Captain Midnight was no stranger to hand-to-hand fighting and, with a few quick moves, disarmed and subdued the man. He discovered Jenkins trussed up in a back room. Clearly, Littman was working for the enemy. He started to the hangers on a run.

Chuck had gone directly to the hangars to check over a second, smaller aircraft that also had a bombsight installed. It was used as an alternate "platform" for certain tests. Chuck was to check it over for evidence of sabotage. However, because of his youth, a guard delayed him while verifying his identification.

The cough of a starting engine alerted Chuck. He asked the guard what was going on, and was told that Mr. Lambert had entered the hangar a few minutes previously, saying he was taking the smaller airplane out for a short flight. Alarmed, Chuck managed to convince the guard that Lambert was still in Jenkins' office. Both raced toward the aircraft.

The plane started to taxi, rolling past them. Chuck ran after it and caught the tail section. He jammed the rudder, even as the aircraft started to pick up speed. This action caused it to swerve into a hangar, wrecking it past flyability. As the pilot tried to get away, Captain Midnight and several guards arrived and caught him.

Word of the attempted bombsight theft reached Ivan Shark within the hour. His operations were in a large underground headquarters close to the city, a remnant of the Prohibition days. Fang entered with the report, handing it to Shark while mentioning that Borgmann was waiting to see him. Shark instructed Fang to admit the agent in five minutes.

The Axis agent was highly irritated because he'd just received word that his attempt to steal the bombsight had failed. Shark regarded the agent. He reminded Borgmann that coordinating activities was the only efficient way to run a combined operation.

The master criminal pushed a button on his desk and instructed Fury to come to his office. When she arrived, she had a small package. Without a word, she handed it to Borgmann.

The Axis agent opened it and was astonished to discover the package contained plans for the bombsight. Shark explained that while Borgmann tried to pull a grandstand stunt, he'd been efficiently gathering sections of the bombsight plans. He lacked only one portion — roughly 16 percent of the whole — to have a complete set. Almost too politely, the master criminal suggested that if Borgmann wouldn't be too impatient, the complete plans would be in the hands of his backers within two weeks.

Once he was alone again, Shark scrutinized the report. He became

6. Pre-War Operations

convinced that the youth who aborted the efforts of Borgmann's hireling was Chuck Ramsay. He also knew that whenever Chuck Ramsay was around, Captain Midnight was likely to be there too.

Shortly thereafter, Captain Midnight received unpleasant news. Marshall discovered that his safe had been tampered with. He'd opened the safe that contained the bombsight plans and noticed that one subset was missing. He'd gone to his chief of security. When he got back, the missing subset had been returned. Marshall added that while officially "Lambert" was a test pilot, the manager thought he should know.

Midnight agreed. It was obvious that the only reason to take *and return* sections of the bombsight plans was to photograph them. What was most worrisome, it was impossible to determine just how many subsets had already been "borrowed." Although security had been tightened further, there was no assurance that all the plans hadn't already been copied.

The other news was even more disturbing. The Squadron base near San Diego had stopped transmitting its regular messages.

The mysterious silence had top priority. Captain Midnight decided to investigate it himself. So he applied for a "short vacation," which, through Marshall, he got.

Shortly before his departure, Midnight received a pleasant surprise. Chuck Ramsay ran into an old and dear friend at Burgess Field, Ichabod Mudd. He'd helped them when Captain Midnight was still a private citizen. Together they'd tangled with Ivan Shark when he'd been directing activities that preyed on private gold mines.

Mudd had proven to be an incredibly adept mechanic, and was Albright's personal mechanic until circumstances separated them. A chance remark made by a friend of Steve Donovan's enabled Mudd to trace Chuck to Burgess Field. He hoped to find Albright through him.

Captain Midnight came to Burgess Field and greeted Mudd warmly. He was delighted when Mudd indicated he wanted his "old job" back. Midnight accepted instantly and had him brought to Secret Squadron headquarters. Time would show just how important that "job application" would be.

While Ichabod Mudd was being processed as a Secret Squadron candidate, Captain Midnight flew to the San Diego area, taking Chuck and Joyce with him. It was dusk as he approached Secret Squadron Base 7. Following established routine, he blinked his navigation lights in a certain sequence; the response from the ground was incorrect. Captain Midnight decided that he'd better be cautious about approaching the base. He flew off and landed elsewhere.

The next morning, the three of them approached the Squadron base with caution. This proved unnecessary. The personnel were there, tied and helpless, and their attackers were gone.

Captain Midnight freed them and, after establishing his identity, questioned them. The attackers caught them off guard by a bold night strike two days previously. It took a little time to reconstruct how they'd managed to evade the base's defenses — and plan how to defend against such an attack in the future.

A quick check of the security safe confirmed Captain Midnight's worst fears. The *Secret Squadron Code Book* had been stolen. And that could only be useful to an enemy.

Midnight immediately alerted the Squadron to switch to an emergency cipher based on a simple formula. He realized that the cipher was a stopgap measure, and that something better had to be developed — quickly. He brooded about it all the way back to Grant City.

Captain Midnight's concerns were well founded. The raid on Base 7 was made by Ivan Shark's agents. When Shark's operatives intercepted radio transmissions in code, he recruited an expert cryptanalyst (a codebreaker) to try to unravel their messages. By the degree of activity of the signals, even without knowing their content, Shark became convinced that the messages involved that new organization that Captain Midnight was connected with.

The cryptanalyst had been making only slow headway with the messages because of their nature. The codebreaker informed Shark that messages from code books were very difficult and time-consuming to solve.

Shark decided to launch a raid to steal the book or books. It was made possible by the heavy traffic between Base 7 and Headquarters. Because it didn't have the full resources of Headquarters, the new base could be located through triangulation.

As soon as Shark received the book, the Squadron had shifted to the emergency cipher. The only practical effect was that Shark learned that the opposing organization was the Secret Squadron. But he also realized that the speed with which the new method of encrypting messages was implemented indicated that it had to be something his cryptanalyst could crack fairly quickly.

Reports from Shark's agents at the Aerial Instrument Company provided Shark with enough information about the new test pilot, Lambert, that Shark suspected that he might be his old nemesis. Correlating his actions with the attack on the Secret Squadron base and its aftermath was particularly telling: The emergency "code" came into effect within three days of Lambert's sudden departure. And he took the youngsters with him — including the one Shark had tentatively identified as Chuck Ramsay. Shark didn't know who the girl was, and didn't care. She was obviously connected to the Secret Squadron. Shark decided that on or about the time he received the final plans for the bombsight, Midnight and those with him should be destroyed — and, most fittingly, in an airplane crash.

6. Pre-War Operations

Captain Midnight's concern over message security continued to nag him after he returned to his headquarters. He'd completed his mission rapidly, and there were several days left in his vacation period. He used them to run the Squadron, but his big concern was still codes and their ilk.

It was clear that an expert cryptanalyst could crack the emergency cipher in a few weeks at most. The new cipher had one decided advantage though: It was easily constructed in the field by an agent. All that was needed was a pencil and paper. What would be ideal would be some means that would enable field agents to construct a number of ciphers quickly and easily.

He was "thinking out loud" about these matters in the presence of Chuck Ramsay one day. Chuck observed that what Captain Midnight wanted sounded like a self-contained gadget for encoding and decoding messages. For field agent use, it should be small so that it could be hidden easily or, if necessary, discarded with a minimum chance of being found.

Captain Midnight was pleased with the concept. He brought the problem to Ichabod Mudd, who had been assigned as Chief Mechanic, since it clearly concerned some sort of mechanical assembly. He outlined the problem and Chuck's suggestions. Mudd fancied himself something of an amateur expert on codes, and agreed to tackle the problem.

It is to the eternal credit of Ichabod Mudd that halfway through his development of the "gadget" he realized he *was* an amateur. He contacted Major Steele and requested that he be allowed to confer with experts. His request was granted, and development resumed.

Captain Midnight returned to the Aerial Instrument Company. He made his way to Marshall's office, where he revealed his actual identity. He didn't reveal the existence of the Secret Squadron. Marshall had heard of him, and was relieved that someone with a reputation as a troubleshooter had been sent. He assumed that Midnight would continue as a test pilot.

Captain Midnight agreed to do so for a short time. A critical test was upcoming, in which the bombsight was coupled to an autopilot. A few observers, each with a different area of expertise, would be along for the flight. They'd form an *ad hoc* team to determine the effectiveness of the arrangement. One of the observers would be Major Steele.

Midnight realized that this sort of V.I.P. flight would be likely to draw trouble. "Make sure that as few people as possible learn of this flight," he said. Marshall agreed.

Lawrence Marshall didn't realize how thoroughly his staff had been penetrated by agents. Within twelve hours of the new flight schedule being finalized, a dossier on each visiting official was on Shark's desk. One of the observers, Major Crane, bore a fair resemblance to a Shark agent named Gleason. With a little work, Gleason could be made into a perfect double.

With the addition of counterfeit documents, Gleason would be in a position to steal a functional bombsight.

Despite his bold plan, Shark was canny enough to continue his efforts to steal the remaining folder of bombsight plans. He had someone who could be blackmailed. He'd found a woman, an employee for many years, who actually was an illegal alien. His people convinced her that because of existing war jitters, if her status were discovered, she'd be deported immediately. (She was actually safe, but Shark's agents were convincing.)

Though not official members of the Secret Squadron, both Chuck and Joyce were privy to the emergency cipher. Chuck had use of Squadron planes. Routinely, Chuck took Joyce on patrol flights.

On one such flight, Joyce spotted a familiar-looking airplane. A quick pass revealed that Gardo was piloting it. He spotted them, and they gave chase. Gardo flew into some clouds and evaded them. Although it was a small incident, it had serious repercussions.

Chuck had Joyce construct a coded message telling of the incident. She sent it as they continued the patrol.

As with previous messages, this one was intercepted by Shark's people. However, Shark's cryptanalyst, Brubaker, managed to crack the cipher. The message, sent as "NORAXAYQIEJKIRPFFPOZLXIZZRHRPBDOLRIQFF-ZLAOALKQRQKBEZO," was the first active message to be decrypted.

Brubaker showed the deciphered message to Shark, which read, "Pursued Gardo but lost him in clouds. Radio instructions at once. Chuck R." Brubaker noted that the message was encrypted as a railfence cipher that had been made more difficult by being superenciphered with a Caesar substitution. Shark was less interested in the mechanics involved than in the message content.

Shark decided to turn the tables on his foes. He believed that Chuck Ramsay could provide a good way to locate Captain Midnight. From previous messages that Brubaker deciphered once he cracked the code, Shark determined that the leader of the Secret Squadron signed his messages "SSwn." Shark had no doubt that SS-1 was Captain Midnight. So he had Brubaker send back a message saying, "Chuck R. Return to SS Headquarters at once. SSwn." Gardo or another aircraft could follow the lad and find the location of the headquarters. Shark ordered another aircraft aloft.

However, interception is a two-edged sword. A startled radioman at Headquarters brought Captain Midnight a copy of Shark's message. It was what Midnight feared: The emergency cipher had been cracked.

Rushing to the radio room, Captain Midnight called Chuck, telling him the message he just received was false. Further, since he shouldn't reveal sensitive information, he should use his own judgment on where to land.

6. Pre-War Operations

(Chuck landed at Burgess Field; the plane didn't have any special markings, so it blended in with other air traffic.) Then the Secret Squadron leader instructed couriers to fly to Squadron bases to bring back the base commanders. A new "code" would be issued.

After all the base commanders had been assembled, Captain Midnight introduced several changes, both in communications and Squadron organization. First was the new "coding" device — a badge called the Code-O-Graph. A cipher disk, the Code-O-Graph was a key element in the new code scheme (detailed in Appendix 3). In addition to its cryptological function, the badge was a form of identification, though it was to be worn openly only within Squadron bases and shown only to other Squadron members or commanders of military bases. A new and different emergency cipher was also detailed.

The first of the Secret Squadron Code-O-Graphs. Undated, this unit not only served as an identifier, but provided a secure means of communication for agents in the field. (Photograph: *Stephen Kallis, Jr.*)

Also, the Secret Squadron was reorganized and extended. With war deepening in Europe and the Far East, the Squadron required backup. A new category of member was created: the General Reserve. Unlike the active field agents and base commands, the General Reserve would be basically unstructured, but could be called up in emergencies.

Finally, Captain Midnight took pleasure in announcing the appointment of both Chuck Ramsay and Joyce as active Squadron members. As he put it later, "I'd tried to discourage Chuck's membership at first, but he faced as many dangers as any other agent, including myself. So I felt he should have the honor as well as the hardships."

As for Joyce, she had a natural aptitude for the work, a love of adventure, and had more than once expressed interest in joining the Squadron. "How could we honestly keep her out?" Midnight said some years later. "At the time, we were the only family she had."

Because of their distinguished "unofficial" services to the Squadron,

Chuck was assigned the designation SS-2; Joyce, SS-3. Besides being the two youngest active agents in the Squadron, they had the only SS designations besides Captain Midnight's below 10. (Ichabod Mudd was unofficially known as "SS-4," but his official title was Chief Mechanic; "SS" designations were reserved for active agents).

Ivan Shark's forces were not idle. Major Crane was intercepted and, in Fury Shark's words, "dealt with." The disguised Gleason, carrying documents that identified him as Crane, arrived at Burgess Field and toured the Aerial Instrument Company.

The other officials arrived. They and Gleason boarded the Flying Laboratory. A Shark agent working as an Aerial Instrument engineer also boarded. The engineer had a concealed weapon; Gleason openly wore one as part of his uniform.

Besides Captain Midnight (still "Lambert"), Chuck, Joyce, and Kelly were aboard. The Flying Laboratory had been outfitted as a bomber so that the bombsight could be demonstrated with small simulated bombs.

After a successful run at low level, Gleason made his move. He surreptitiously locked the pilot's compartment. Then he and the Shark agent posing as an engineer drew their weapons and, covering everybody outside the pilot's compartment, forced the other engineers to don parachutes and jump. He advanced on Kelly, who was one of the few left. Gleason's assistant suggested that he be made to jump — but without a parachute. The false major agreed with him.

A few moments previously, Captain Midnight received a message in the new cipher. It was so short it wasn't superenciphered. Shortly after the Flying Laboratory's takeoff, the real Major Crane's body had been found. Not wanting to tip their hand prematurely, Headquarters sent up a simple message: "CRANE IS SPY."

Everything happened at once. Placing the aircraft on autopilot, Midnight helped force open the door just as the two spies made a grab for Kelly. Joyce screamed to create a diversion even as she reached for something to use as a weapon.

In the brief hesitation resulting from Joyce's scream, the Shark agents lost the few seconds they needed. Then Kelly, Captain Midnight, and Chuck all sprang into action at once. The spies were quickly subdued.

Under questioning, Gleason indicated that Shark had succeeded in getting the plans for the bombsight. He was actually guessing, but his guess was correct.

Shark had been forced to work with haste. A special aircraft, piloted by an Axis courier, was waiting for the plans. On microfilm, the plans were to be flown to a yacht lying off the Bahamas. Even as Gleason was telling this to the Secret Squadron agents, the courier aircraft took off.

6. Pre-War Operations

Gleason knew the rendezvous point with the yacht. He had a chart, printed on silk, in case he'd been able to gain control of the Flying Laboratory. If he had, he would have flown to the rendezvous to receive a bonus by delivering the actual bombsight.

A delaying plan was developed. Chuck was to fly the Flying Laboratory to the rendezvous point, with Joyce acting as unofficial co-pilot (she still had no license, but could handle the plane), accompanied by Kelly. Captain Midnight and his prisoner were to bail out near a Federal installation along the route. He would requisition a fast fighter plane there. He would then race to the rendezvous point, leading enough forces to intercept the yacht.

Although the plan was good, the master of the yacht was suspicious. The Flying Laboratory made exceptional time with respect to the slow amphibious aircraft the courier used. The amphibian landed only a short time previously. The signalman on the yacht flashed a special recognition sign. When the Flying Laboratory didn't respond correctly, guns were uncovered; these began to fire (ineffectually) at the circling aircraft.

Those onboard the yacht realized that, because it was out of range, the Flying Laboratory could "orbit" the boat for some time. The aircraft could keep track of the yacht's position and help lead reinforcements to the location. A Shark agent aboard the yacht radioed for aircraft to shoot down the Laboratory or, at the very least, chase it away.

Captain Midnight turned Gleason over to Federal authorities. He obtained a fast fighter. As soon as he was airborne, he directed a U.S. Navy destroyer to proceed to the rendezvous point. Shortly thereafter, Squadron aircraft joined up with his plane, and the whole Squadron formation raced toward the Bahamas.

A short air engagement ended it. Outclassed, the harassing Shark aircraft broke off; after a halfhearted attempt to engage, they fled. The fighters "herded" the yacht in the direction of the destroyer, and that was that.

The search of the yacht recovered the film. The Axis agents were arrested on a technicality and — very unofficially — turned over to the British, with whom they were already at war.

But Captain Midnight was far from satisfied. Although Chuck remarked that the arrival of the Squadron had all the flavor of the last-minute arrival of the Cavalry in a B-grade Western movie, Midnight didn't even crack a smile. The plans were recovered, but the mastermind behind the events was still at large. Shark could be expected to do anything.

There have been many things said about Ivan Shark, but no one ever denied that he had a first-class mind. He was far from impotent, even if he lost a round to his old foe.

Shark was conscious of the threat his old enemy posed, particularly since his foe headed an organization that had thwarted more than one of his plans. He decided to eliminate Captain Midnight and neutralize the Secret Squadron.

Various attempts to eliminate Captain Midnight in the field had failed. Shark decided to concentrate on the Squadron. He deduced that Squadron Headquarters were not too far from Grant City. Spotters traced the flights of many aircraft to and from a nearby valley. Shark believed that the valley was the location of Secret Squadron Headquarters.

While Shark's people were delivering the microfilmed plans to the Axis courier, Shark began his move against the Squadron. By the time Captain Midnight had his fighter refueled, Shark's forces had Headquarters completely surrounded.

An encrypted message was sent to Captain Midnight, informing him of the basic situation. He raced back, leaving the Flying Laboratory to return at its own pace. Shark hadn't yet launched his attack when he "greased in" a landing on the Headquarters' runway.

A battle erupted, but the Squadron forces beat back all attempts to invade the stronghold. A carefully initiated feint by the Secret Squadron resulted in the discovery of a weak spot in Shark's forces, prompting a decisive counterattack. A few key agents were caught by Squadron forces, and the others scattered.

Captain Midnight decided the best strategy would be a counter against Shark's stronghold. Fortunately, the Secret Squadron had an ace to play. They'd discovered the location of Shark's lair. Armed with the information, the Squadron launched a raid.

Shark's headquarters in Grant City were underground, for the most part. Shark's agents had found a small underground hideaway from Prohibition days. After setting up a small operation, they discovered that a back wall sounded hollow. The agents discovered that behind the wall was a complex of underground tunnels. The tunnels (and associated chambers), forgotten over time, were converted into a labyrinthine base with numerous secret exits and entrances.

The attack on Shark's headquarters was no picnic. Though Shark's agents were mercenaries, they were tough fighters. Further, they had no illusions about what would happen to them if they were caught. So it took a great deal of effort, and some wounded, to reach the innermost sanctum.

Even as the raiding parties were forming, Shark, Fury, and Fang had departed aboard one of Shark's powerful four-engine amphibians. Both Shark and his daughter could fly aircraft.

Ironically, Shark's flight had little to do with escaping the Secret Squadron; the raid just accelerated his schedule a little. He'd proven his value to his Axis contacts by obtaining the bombsight plans. It wasn't Shark's

6. Pre-War Operations

fault that Borgmann bungled his part of the affair. Shark, working for the Axis agenda, had merely departed when the raid started.

Having decided that Shark was a valuable resource, extra funds and equipment were placed at his disposal. These included some ships, a nearly finished base, and easily accessible monetary sources. It was toward the base, which was in its last phase of completion, that Shark and his inner circle were headed — on a scheduled inspection trip.

Upon arrival, Shark and his party inspected the new base and were delighted. The base was situated on an island in the Caribbean; most of the base was concealed beneath the surface. It had a vast pen area for submarines to dock, quartering space for many agents, and an elaborate radio room with wideband sending and monitoring equipment.

Shark was given full control of the base. One of the conditions for him receiving the base, however, was Shark's agreement to smuggle Axis agents into the United States from time to time. The master criminal was perfectly happy to do so, since the Axis agents wouldn't know the location of the base (a stipulation of the agreement), and it would put the Axis further into his debt.

As the battle at Shark's Grant City headquarters continued, it became clear that the Squadron had the advantage. One of the senior Shark agents radioed for instructions. Fury Shark took the message en route to the Caribbean base. She responded, "Execute Plan E."

"Plan E" called for senior staff members to gather in a certain room. If it appeared that a raid would succeed, the senior agents should try to escape via a hidden passageway. They were to lay low until contacted. They should look for certain advertisements in the "personals" section of the *Grant City Courier*.

Having bottled up the enemy agents, Squadron operatives flooded the headquarters with tear gas, forcing most of the base personnel to surrender. Captain Midnight led the forces to Shark's office, where they recovered Shark's records.

Major Steele was elated. With the majority of the base personnel captured and many of his records confiscated, the master criminal seemed to be on the run. But Captain Midnight was cautious.

"Let's not get too confident," the Secret Squadron leader said. "It's true we made a clean sweep of the base — but is this his only base? As long as Ivan Shark is on the loose, we can't afford to relax one bit."

When the Squadron examined Shark's records thoroughly, it became clear that they dealt only with Grant City matters.

The Secret Squadron leader suggested they launch a nationwide dragnet for Ivan Shark. This would require a public announcement of the Secret Squadron, but this didn't bother Captain Midnight. "Our principal enemies have known who we were since our code book was stolen. So what's the harm if the public knows?" he said.

"What about the name?" someone asked. "If we go public, the Squadron won't be very 'secret,' will it?"

Captain Midnight pointed out that the Secret Service had a very good reputation without bothering about its name. "Our name is a good one, too. There's no reason to change it." So the Secret Squadron has retained its name to the present.

Agents on the lookout for Shark's amphibians spotted several in the Caribbean, suggesting to Captain Midnight that the master criminal might have a major base in the region. He decided to mount a personal expedition to try to locate it.

He took his regular crew of Joyce and Chuck, and added Ichabod Mudd. Both Chuck and Joyce were familiar with Shark's aircraft. Joyce, besides exhibiting a flair for flying, had extraordinary eyesight. Squadron medical personnel, checking her vision as part of a routine physical, discovered that it bordered on the superhuman — better than 20/10 for both eyes — the keenest eyes in the Squadron. Coupled with a natural ability to shoot any type of gun accurately, her vision made her a great asset. Captain Midnight's main reason for bringing her was that he thought she'd be the most likely to spot a Shark plane.

Mudd was brought along to effect any necessary repairs to the Squadron aircraft, should it become damaged. Midnight said more than once, "Ikky's the most important piece of survival gear we can bring on any mission."

The team used a fast four-place aircraft to reach a Squadron base near Jacksonville. There they transferred to a lower-speed, long-range, twin-engine amphibian. The following morning they departed, heading toward the Caribbean area where the Shark planes had been spotted. Rough projection backwards from the Shark planes' flight paths indicated a small region, trapezoidal in shape, which was the most likely area for the base.

When they reached the region, Captain Midnight and Chuck took turns at the controls, flying the amphibian in a standard search pattern. As they continued, the weather started to look ominous.

Just as they spotted a small island in a likely position, the weather degenerated into a tropical storm. The island they'd just spotted couldn't be used as a shelter, since there was a distinct possibility it was a Shark base. They would have to fly to some place where they would feel secure. This forced them to fly into the storm.

"I wasn't too pleased at the prospect," Midnight recalled many years later, "but it was a matter of fuel and available friendly locations. After all, the world was at war. And riding out a storm on the surface is hardly the

6. Pre-War Operations

best procedure for amphibian aircraft, so we had little choice." They landed at Trinidad.

The Squadron members rested. Then, while Mudd inspected and arranged for refueling of the amphibian, Captain Midnight made some inquiries of a British official, a friend from World War I (and a man who, because of the peculiar nature of Albright's mission, knew him *only* as Captain Midnight). This official, Captain Bostwick of the Royal Navy, had become aware of various activities in the Caribbean. He heard speculation that the base of the amphibians in question was located somewhere along the South American coast.

Captain Midnight realized that a Caribbean base didn't preclude a second base on the South American continent. In fact, a South American base would probably be easier to find.

Thus it was that when the amphibian took off, it climbed to near its service ceiling and headed South. Shortly after reaching altitude, Kelly radioed information that at least one Shark amphibian was reported to be heading in a great-circle route that was projected to end in—or over—South America. Captain Midnight, with the information supplied by Captain Bostwick, decided to see whether he could spot, then trail, the Shark plane.

It was through Joyce's phenomenal eyesight that the quarry was first spotted. The others saw it a few moments later, and Midnight turned his craft to fly a parallel course until he could be certain of the identification.

When he was assured that it was a Shark aircraft, Captain Midnight followed it through the skies above the Caribbean and on over the interior of South America. A stratiform cloud layer spread like a white blanket beneath the two aircraft, blotting out the features of the ground below.

With startling suddenness, the Shark plane dived into the cloud. Captain Midnight was certain that the other aircraft hadn't detected his presence, and deduced that somewhere below the clouds was Shark's South American base.

To follow the aircraft would be foolhardy, to say the least. Instead, he opted to head for an airfield in British Guyana so that he could search again when the weather conditions improved.

Then trouble struck. The engines quit: first one, then the other. Mudd later traced the malfunction to fuel contamination, but it wasn't immediately obvious. However, it forced a deadstick landing.

When the aircraft broke out of the clouds, directly beneath them were trees that extended in all directions. Then Joyce spotted a lake at the nine o'clock position. Captain Midnight banked the amphibian and set it to glide toward the lake. Fortunately, he had enough altitude; he landed on the lake, which, unfortunately, was just a bit too small. The aircraft sustained minor damage. To fly again, it required repair, clean fuel, and a larger lake to take off from.

Not only was his aircraft downed, but in his geographic position he was unable to raise Kelly on the radio. He set up a transmission schedule, calling once every few days to conserve what electricity was in his batteries.

Although Captain Midnight's transmissions didn't reach Kelly, one of Ivan Shark's radiomen got them. They couldn't decipher the message, but they were able to identify the initial message of transmission as coming from "SS-1." The enciphered message was long enough to get a directional fix on it. From this information Shark was able to deduce that his archenemy was in the jungle, doubtless downed. He decided to send search aircraft to ferret out the downed plane.

Fortunately, as Mudd was completing what he needed to make the aircraft flyable, the party discovered an inlet on the lake, invisible while they were airborne, that formed a natural canal to a second lake that had been beyond the glide range of the unpowered amphibian. This second lake was large enough for the amphibian to take off. By the time Shark's planes located their old position, they were ready to take off from the new one.

Shortly before they did, two things took place. First, friendly natives discovered an unconscious white man. They brought him to the Secret Squadron party, and Midnight soon learned that the man had been a prisoner of Shark's forces.

The man was a British Intelligence agent named Hall. He'd been investigating the area when he was captured. During their interrogation, Shark's men tried to break his morale by letting him know of some of their organization's accomplishments. One of the things they told him was that Shark had contracted to bomb the Panama Canal.

If Shark launched an attack on the Canal, Midnight realized, it wouldn't be grounds for war. Shark was not diplomatically affiliated with any country. Without proof of collusion, there could be no official retaliation against any country. However, such a move would be highly advantageous to the Axis. A successful attack could ruin the locks, thus paralyzing a significant portion of Western Hemisphere defense. It became important to get to a Squadron base as soon as possible.

Secret Squadron radiomen were able to detect faint radio signals on a frequency generally used by Captain Midnight. However, reception had been so poor that they had been unable to extract the message. One of the technicians indicated that taking a more powerful transceiver to a better position would enable the Squadron to reestablish contact with their leader.

Agent Kelly flew with an appropriate transceiver to Puerto Rico. Once there, he was able to contact Captain Midnight. The Secret Squadron

6. Pre-War Operations

leader exchanged information briefly (because he had to conserve battery power) but primed Kelly about what might have to be done to defend the Canal.

Captain Midnight's amphibian became airborne just in the nick of time. Shark's forces, as noted, had located his old location via triangulation. They were able to determine by air that the Squadron amphibian wasn't there; and they couldn't see the inlet from their perspective. There were several overflights of the old lake, but it was obviously empty.

When Kelly reestablished communications, the Shark forces were able to determine the new location. Ivan Shark ordered his entire air fleet, including the bombers, to destroy his old enemy. But by the time they got to the location, the Squadron amphibian was gone. Not able to see the campsite from the air, the Shark forces made pass after pass over the site, raining bombs down on uninhabited jungle.

After they became airborne, Ichabod Mudd reported he'd not been able to salvage much fuel in his straining operations; they had less than an hour's fuel remaining. They couldn't make it to a friendly base or neutral airport, yet it would be disastrous to be forced down in the jungle again by fuel starvation. They wouldn't be so lucky next time.

Captain Midnight's mind raced, and he came up with a bold plan. Banking on the psychology of the international criminal — and intercepting some radio chatter — he gambled that there would be nobody of importance left at Shark's South American base. He located it easily and landed there!

The Squadron amphibian looked enough like a Shark plane to the guards that they assumed it was just an early returnee. This assumption was reinforced by the aircraft taxiing up to the hangar area.

Ichabod Mudd, grease-covered and wearing stained coveralls, looked from a distance like any other mechanic. He hopped out and filled the amphibian's tanks from Shark's store of aviation fuel. Chuck nervously, though inconspicuously, manned the amphibian's machine gun.

They got away with it. With tanks topped off, the amphibian taxied to the runway and took off.

However, just as they were climbing out, another aircraft, a bonafide Shark plane with engine trouble, flew into the pattern and landed. Because it had engine trouble, it couldn't give chase. As soon as the pilot learned what had been done, he got on the radio.

The airwaves became filled with messages. Captain Midnight called Kelly, giving him the location of the base he just left and instructing him to pass the information to the appropriate officials (Midnight determined the base was in Brazil). Meanwhile, Shark conferred with the pilot and learned of Captain Midnight's trick. Shark's old enemy had once faced him in

Mexico and had stolen fuel from him back then; the repeat was an insult not to be borne.

Shark was airborne during the exchange, heading toward his South American base. He learned that the Squadron amphibian was fairly close to his location, and turned to engage Captain Midnight. He called his fighters in case he needed reinforcement. And as he was doing that, Kelly called the Brazilian air arm.

Shark's plane was close to the Squadron amphibian; his fighters weren't. He spied his quarry about the same time Captain Midnight spotted his aircraft. The two amphibians waltzed around in a slow-motion version of a dogfight. Although Shark tried every form of trickery to shoot down his foe, he didn't prevail. He was a pilot, but not even in Gardo's class, to say nothing of Captain Midnight's. Thus, Shark's plane went down in flames.

As it fell, those with Midnight said the equivalent of "good riddance." Captain Midnight pointed out that both he and Shark had escaped many times from what appeared to be deathtraps. "We may have seen the last of him," he said, "but I doubt it."

As Shark's plane went down toward the jungle, trailing smoke, Joyce called out that other aircraft were approaching. She identified them as Shark aircraft.

Almost as soon as the Shark force was sighted, Joyce spotted more aircraft. The newcomers were units of the Brazilian air arm, and their very presence caused the Shark planes to scatter.

The Brazilians appropriated the airfield, including the bombers. This effectively ended Shark's planned air raid on the Canal.

Although it appeared that Shark's Caribbean activities had been stymied, Captain Midnight was still concerned about the mysterious island they'd spotted. The island was at the focus of several extrapolated paths of Shark aircraft. It was worth investigating.

Fury Shark was in charge. She'd heard enough of the radio exchange to realize her father was shot down. Perhaps he was dead, perhaps not. She might not have had the genius of her father, but she had a superior intellect and was easily qualified to head the organization in her father's absence, temporary or permanent.

Even as Captain Midnight and his companions were leaving the coastline of South America behind, a signal was being received at Ivan Shark's island base. The base was understaffed, as Shark had brought a large force with him to set up the Brazilian airfield. There was enough left to man a submarine, and the signal urgently required the dispatch of a submarine.

This left Fury Shark on a virtually deserted island. She only had a few guards left and was all too aware that the island base was highly vulnerable.

6. Pre-War Operations

Impatiently, she awaited the return of the submarine and the agents in Shark's air fleet who had been driven away by the Brazilians. She expected the airmen to straggle in over the next few days; meanwhile, she told her skeleton crew to be especially vigilant.

Captain Midnight's original intent was to bring the rescued Hall to Trinidad, but the strange island wasn't too far off his course. Since he had plenty of fuel, he thought it worthwhile to detour slightly.

The island still looked deserted, but Captain Midnight, Hall, and Chuck all spotted an odd-shaped object in the water below. They weren't sure, but it seemed to have the approximate outline of a submarine.

Since the object was moving away from the supposedly deserted island, Captain Midnight decided that he'd better inspect the island more closely. Spying a small, sheltered bay, he set the amphibian down on the surface so adroitly that he surprised Hall.

Realizing that as an intelligence agent, Hall could take care of himself, Captain Midnight allowed him to join the investigation. The Secret Squadron leader took Chuck with him to investigate the island's interior. Hall and Mudd were to explore along the shoreline. Joyce, who had a highly accurate and powerful rifle (along with the machine guns) and the sharpest eyesight of the five, remained behind to guard the amphibian.

The drone of an aircraft overhead caused Captain Midnight and Chuck to cut short their investigation. They raced back to the amphibian, which became airborne to trail the other aircraft. But the small plane seemed to sink out of sight after floating over a ridge down the center of the island. When the amphibian reached the spot, the smaller craft had disappeared completely.

Perplexed, the trio returned to the landing spot to retrieve Hall and Mudd. The two had disappeared. And after a long search, only Mudd was found.

He was in bad shape. Mudd was semiconscious, wounded in the head. He attempted to tell the others where he and Hall had been, but he couldn't. They cast around, but couldn't find a trace of the missing agent.

Because Mudd's condition was becoming serious, and because they'd exhausted the places to look for Hall, Captain Midnight reluctantly decided to rush his injured Chief Mechanic to a medical facility in Puerto Rico. He or other Squadron pilots would investigate the island again, soon. Mudd was a known casualty ... but of what?

Mudd was a casualty of the "shadow" crew of the Shark base. Fury Shark had ordered a small party to intercept the interlopers, capturing them if possible. Both Mudd and Hall had put up a good fight, but they were overwhelmed. Mudd was left for dead, and Hall was brought below the surface to the base.

With the base so understaffed and the armament of the amphibian an unknown quantity, Fury Shark was not ready to launch her pitifully small force against it. She wasn't in a position to prevent it from leaving.

Within hours of the time Captain Midnight's amphibian lifted off the smooth surface of the sheltering bay, a dark shadow swept through the water surrounding the island to an undersea entrance. It surfaced, and the crew poured out, followed by a grim but triumphant Ivan Shark.

Shark's escape was narrow. He and Fang had taken to parachutes when the aircraft was barely high enough for deployment.

Fortunately for the master criminal, he landed fairly close to a cache he'd established in the jungle. Included was an emergency radio transmitter. He ordered the dispatch of a small airplane to drop him a few special supplies, and for a submarine to pick him up.

The airplane that lured Captain Midnight's party to investigate was the messenger aircraft returning from dropping supplies to Shark. The search for Hall had consumed so much time that Captain Midnight was not long departed from the hospital where he'd taken Mudd when Ivan Shark resumed command of his island base.

Kelly was not alone when Captain Midnight met him in Puerto Rico. Major Steele was with him. The major explained that he was soon to go on a special mission to the Far East, and he wanted to confer about the Shark situation, as well as to brief the Secret Squadron leader on other possible trouble spots.

They went to Captain Midnight's hotel room, where the Secret Squadron leader briefed his superior on all that had happened and outlined a plan to rescue the British intelligence agent. As he was talking, something caught his eye and, still talking, he walked over to a lamp. He examined it and found a hidden microphone. The room was bugged!

Still talking so as not to arouse the suspicions of the eavesdroppers, Captain Midnight scribbled a quick note to Major Steele and passed it to him. Steele nodded, and shortly they found a pretext to leave the room. They went to a secure area and resumed their talk.

Because it was overheard, the rescue plan Captain Midnight had put forth would have to be abandoned. Doubtless, the information on that plan was already on its way back to Shark's forces. Since the island was a major Shark base, it would have to be neutralized.

The job wouldn't be easy. The base was obviously below the island's surface and could be quite formidable. If the shadow they saw was really a submarine, the base had docking facilities. This implied that the base was extensive and a very tough nut to crack.

Captain Midnight suggested that the best policy might be a war of nerves. There would be overflights, brief exploratory landings with air cover, and equivalent overt actions to keep Fury Shark, or whoever was in charge, off balance.

Major Steele reviewed the Squadron leader's overall plan and approved. Then he changed the subject to his forthcoming Far East mission. He reminded Midnight that the expansion of the Japanese empire into China did not bode well for that part of the world. He'd received word of some independent actions that could be furthering Japanese aims.

A Chinese general had contacted Steele through indirect means and indicated that he had information of interest to his government. With suitable preparations, Steele was to meet with this general somewhere in Free China. So he would be out of the picture for a while.

"We'll finish up with this Shark business, sir, then join you in China," Captain Midnight said.

"I hope your mission is short," Steele answered, "but I hope I'll be back from China before you've finished here."

In the absence of Major Steele, agent SS-11 (Kelly) was to act as temporary liaison between Captain Midnight and "Mr. Jones" in Washington.

Shortly, Steele was to fly to Washington. It would take him some time to make the required connections for his trip into China, but he would have to handle all the operations from the Capitol. "Although I'll be out of the direct chain for a while, I'll keep an ear to the ground," Steele promised. "Anything really important will be relayed to Kelly."

It was essential to determine who bugged the hotel room. Obviously, there was significant espionage activity on the island. "It would be worthwhile to set up a base on this island," the Secret Squadron leader said. Steele gave him a green light to do so.

A small but adequate Puerto Rican airstrip was located and purchased. A detachment of Squadron planes, mostly land craft, was sent quickly to form the nucleus of the new Squadron base. Since the existence of the Secret Squadron was public knowledge, there was no effort to conceal the base, even though its dealings were restricted to those with a need to know.

The first operation of the new base was to set up an aerial patrol around the island to try to prevent spies from leaving clandestinely. Security was subtly increased for travelers taking conventional means of transportation.

None of these activities seemed out of the ordinary for the average Puerto Rican citizen. War was raging in Europe, the high seas were patrolled by submarines, and, despite American "neutrality" declarations, material was being sent from the United States to Great Britain via convoys. The Lend-Lease Act had been passed. German operations had increased in Mexico, and Central and South America. And American defenses were being beefed up, including those in Puerto Rico. Just in case.

Ivan Shark was extremely busy, which is perhaps the only thing that saved Hall from drugs and intense torture. Being a criminal genius of the first order, Shark was becoming aware of some below-the-surface activities that could spell trouble for his Axis clients. Clever questioning of Hall had led Shark to suspect that the Englishman didn't have a very wide perspective of intelligence activities; with so many other pressing items, he decided to ignore the agent for the moment.

Shark's plan to bomb the Panama Canal locks had been scuttled by Secret Squadron intervention. Rather than rail uselessly at a lost opportunity, Shark decided to see whether he could salvage the essence of the plan.

A slate-gray amphibian from Central America arrived at Shark's island late one afternoon. Its sole passenger was Rogart, an Axis agent who was sent to the base as a "liaison observer." Shark knew that it really meant that the Axis wanted to keep an eye on its investment.

Shark showed the agent the extensive workings of the underground base. "We have done a lot with it," Shark said simply. "We have extended the capacity of the submarine pens so that this has become the finest submarine base in the world. That alone has been worth the investment made by your masters."

Though impressed, Rogart replied, "If that is what we desired, we would have retained this for our own use. What my superiors are interested in are your plans since you lost your bombers."

Ivan Shark smiled maliciously. "We still plan to paralyze the Panama Canal. We will just use more finesse." He explained that his technicians were developing an underwater explosive device that could be attached easily to ships. The device had sufficient power so that it could damage the locks to prevent their use for months, if not years. Personnel exiting from a submarine below the surface, from a modified torpedo tube, could emplace the necessary explosives. There were a few details to be worked out, even as one submarine was undergoing necessary modifications, but the plan soon would be ready for execution.

Rogart was satisfied. Also, since he was carrying a forged Swiss passport and other credentials, he wanted to conduct one or two side investigations in Puerto Rico.

"I would advise against it," Shark said. "It becomes a temptation to try a little uncoordinated action. That is why Herr Borgmann currently languishes in a British cell."

Rogart snorted. "Borgmann was a fool."

"As you say," Shark said. But he did not volunteer to take Rogart to Puerto Rico immediately.

However, Fury Shark went. And she did not go alone. Shark's previous agent on Puerto Rico, code-named "Operator 23," sent word some days previously that he'd spotted Captain Midnight at an airfield. He'd learned

6. Pre-War Operations

where the Secret Squadron leader was going to stay, and would try to slip a microphone into his room for a bit of eavesdropping. That was the last he'd been heard from.

The tightened security around the island, immediately evident to one like Shark, suggested that Operator 23's activities had been uncovered, but that he'd not been captured. Therefore, Fury Shark was accompanied by Clyde Russell, another Shark operative. She'd conduct a clandestine search for Operator 23. Russell, under the guise of Holbrook, a news correspondent, would keep an eye on the Secret Squadron. (In the radio drama, "Holbrook" had infiltrated into the Puerto Rican Squadron base; the Squadron was exceedingly sensitive to possible infiltration, and such a scenario would have been almost impossible.) A journalist could ask a lot of questions without arousing much suspicion. With the disclosure of the Secret Squadron's existence, a new base would naturally attract newsmen.

It wasn't publicly known that Captain Midnight was in Puerto Rico, even though the new Secret Squadron base was. There were few pictures of the Squadron leader available, and since those that were did little to reveal his features, he decided — as a precaution — to operate under an alias for a while, using the name "Mr. Lambert" once more.

As Pilot Lambert, Captain Midnight ran the base and directed overall activities. And (as Pilot Lambert) he was introduced to a journalist named Holbrook at one of those functions one is forced to attend if one is a base commander. For the rest of the evening, Captain Midnight artfully dodged questions posed by the supposed reporter.

The next morning, at an out-of-the-way cafe, Russell met with Fury Shark. Russell reported on having met Captain Midnight, operating under the name of Lambert. Fury informed her field partner that she had a lead on Operator 23 that she'd follow up in the evening. Each would follow their own lines of inquiry and meet at the restaurant the next morning.

As they were finishing their breakfast, Fury told Russell to move his chair so that he faced the interior of the restaurant. As he did so, Fury explained: Chuck Ramsay and the girl, Joyce, were walking down the street, sightseeing. She was certain that Chuck would recognize her instantly. It was too late for her to maneuver her chair or leave the restaurant without catching young Ramsay's eye. Since the youth was known to work with Captain Midnight, it would be prudent if he didn't catch sight of Russell's face.

Russell agreed. Even though Chuck might not even see her, it didn't pay to take chances. He added that it might be a good idea for Fury to return to the island base.

Fury demurred. A Secret Squadron party nearly captured Operator 23 the previous night. They'd found a transmitter at his hideout; but it was obvious that he hadn't had time to send any data to the base. Fury estimated that without her intervention, he would be caught within 24 hours. For the sake of mission security, she would take her chances.

That morning, Captain Midnight received reports on the Operator 23 raid. It confirmed his suspicion that Shark's Caribbean activities included espionage as well as sabotage. Physical evidence suggested that a spy, identity unknown, had departed just as the agents broke through the door. (In the radio dramatization, Captain Midnight was supposed to have led the raid. In reality, it was a crack team he assembled, led by an agent with extensive police experience. Captain Midnight wanted the squad leader to be someone capable of finding meaningful clues.) The report concluded that the degree of haste involved in the escape suggested that the spy would be relatively easy to track down from that point on.

The only unresolved problem was the island where Hall had been captured. Captain Midnight decided it was about time he overflew it again. He was convinced that somehow it was central to all the recent activities. This was underscored when it was linked to a radio frequency used almost exclusively by Shark and his forces.

Several things about the island puzzled him. Primary among them was the small aircraft he, Chuck, and Joyce had seen. The way it disappeared was an as-yet-unsolved mystery. He decided that a photographic mission might disclose details the unaided eye might not pick up. He ordered a camera plane be made ready, and to make sure it had armaments—just in case.

Before going on his mission, Captain Midnight wandered over to the repair hangar, where he found a mostly recuperated Ichabod Mudd. The Secret Squadron's Chief Mechanic was working on something that looked a bit like a large model airplane with vertical as well as horizontal wings. Puzzled, Midnight asked what Mudd was up to.

"Well, Cap'n, it's this way," Mudd began. "I've got this idea on making bombing runs more accurate. I've got this almost designed. I call it my 'flying bomb.'" The mechanic explained that the bomb didn't really fly; rather, the "wings" acted to steer it to its target. It could be done through radio control. A super-accurate bombsight would no longer be necessary.

"I'm making up a bunch so I can test a few," Mudd said hopefully.

"Don't worry," Midnight responded. "I've got an idea that you'll be able to test them out fairly soon. I have a target area in mind."

The Secret Squadron leader then went to his aircraft, preflighted it thoroughly, and took off on his photo mission. He was back in less than an hour, with all his film expended.

As he landed, he noticed a civilian car near the base gates by the airstrip. After instructing a ground-crewman to have the film unloaded, he strolled to the Operations shack, near the gate. After spending a few moments inside, he emerged and paused.

"Oh, Captain ..." someone behind him called.

Captain Midnight turned. It was Holbrook, standing just outside the gate, by a guard. "Eh?" Midnight asked the bogus reporter.

Staying outside, Holbrook said, "I see you've just returned from a flight somewhere. Is it something you can talk about? Ever since that *Bismarck* business ...."

The guard at the gate intervened. "Shall I tell this man to get lost, sir?"

Captain Midnight waved his hand in a short, negative gesture. "No, it's all right. I'll take care of this." Turning to the bogus reporter again, he said, "Surely, Mr. Holbrook, you must realize that the United States is a neutral country. My flight was strictly routine. While I appreciate the attention, I'm afraid that there's very little I can say." He excused himself.

When he returned to his office, he found a very excited Chuck waiting. The youngster related that he'd seen Fury Shark in a downtown cafe. "I pretended I didn't notice her, but that was Fury, no question," he said.

"That clinches it," Midnight said. "Ivan Shark's still alive. Fury wouldn't be acting as a field agent, otherwise." He paused, then added, "And I believe we'd better keep a sharp eye on our Mr. Holbrook."

Chuck asked why, and Midnight said, "Just a few minutes ago, he addressed me as 'Captain.' As far as he's supposed to know, I'm 'Mr. Lambert.'"

Soon, Captain Midnight was studying the processed aerial photographs. He was able to determine that though the island seemed deserted, it had a short landing strip, cleverly concealed by camouflage. He guessed that the pilots lined up on it via a radiodirectional "beam" (such as was used in civil aviation) that guided them in. If Shark ran true to form, the main base would be established well below the surface.

After a few moments of thought, Midnight decided that the best way to start his war of nerves against Shark was to announce that the Squadron would conduct a series of tests on a deserted island, and warn ships to avoid the area. Then he'd use Mudd's experimental bombs as the first thing to be tested.

After contacting Kelly and instructing him to have Holbrook investigated, he went back to see how Mudd was doing. He decided that Mudd might have underestimated the number of bombs to be tested, and indicated as much to the startled mechanic.

That evening the pace of events quickened. Midnight learned that a Shark operative had been captured. It was the very agent who had bugged his hotel room. He was able to verify that Ivan Shark was alive. Further, the master criminal was working with or for somebody named Rogart. The captured spy received written instructions from a "drop," and was trying to set up another transmitter when he'd been captured. He knew that Fury Shark was involved in current Puerto Rican operations, perhaps with another agent.

As he was leaving the building, letting an interrogation team see what else they could wring from the Shark operative, Midnight ran into Kelly. SS-11 had news. An investigation team had managed to break into "Holbrook's" room in his absence. They discovered a makeup kit among his effects, indicating that the man was operating in disguise. This verified Captain Midnight's suspicions.

Kelly accompanied Captain Midnight to his office. The Secret Squadron commander was about to start a memorandum when his "priority" telephone rang. It was Major Steele. All he said was that Midnight was to come to Washington immediately.

Captain Midnight rounded up Chuck and Joyce. Leaving Kelly temporarily in charge of Puerto Rican operations, he bundled the youngsters into the fastest four-place aircraft he could get his hands on and took off for Washington, D.C.

Dawn was breaking when Captain Midnight's aircraft turned to its final approach leg for Bowling Field's active runway. Chuck Ramsay was at the controls; though he was a competent pilot, he was tired, so his guardian kept an eye on him. Yet Chuck stuck to the proper glide slope as if the aircraft were on wires. The wheels touched the runway with the comforting double *chirp* of an optimum landing.

While the youth "cleaned up" the aircraft on rollout, Midnight looked for any indication of a welcoming party. Scanning the field, he saw a small gathering close to one taxiway and indicated to Chuck to head in that direction. It was Joyce, with her incredible eyesight, who first recognized Major Steele.

Steele made quick introductions. He indicated that Captain Midnight should accompany him, and that the others would help Chuck and Joyce go to a transient hotel where the Secret Squadron leader would meet them later.

Steele took Midnight to a large car that looked as if it might belong to a diplomat. They climbed into the back seat. As the door closed and the major leaned back, the car started up. Captain Midnight noticed that there was a glass partition between the passengers and the driver; the back seat area was soundproofed.

In time, they arrived, and Captain Midnight was led into a large and well appointed room. Seated behind a desk was a smallish but intense looking man. This individual wasn't introduced to the Secret Squadron leader by name. Major Steele merely said of him that he was one of the most important men in the world right then, though the public might forever remain unfamiliar with his activities.

The stranger, who seemed to radiate a sense of controlled power and massive intellect, spoke carefully, reminding Captain Midnight of his meeting in the Slater farmhouse with "Mr. Jones," though he used the man's real name. He pointed out that un–American activities had continued to increase, even with the Secret Squadron countering many of them. Much of the activity had been blatantly pro-Axis.

"Soon," the intense-looking man said, "the President is going to formalize the formation of a central agency for intelligence coordination. It will help tie all the ends together and perhaps minimize the duplication of effort between different agencies."

Major Steele, nominally of Military Intelligence, would act in concert with the new group. And the Secret Squadron's role would be changed slightly.

"These are odd times," the stranger noted. "All but officially, the United States is at war with the Axis powers already. Intrigue has reached the point where your organization, meant to fight internal subversion, is currently acting internationally, as are others."

"Sooner or later, the United States will be drawn into this war—officially. Then the Secret Squadron's duties may change again. For now, it would appear that your specialty should lie in fighting the type of chap you are fighting now."

The stranger went on to point out that there were those, like Ivan Shark, with effective independent organizations that would be hired out to those with few scruples—primarily to Axis agents. While Captain Midnight was fighting one such group, Major Steele was to be dispatched to the Far East. His purpose was twofold: to contact certain forces in Free China and, as relevant, to gather information on another such "freelancer," whose activities were helping the Japanese.

Midnight was briefed on the new organizational relationships. Then, after they took their leave of the man, he asked Major Steele how their late host fit into the overall picture.

"I don't know all the details yet, Captain," Major Steele said. "But I can tell you this: He has the support of our highest leaders. Currently he is the busiest man on either side of the Atlantic Ocean."

That evening Major Steele conversed briefly with Captain Midnight. He pointed out that the new status of the American intelligence operations would merely extend the scope of the Squadron's activities. His mission to China would begin in a few days; and, in due course, he expected to see Captain Midnight in the Far East. He was certain that the Secret Squadron leader would make short work of Ivan Shark. Then the Squadron leader would be free to take over the new and delicate mission.

With that, he left Captain Midnight to his thoughts.

The following morning, the fast Secret Squadron aircraft took off from

Bowling Field. Once clear of the traffic area, its nose pointed toward the great circle route to Puerto Rico, and action.

While en route, the aircraft was diverted to the Bahamas. This caused a delay, but little else. Thus, it wasn't until well past dusk of the following day that the Squadron plane droned over the waters of the Caribbean.

While en route, Chuck noticed some mysterious flashes on the water below. He called it to the attention of the others. Joyce studied the scene and said the lights looked like some sort of signal flashes. Captain Midnight agreed and spiraled down for a closer look.

Suddenly, the lights disappeared. Recalling the approximate position of one of the flashes, Captain Midnight instructed Chuck to fire off a flare.

And below was a sea that was empty, save for an oldish-looking tanker, which suddenly turned on its running lights. Being without running lights on the high seas was dangerous and contrary to maritime regulations. But the tanker was the only thing visible.

As Captain Midnight resumed his course to Puerto Rico, he expressed regret that he'd ordered Chuck to deploy the flare. If the waters had remained darkened, the luminous traces left by a ship disturbing the plankton would have verified the presence of a second vessel, such as a submarine; the flare light would have drowned out any plankton glow.

They flew on to Puerto Rico without further incident.

The next morning, Captain Midnight alerted his pilots to be on watch for submarine activities. Subs were important at that time; and they generally belonged to the wrong side. Any sightings were to be radioed in, immediately, and unenciphered. Other patrolling aircraft were to converge on the sighting. And just in case of trouble, each patrol aircraft was to be fitted with small bombs. When possible, there would be patrol-boat backup; when not, amphibians would be used. Strange submarines would be investigated if on the surface. Those clearly part of any nation's patrol forces would be noted, and nothing more.

As the patrol aircraft took off on their missions, Captain Midnight decided to check on the progress being made by his Chief Mechanic. He found Ichabod Mudd in a hangar, surrounded by large numbers of his prototype flying bombs.

"You certainly made enough of them," said the Secret Squadron leader.

"Well, Cap'n, it was you that said we needed more'n I was making," Mudd said. "And since you said we'd have a target pretty soon, I feel that if I'm going to check these things, I'd better do it right."

Laughing, Captain Midnight said he'd have his targets soon enough.

The first phase of his war of nerves was Ichabod Mudd's "flying bombs." It was common knowledge that the Secret Squadron was using an "uninhabited" island for tests. Mudd took great delight in guiding his first few

6. Pre-War Operations

bombs toward a preselected spot. After satisfying himself that the control principle was sound, he let others continue the experiment.

The radio-controlled devices performed well. After being released, they could be guided with precision by an observer using a small radio transmitter coupled to a joystick. Even bombs that were dropped too late could be guided back to their target.

Regrettably, the runs proved Mudd's device impractical for conventional bombing. The control gear in the bomb took up space that could be used for explosives. Dropping more than one bomb at a time required multiple control channels; otherwise, they would all fall "in formation." Standard multiple-bomb drops were as good; the wings on Mudd's bombs took up space, so a bomber couldn't hold as many of them as conventional bombs.

(After World War II, when a single bomb could contain much vaster amounts of explosive power, the "guided bomb" idea surfaced with the AZON device, a controlled bomb that the Air Force was experimenting with. The advent of guided missiles curtailed much interest in that sort of device; however, "guided bombs" could easily be considered ancestors to the "smart bombs" used decades later in Iraq.)

Though the bombs proved less than ideal for their design goals, the effect of repeated concussions overhead unnerved the underground base's personnel. Ivan Shark could travel only under cover of darkness.

Once, flying night patrol, Chuck and Joyce encountered one of Shark's planes. The strange aircraft engaged the Secret Squadron airplane in a dogfight and shot it down.

Joyce and Chuck were forced to bail out, even as Chuck was radioing an SOS to Squadron listeners. The only way to save themselves from being gunned down (Chuck Ramsay had no illusions when it came to Shark's gang) was a delayed-opening drop. The parachutes opened close to the water's surface; Chuck had no trouble, but Joyce was knocked unconscious.

When she came to, Joyce reported that she knew who she was! The shock she'd experienced had broken through a mental block, apparently. She was Joyce Ryan. Her mother was still alive; her father was recently deceased.

An air cover flew out and protected the pair until they could be retrieved by a patrol boat. Chuck was none the worse for the adventure. Because of her regained memory, Joyce could be said to have profited from it.

Back at the Squadron base, the excited youngsters brought the news to Captain Midnight. He nodded, then asked Joyce whether, now that she had a past once more, she wished to leave the Squadron, or stay on.

Joyce considered. She had a family — two, really. Her natural family and the Squadron. She thought of the war in Europe and the subversion at home. She thought of the adventures she had had with the Secret Squadron, and of those she'd like to protect. "Well," she said, "I'd like to stay with the Secret Squadron."

Both men were pleased. Midnight added that he was proud of her spirit.

Joyce's decision, and the sincerity with which she made it, galvanized the Secret Squadron leader into action. He organized and launched an amphibious and parachute assault on Shark's island. He led the assault himself, declaring that there had to be ways to enter the base from the surface, and that he'd find them. Chuck and Joyce insisted on going along as part of the strike force.

This nearly did Captain Midnight's plan in. Shortly after he and the youngsters landed, agents sprang from a secret entrance and captured Chuck and Joyce, though they didn't get Midnight. Ivan Shark, who had been monitoring the landings using a primitive but effective television surveillance system, had Chuck and Joyce intercepted because he realized he could use those two hostages like no others.

His cunning worked. With his hostages, he was able to force Captain Midnight to pull his troops back 50 miles for three days. This gave Shark time to take action.

A rescue was essential. Analysis of Shark's island revealed a great deal of submarine activities, now curtailed because of the raids. Captain Midnight decided to take a calculated risk. With a United States Navy submarine, he could get into the underwater entrance. It was the only way he could see to effect an entrance, particularly if Shark's observers were alert.

A submarine was placed at his disposal. Its skipper, Commander McCaffrey, was considered one of the finest submariners available. A voyage that was both cautious and daring — that could almost make a book itself — got them safely into the submarine pen.

Fortunately, the area was deserted. While Captain Midnight and Ichabod Mudd went in search of the youngsters, Commander McCaffrey maneuvered his submarine around for a quick escape.

The search party found Joyce, Chuck, and the British Intelligence agent, Hall, in a small cell complex. While Captain Midnight stood guard, Ichabod Mudd worked on the locks. In a surprisingly short time, the prisoners were freed. They returned to the submarine for a getaway.

They almost didn't make it. A crew had been dispatched to board Shark's submarine. When they reached the area, they saw a second submarine, and a crew member alerted Shark. The master criminal sped to the scene, and when he got there, he ordered the submarine crew to stop the interloper. Shark's submarine was manned but wasn't fully powered up. It fired a torpedo to stop the Navy sub.

The torpedo missed, crossing just inches in front of the American

6. Pre-War Operations

U-boat. But that miss was more than just unfortunate for Ivan Shark; it was a disaster.

The torpedo picked up enough speed to "skip" without detonating, after striking a partially submerged object at a highly oblique angle. It arced out of the water and smashed into a small munitions storage area.

Then it detonated. This precipitated a series of explosions that initiated the death throes of the island, as munitions area after munitions area was affected. Ironically, this wouldn't have happened except for the production and storage of extra explosives intended to cripple the Panama Canal locks. For once, Shark's preparations did him in.

In the confusion, Captain Midnight was able to leave the American submarine and capture Ivan Shark, along with his servant, Fang. With the island "sinking" around them, Commander McCaffrey blasted a way out of the closing pen entrance with torpedoes, taking the Secret Squadron party and their prisoners to safety.

Ivan Shark and Fang were imprisoned. The base and its submarine were destroyed. Ivan Shark's gang seemed, for the most part, dead. But Fury Shark wasn't found.

Captain Midnight summed it up to Kelly. "We got the head of the group, and both of his senior lieutenants. With these incarcerated, the group is ineffective. The present danger to Western Hemisphere defenses has been curtailed. We have a breathing spell."

But the Secret Squadron leader knew his organization would have a very *short* breathing spell. The war would come to the United States one way or another. It would come through attack or further subversion and sabotage.

He also realized that Shark wasn't the only outlaw who posed a threat to the United States. There was something behind Major Steele's trip to the Far East. Captain Midnight was determined to follow him there and find out what it was and to provide his help.

7

War Clouds Thicken

Nineteen forty-one was a year in which the war spread and deepened. It was also a time when international freelance criminals flourished. International freelance criminals didn't originate in the period just prior to World War II (Shark himself was active during World War I, after all). Most famous of the breed was the great Professor Moriarty, whose pan–European influence was as effective as it was unknown to the public at its height. Moriarty, who was totally amoral in his business dealings, pioneered in selling his services internationally to the highest bidder. While others before him had done likewise, Moriarty's genius was the development of an efficient, multinational organization that could act without "nationalistic" difficulties.

Several others who were tagged "criminal" developed organizations of equivalent scope. However, many of these groups — such as the Si Fan, led by Dr. Fu Manchu — were organized for specific goals rather than working for whomever would pay the most.

Ivan Shark, despite his Oriental-tinged philosophy of fatalism, was primarily Occidental in thought and action. His organization, consequently, was organized along Western lines. Yet Shark's approach wasn't the only way.

In the Far East another such freelancer flourished. The man heading the organization had been active for many years, but he was initially a very shadowy figure. He was virtually unknown, even to law-enforcement agencies, until he was firmly established. Even then, his name was whispered in clandestine exchanges, rather than spoken in normal conversations. Although a Caucasian, he was for all practical purposes a product of the

Orient. To both friends and enemies, he was known simply and solely as The Barracuda. He had two parallel organizations: an equivalent of an armed force (more or less a private army) and a society — a tong — adapted from the Chinese and used primarily for criminal activities.

The Barracuda had agents spread wide. Even as Major Barry Steele was preparing to travel in the Far East, news of his impending trip reached the Oriental criminal. The Barracuda, though selling his services to the highest bidder, was emotionally an Oriental. He saw the trip to China by a senior American intelligence agent as an opportunity to aid the most active Asian movement of the time — the expansion of Imperial Japan. He also saw it as a chance to line his own pockets with gold. So, he set certain forces in motion.

Communication with Free China was difficult. Captain Midnight was unsure about the precise whereabouts of Major Steele or of his mission's progress.

The aircraft crossed the Pacific and stopped at Hong Kong, both for fuel and for any information obtainable about Major Steele. They got fuel. Continuing from the British Crown Colony, Captain Midnight exercised caution, for he had to fly over Japanese-occupied areas of China. While the United States was neutral, the presence of an American aircraft over such territory would lead to complications — if the plane were detected.

Captain Midnight took off at night and was flying over stratiform clouds at 7,000 feet. But shortly after takeoff, he was not alone. Three dark aircraft — one cabin plane and two fighters — flying in formation, intercepted the flight path of the Secret Squadron ship. They approached it high and from the rear.

In the lead aircraft was The Barracuda; with him was a Colonel Goto, recently of the Imperial Japanese Army. The Barracuda's aircraft wasn't visible from Captain Midnight's amphibian. The other two were only barely visible — if one knew exactly where to look.

The Barracuda was reasonably certain that the mystery plane was piloted by a Secret Squadron agent, perhaps the famous Captain Midnight himself. He ordered an immediate attack, instructing the pilots in his escorting fighters to disable the amphibian's engines and to spray the cockpit with bullets.

It was Joyce Ryan's extraordinary eyesight that saved their lives. The two fighters had spread to permit diagonal "runs" on their target. Joyce, looking out a side window, saw the flicker of hot exhaust gases from the engines of one of the diving aircraft. Recognizing it as an attack, she cried out to Captain Midnight.

Calling for the Squadron members to strap themselves in, Captain

7. War Clouds Thicken

Midnight tried evasive maneuvers. Though his flying was brilliant, his aircraft was simply outclassed. Soon, both engines were disabled, and one was beginning to catch fire.

There was only one action to take: bail out. The Secret Squadron leader put his ship into a dive, apparently out of control, until it penetrated the clouds. Then he leveled it off.

The Secret Squadron members bailed out in the clouds, with Captain Midnight the last to leave. All agreed to rendezvous one-half mile north of the crash site. "With the night as dark as it is, the flames should be visible for miles," Midnight had said.

Neither The Barracuda nor his followers saw the Squadron members bail out. Nor, since he was above the clouds, did he see the parachutes.

During the time Midnight was leveling the plane, Chuck and Joyce jumped together, and Mudd jumped as soon as he saw the Secret Squadron leader was coming. This caused a spread between the youngsters and the two adults.

Even beneath the clouds and in a relatively dark night, the contrast of a snow-white parachute over the dark soil of China was sufficient so that Chuck could see Joyce's parachute from above. He slipped his shroud lines so that he drifted near her, and the two landed together.

In a similar manner, Captain Midnight maneuvered so that he would land next to Ichabod Mudd. The Chief Mechanic expressed extreme regret that the aircraft was lost, not so much because they were stranded in China without transportation, but because he'd worked so long and hard on making the plane run perfectly. He was also more than a little puzzled about the unprovoked attack. As he was talking about it, Captain Midnight warned him to be silent and stand still.

Soldiers were all around them. In the glow of the distant flames, Midnight couldn't determine whether they were regular forces or an auxiliary arm. He realized, though, that so many soldiers could only be part of, or in league with, the Japanese forces. It seemed certain that the two of them would be captured.

But fate intervened. As it happened, the soldiers were attracted to some other event. Following the soldiers cautiously, the two were able to determine that the troops had captured Chuck and Joyce!

Captain Midnight weighed the alternatives carefully. The two youngsters were unarmed, and the only weapons he and Mudd had were their automatics. Direct action would almost certainly result in their capture (at best), without effecting an escape by Chuck and Joyce. The decision was hard, but he didn't see that he had any other choice.

"Ikky, this is our only chance to get away," he said. "We can't help Chuck and Joyce without more than we've got with us. The soldiers might think they were the only two on the plane. If we can get away, we stand a chance of rescuing them."

"But Cap'n," Mudd protested, "what can we do then? And Miss Joyce is young and pretty. Mightn't the soldiers ....?"

Midnight nodded grimly. "It's possible, but I doubt anything like that would happen right away. These troops are under somebody's command, and the kids are obviously Westerners. I'll bet the soldiers will deliver them — unharmed — to that commander. And since many Orientals believe in a patient, waiting game, they'll probably be safe for a day or two. And that's all the time I'll need."

"Let's get out of here," Midnight concluded. The two of them, not without misgivings, did.

Chuck and Joyce were seized at once by the soldiers and were searched for weapons. The troops did treat them carefully. Since the youngsters were obviously Occidentals, and were wearing civilian clothes, their status was uncertain.

A small car pulled up, and a man in a military officer's uniform stepped out. Identifying himself as Captain Ishii, he demanded and obtained the youngsters' names. Upon hearing that the two had been flying overhead and had been inexplicably shot down, the Japanese captain expressed regret to the two young Americans. Saying that the incident could have been the work of Chinese pilots, he asked a few other questions, all reasonable for someone encountering strangers in a war-torn land.

Chuck suspected that the Japanese officer knew more about what happened than he said, so telling him the truth might help allay suspicions. He avoided mentioning Captain Midnight and Ichabod Mudd. By sticking close to the truth, he hoped they might get by; it would be easier to break a fraudulent story than one that was mostly true. He gave his nationality as American; status, civilian. He said that he and Joyce were traveling to meet an American friend of theirs in Chungking.

"So," said Captain Ishii. "Come with me." He gestured toward his car. "We will help you," he said with a laugh.

As Chuck and Joyce were hustled toward the car, they realized that they would be in for a rough time.

Captain Midnight and Ichabod Mudd stole along the countryside, keeping out of sight as best they could. Just as the first gray-blue tinges of dawn were bathing the ground in a near ghost-light, the two of them found a large, open plain. On this they could see an immense tent. Light leaking from within suggested activity inside.

Both of them instantly recognized the structure as a tent hangar. As they crept close, they exchanged whispers. It was a fantastic stroke of luck: If there was an aircraft they could "appropriate," they might have just what was needed to rescue the youngsters — or a means of going for help.

The front of the tent was facing away from them, so they couldn't see what was going on. But they heard an engine kick over; once it steadied, they heard another. The rear flap of the tent was raised to let prop wash escape. It became apparent that mechanics had been working on a plane and had decided to taxi it out so they could work on another.

Mudd opined that after it was out of the tent and some distance away, the mechanics might give its engines a final dynamic test.

Both men realized that the situation was the chance of a lifetime. If the crew quit the plane, they could capture it. It would be all warmed up and waiting for them to take off. Tensely, they watched to see what would happen.

Their wishes were granted. The crew did leave the plane, just as Mudd surmised. Timing their actions with the patrolling of a lone sentry who hadn't spotted them, they sprinted across the field and clambered aboard — to find there was still a mechanic onboard.

The mechanic shouted as Captain Midnight wrenched him out of his seat and threw him out of the cockpit. Mudd threw him the rest of the way out of the aircraft as Captain Midnight climbed into the pilot's seat. The Chief Mechanic scrambled to the gunner's position even as Captain Midnight advanced the throttle.

"Err, Cap'n, there's just one thing," Mudd said. "Can you fly this crate? The placards and labels I see here are in Japanese."

The sentry started to shoot at them as Midnight released the brakes and started a taxi that turned into a takeoff roll. "Yes, I can," he said. "I was in China shortly before the Secret Squadron was formed, and I learned a bit about Japanese aircraft. This is a Mitsubishi Ki-2, derived from the Junkers K-37 design. I can get it into the air and away from here. Then I'll feel it out." (In the radio version, the aircraft was supposedly copied from an American design, which was not the case.)

The twin-engine bomber lumbered across the field and into the air, pursued by rifle bullets. Fortunately, none hit; and the fuel tanks were nearly full.

Luckily for the Secret Squadron leader, the field he departed was restricted to bombers. No fighters were on hand to "scramble." He got away cleanly. (In the radio dramatization, his supposedly "American replica" aircraft was loaded with bombs — a highly unlikely set of circumstances for a craft being worked on by mechanics. In the show, after being fired upon by a machine gun, Captain Midnight supposedly turned back and put the opposition out of action. In a mostly unfamiliar plane, such an action would be stupid.) Once familiarized with the characteristics of the Ki-2, he headed it toward Free China.

Chuck and Joyce had been driven over scarred roads in country grimly pockmarked by recent battles. The ugly reality of war was brought home to them; from the air, most of the signs of fighting wouldn't have been visible.

Finally, the car arrived at its destination, a squat building that seemed to be a headquarters: uniformed Japanese soldiers or militiamen guarded the entrance. Captain Ishii escorted the young Americans from the car into the building.

Their destination was an office. A short but powerfully built Japanese officer, seated at a desk, looked up as they entered. Not bothering to rise, the officer, speaking English, introduced himself as Colonel Goto.

Neither of the youngsters had any idea that Colonel Goto witnessed the attack on their aircraft. When told of their nationality, Goto asked Chuck if he were an American Army officer.

Chuck said that he and Joyce were civilians, which was technically correct, since the Secret Squadron was not one of the armed services. He added that the two of them were flying to Chungking to visit a friend of theirs.

When asked to name their American friend, Chuck replied he was a "Mr. Steele." Goto countered with, "You mean, perhaps, one Major Barry Steele, who is connected with American intelligence?" Chuck could only stand mute.

Although Joyce tried to cover, saying something about being social friends, it was obvious that Colonel Goto knew of their mission, at least in part. The colonel said he knew that Captain Midnight and three companions were scheduled to rendezvous with Major Steele in Chungking, and opined that perhaps the two were among the ones accompanying Midnight. Since they were civilians in a war area, they could be considered spies — and shot. He said some words to Captain Ishii in Japanese, and the youngsters knew that they'd been dismissed.

Captain Ishii led them to a building wing that contained a cell block. He said that Colonel Goto had ordered a surprise for "the American spies." He brought them to a cell and, at gunpoint, ordered them to enter. He locked the door and departed, leaving Chuck and Joyce standing in the gloom of the unlighted cell.

As their eyes grew accustomed to the dim lighting, they realized that they were not alone. In the cell with them was a thin and exhausted Major Barry Steele!

While Captain Midnight's getaway with the stolen bomber was successful, his troubles were far from over. With the Japanese having both land lines and radio available, the theft of the bomber couldn't be kept a secret long. Midnight was certain that fighters would be sent to intercept him. Also, the aircraft he was flying had Japanese markings, and the antiaircraft guns of Free China would make safe flying over unoccupied territory difficult.

Nevertheless, he had to try. He called to Mudd to try the machine guns, which proved to be in good working order. Mudd informed him that there was plenty of ammunition.

Trouble came in the form of three fighters. They closed in what Captain Midnight's experienced eye informed him was the beginning of an attack: Three swift planes pouncing on a lumbering old plane with a top speed of only 140 miles per hour.

Ichabod Mudd commented on the dogfight later on. "I was busy firing at the fighters under Cap'n Midnight's direction. But even so, the Cap'n did things with that old crate I still don't believe. Anyway, we managed to get all three planes with only some chewed-up control surfaces in return."

When Midnight was asked about the fight, he shrugged. "Speed isn't everything. The other pilots thought we'd be a pushover, and in air battles, overconfidence can be a big handicap."

Captain Midnight resumed his flight toward Free China. The only thing he was sure of was that they hadn't seen the last of Japanese interceptors.

When Chuck and Joyce found Major Steele in the cell, he was unconscious. He'd obviously been through an ordeal, had lost weight, and looked generally unwell. Chuck managed to rouse him.

The major explained that he'd been captured by Colonel Goto, whom he described as, "one of the worst kinds of Japanese officer." He explained that the colonel and his troops were actually mercenaries who'd lately attached themselves to one of the most dangerous outlaws alive.

"Ivan Shark?" Chuck asked. He was puzzled because of the recent capture of the international criminal.

"No," Steele said. "Ivan Shark is an opportunistic man of the Occident. By contrast, The Barracuda has all the subtlety and patience of the Orient, with a cruel streak in the worst tradition of the Far East. He is extremely dangerous."

As Steele was beginning to discuss The Barracuda's troops, there was an interruption. The cell door swung open and Colonel Goto strode into the cell, followed by a man who could be none other than The Barracuda. He was a small, slightly built man with a penetrating gaze that was hard to meet. His eyes seemed to burn with a greenish fire.

The Barracuda greeted Major Steele, ignoring the youngsters. He told the major that he was not impressed with Steele's activities, but that sending for Captain Midnight brought things a bit too far. It would be a simple thing for Steele to win his freedom if he were just to order Captain Midnight to leave Asia. "There is no room here for the Secret Squadron," he said evenly.

Steele indicated that he couldn't do that. Both Joyce and Chuck gave their enthusiastic support for the sentiment.

The Barracuda smiled. "A most unwise decision," he said. He then left the prisoners to their thoughts, after telling them that they had but twelve hours to change their minds.

Realizing that their cell might be wired, Chuck and Joyce huddled close to Major Steele so that they could talk in low tones. Chuck again congratulated the major for being so resolute.

"These waters are deeper than they might appear," the major responded. "This business about my leaving as a free man by ordering Captain Midnight away — don't take it at face value." The request was a litmus test to determine just how far Steele could be made to do the bidding of his captors. He added that the 12-hour limit was just another example of the cat-and-mouse game his captors were playing in order to wear down his resistance.

Steele didn't add that the presence of the two young Secret Squadron agents made it more difficult for him. He knew, and realized that The Barracuda understood, that the youngsters could be used to reach him.

The 12 hours given for "reconsideration" were to end at midnight. Perhaps this was meant as a calculated subtlety to drive home the helplessness of their situation; but more likely it was the simpler trick of lowering resistance through sleep deprivation.

Eventually the deadline came. Footsteps of guards could be heard to echo, perhaps more than was strictly necessary, as the hour approached. And the tower clock began to strike twelve.

All Hell broke loose. First, the drone of an aircraft could be heard over the clock's bell. (Steele exchanged surprised glances with Chuck and Joyce. Could it be?) Then, explosions and the drone of other aircraft.

The sound of footsteps in the hall ceased; this was replaced with sounds of confusion. These dwindled, and, save for far-off battle sounds, there was silence.

Joyce ran to the cell window and looked out. Searchlights were probing the sky. Aircraft were dropping bombs and flares. A few antiaircraft guns began to roar, but these were silenced quickly; the sky was dotted with parachutes. Some force was doing battle with the soldiers guarding the building. Because of the hour, Chuck was absolutely convinced that Captain Midnight was behind it.

It took more than an hour to verify Chuck's belief. The battle raged on for what seemed to be an eternity, then subsided to the occasional crack of rifle fire. Footsteps were heard along the corridor once more, but this time they were rapid. To the relief of the three prisoners, the face that appeared at the cell door was Captain Midnight's.

7. War Clouds Thicken

The door was opened in a trice. The three freed prisoners saw that Captain Midnight was accompanied by an Oriental in uniform. Major Steele recognized him as Major Sun of the Chinese Air Force, a friend of his.

Ichabod Mudd explained how he and Captain Midnight "appropriated" the Ki-2 aircraft, and detailed the air battle that followed. After that, there were clear skies until they almost reached the area of Chungking. A Japanese fighter group of about a dozen planes intercepted them. They were taking evasive actions when a second group of planes joined the fray — Chinese planes. The newcomers engaged and disposed of the enemy in a quick but intense dogfight.

The captured Ki-2 was escorted to a Chinese airfield. Upon deplaning, Captain Midnight met Major Sun. The friendly officer explained that the Chinese had been monitoring Japanese radio bands. They'd picked up the report of a bomber being stolen, plus the orders for its interception. They decided to lend a hand to the renegade bomber.

Captain Midnight explained his problem. From the approximate location where the Squadron amphibian had been attacked, Major Sun felt fairly certain that The Barracuda was mixed up in it.

A rescue operation was organized. Captain Midnight decided to time the strike for twelve at night — usually a "lucky hour" for his activities. That they found Major Steele with the youngsters was serendipity.

The raid was a rescue mission only. However, there would be an hour or so before reinforcements could be gathered for a counterattack. Captain Midnight suggested that the time be put to good use.

Major Steele pointed out that all the leads he'd been following pointed to The Barracuda. A search might turn up something interesting. And it did.

It was Captain Midnight who first noticed the teakwood table in The Barracuda's quarters. He remembered seeing a similar table years previously. With great caution, he prodded and poked it. Turning one of the legs did the trick.

A section of the seemingly solid inlaid marble slid back, revealing a shallow compartment. An oilskin pouch or packet could be seen inside the cavity.

Captain Midnight warned the others not to reach into the compartment with their hands. He opened a long-bladed pocket knife and used the blade to flip the packet out. (His warning wasn't idle: As the packet was removed, a long needle, doubtless coated with a fast-acting poison, sprang out. Triggered by reduction of weight on the compartment's base, the needle would have struck any unprotected hand that might have grabbed the packet.)

The pouch was opened. It contained papers and a small roll of microfilm sealed in a light-tight canister. Major Steele and Captain Midnight realized that this was an important find.

"We'd best go to Hong Kong," Major Steele said. "This microfilm might be undeveloped, as a safety precaution. If anybody might try to examine it without taking the proper steps, it would become light-struck and useless." Since both Steele and Midnight were known to various members of British Intelligence, they were confident that they would be able to get help in having the microfilm processed.

Major Sun was sorry to hear that they wouldn't be returning to Chungking with him, but after the find was explained to him, he nodded. "We regret the tools you need can only be found in Hong Kong or beyond. But that which you find will help in the struggle against China's enemies."

As dawn was breaking, the Chinese forces and the Secret Squadron's KI-2 took off and parted company. The Ki-2 had been lightened as much as possible (it was a relatively short-range aircraft); though its ammunition was replenished, what bombs remained after the raid were unloaded. Its fuel tanks were topped off, and Captain Midnight and Ichabod Mudd comprised its crew. Chuck was checked out in a "liberated" Kawasaki Type 88 biplane captured at the field. He and Joyce manned the smaller aircraft, flying "escort" for the bomber. Both the Mitsubishi and the Kawasaki had service ceilings above 20,000 feet; while they didn't fly that high, both flew high enough to require supplemental oxygen.

They landed near the outskirts of Hong Kong, having decided that landing at a conventional airport in two stolen Japanese aircraft might cause a stir. They made their way into the city proper and sought out Major Steele's friends in British Intelligence.

When presented with the film, the Intelligence personnel promised that they'd process it, but that it might take a day or more. "We just can't be certain that the film's a standard type, y'know," a photographic expert explained. "I believe I will have to take a small snip or two from the end and analyze them. Then I will know how best to develop the film."

Captain Midnight's party made the most of the time. The Secret Squadron members and Major Steele picked up some articles of clothing and checked into a hotel where they could freshen up. After a massive meal, the entire party, save for Captain Midnight and Ichabod Mudd, turned in to catch up on sleep.

After Captain Midnight sent an enciphered message to the nearest Secret Squadron base directing that a long-range amphibian be delivered to him, he turned in, too, as did Mudd. All needed rest in great quantities.

The Barracuda and his troops approached their headquarters building warily. It seemed evident that the invaders had departed, probably taking

7. War Clouds Thicken

Major Steele and the two youngsters with them. However, they may have left rearguard troops, or they may have set booby traps.

The Barracuda went directly to his living area, even as Colonel Goto headed for the prison area. The most important thing, as far as The Barracuda was concerned, was not the prisoners, but what was concealed in his quarters.

Colonel Goto found him staring at the empty compartment in his teakwood table. That the prisoners were now free was of only minor importance. The other loss was critical. The microfilm had been prepared for a day not too far off and was intended for a certain meeting as proof of being able to make particular connections. And with things so close to fruition, neither Steele nor any member of the Secret Squadron could be allowed to leave China.

It hadn't been too difficult for The Barracuda to deduce where the aircraft with the escapees had gone (later verified by the discovery of the abandoned plane). If it had been a matter of Major Steele getting away, and nothing else, the logical place he would have tried for would have been Chungking. But with the microfilm gone, the picture changed.

The Barracuda had no doubts who rescued Major Steele. He'd heard about the exploits of Captain Midnight from reliable sources.

Possession of the microfilm would make the logical destination Hong Kong. Either they would find resources there to process the film, or, since the colony was still under British control, it would be a friendly gateway to reach resources elsewhere.

The Barracuda wasn't too concerned about Captain Midnight getting immediate information from the microfilm. He presumed that Midnight, if smart enough to avoid the table's death trap, was smart enough to assume the microfilm hadn't been developed. But Captain Midnight might *not* be smart enough to realize that the film used was special, and that processing it as if it were ordinary microfilm would render it useless.

After a good rest, Captain Midnight's party went to British Intelligence. The microfilm had been developed successfully. It consisted of a short roll with several diagrams on it, all apparently of some sort of naval installation.

"Can't say for certain," said Commander Barkley, "but that base looks familiar. As there is no writing on this, I'd be guessing."

After a moment's consideration, Captain Midnight recognized it. "Great Scott! That's a diagram of Pearl Harbor! I'm familiar enough with its layout."

All were surprised. If The Barracuda had been part of the Japanese military, a diagram of the naval facility would have implied that some sort of attack was being planned for the base. Yet The Barracuda was most certainly a freelance criminal. And yet...

Commander Barkley made a suggestion. It could be that The Barracuda might have been hired to smuggle saboteurs and equipment to the Hawaiian Islands. This action could help delay or partially disable ship actions as Pacific tensions tightened.

"That sounds reasonable," Captain Midnight said, "but then why the high-security microfilm? Whether sabotage or worse, I'd better get over to Hawaii to check things there."

The Barracuda was aware of a British Intelligence operation in Hong Kong, but he had no idea of its capabilities; so he was unaware that the microfilm had been developed.

Ideally, he would have liked to loose his Tiger Pilots on Captain Midnight as soon as he lifted off the ground, but that was not practical. But there was another way.

He mused that much of his most effective work was done by subtle means. He picked up a small hammer and struck a gong. A servant appeared and he issued instructions.

Captain Midnight had weighed sending out an enciphered message about the contents of the microfilm and finally decided against it. What was needed was investigation *at* Pearl Harbor, where Squadron and select Armed Services officers could review the actual diagrams. His instincts impelled him to get going as soon as possible.

However, before he departed, he thought he'd better hedge his bets. He requested that the British Intelligence technicians make duplicates of the microfilm: at least one copy for Major Steele, who wouldn't be accompanying his party, and one to be sent via normal diplomatic channels to Washington, D.C. Colonel Barkley asked whether they could retain a copy for their own analysis. Major Steele and Captain Midnight had no objections.

Since the microfilm was processed, making duplicates was a routine operation, though time-consuming. Captain Midnight used the time to check out radio reports about weather and other flying information. He laid out his flight paths carefully. With his fuel, he could go directly to Guam, where there was a Squadron base.

They departed the following morning. The heavily guarded plane was taxied out. The fuel tanks were topped off, the hatches closed, and the still-warm engines were fired once more. The aircraft, heavily laden with fuel, took nearly the full length of the runway and climbed for altitude slowly.

High above and behind the Secret Squadron aircraft, another airplane flew. It, too, was an amphibian, but it wasn't provisioned for an extra-long flight to Guam. In its cockpit was The Barracuda. He'd instructed the pilot to fly so as to remain always within the blind area of the other plane. The pilot, as dedicated a servant as one could find, didn't disobey.

The Secret Squadron amphibian finally reached an altitude of 10,000 feet. While not absolutely necessary, to ensure the sharpest possible mental acuity, Captain Midnight ordered everyone on oxygen for the hop to Guam.

Somewhere over the South China Sea, one of the engines began to sputter; then, the other. Then, one after the other, both quit. Since all were familiar with "engine-out" procedures, nobody was alarmed at the turn of events. The plane was put into the best-angle-of-glide attitude after a few unsuccessful attempts to restart the engines. With the altitude the aircraft had, there was plenty of maneuvering room on the way down.

Joyce was the first to spot the islands ahead of them. She asked whether they were part of the Philippines, and was told that they were associated with the Bubayans. It would be better to land close to an island than in open seas.

As they continued to descend, Captain Midnight pointed at one of the islands and remarked that it appeared to have a natural harbor into which, with careful maneuvering, he should be able to guide the amphibian, giving Mudd a sheltered area to work on repairs.

It was Joyce again who spotted signs that the island was inhabited. "Captain Midnight! There are a lot of boats down there. They appear to be junks," she said.

Captain Midnight judged that it could be a fishing colony. They might be able to enlist help there, for as a rule, junks were Chinese, not Japanese.

Above and behind them, The Barracuda smiled in satisfaction. His plan had worked better than he'd hoped. It took all his resources to get an agent to the airfield in Hong Kong to sabotage the amphibian.

"Do you see where he is going down?" he asked Colonel Goto. "That is the lair of Cho Yuk, the pirate. This is better than having them at sea. Cho Yuk will make them prisoners. I will not have to call up reserves — a little gold will do." He instructed his pilot to divert to a base of his own on Taiwan; the bargaining for prisoners would take several days.

(In the fictionalized radio drama of this adventure, the Squadron aircraft was supposed to have been forced down because of a poison gas bomb placed onboard. Since the Squadron members were on oxygen at the time, the poison gas would have been a waste of time.)

The Secret Squadron amphibian came to a stop inside the harbor, near the fleet of junks. While Captain Midnight tried to attract some attention, Ichabod Mudd clambered out and inspected the aircraft. He determined quickly that a sizable amount of water had been put into the gas tanks — obviously sabotage.

Junks had managed to surround the amphibian. Soon the Secret Squadron members were startled to learn that they were "guests" of Cho Yuk and would remain so until they paid a ransom of $10,000. "Cho Yuk, he like 'Merican," a pirate lieutenant explained, "otherwise cost much more money."

Of course, the Secret Squadron members were traveling light — particularly with respect to cash. Among the four, there was a total of less than $600. With the peculiar ethics of the old-school Chinese pirate, none of the Secret Squadron members were treated as other than guests, nor did any pirate try to relieve them of their cash. Ransom money was considered something different from personal funds.

The Squadron members were not permitted to use the radio (Cho Yuk didn't want anyone calling for a rescue force). Captain Midnight was reduced to writing a letter explaining their situation. The letter would be delivered to American authorities in the Philippines, who in turn were to forward the message to the Secret Squadron base in Guam. Midnight told the pirate who'd captured the squadron members, a small but tough individual known simply as Mong, that the message would take time to reach its addressees. "That all right," said Mong, smiling politely. "We not mind wait."

Events were to shorten the wait. The Barracuda's amphibian, flanked by supporting fighters, flew over the area in a typical show of force. The fighters, being land craft, flew off, and The Barracuda set his amphibian down outside the bay proper.

After some consultation, Cho Yuk dispatched a boat to see what the stranger wanted. Mong brought the news to Captain Midnight. "Man in plane want all Cho Yuk guest. Him offer money. We no like him — he work with Japanese. We tell him fifty thousand dolla. He say he pay."

Captain Midnight's identity was not unknown in the Orient, nor was it unknown that he was a friend of China. He told Mong his identity and requested an audience with Cho Yuk.

Mong interpreted, since the pirate chief spoke no English. Cho Yuk, though a pirate and geographically removed from China, said he was honored to have so illustrious a person as his guest. He indicated that he would still honor his guest's ransom price of $10,000. But he'd have to receive money from *someone* before he'd release the Secret Squadron party.

Captain Midnight reminded the pirate chief of The Barracuda's overflight with fighters, and said, "Since when does a man draw a sword before doing business? It is not good." The Secret Squadron leader outlined a plan that would enable Cho Yuk to get his money while the Squadron party would obtain their freedom.

The pirate chief considered the plan, then indicated agreement. Cho Yuk would have to trust him. But the chief considered Captain Midnight an honorable man.

The Pirate chief let it be known that if The Barracuda would bring the agreed-upon sum, the prisoners would be produced. Just under an hour later, The Barracuda arrived, accompanied by Colonel Goto. Both were carrying briefcases with the necessary cash.

7. War Clouds Thicken

After receiving the money, Cho Yuk gestured.

Captain Midnight stepped out of the shadows, flanked by two fierce-looking pirates. Others of the party were brought out, under lesser guards.

The Barracuda studied Captain Midnight, who returned his gaze grimly. Neither man had met before; each seemed to sense that the other was an extremely dangerous man.

"At last we meet," The Barracuda said. "It is most unfortunate we meet under such circumstances." He switched to Chinese and addressed some words to the pirate chief.

Mong translated. "He ask why not more people here."

"I can answer that, Barracuda," Captain Midnight said. "Those I rescued split up. Major Steele, for instance, required hospitalization, thanks to you."

"I see," said The Barracuda. "You wrong me, my dear Captain. I do not believe you have fully appreciated the beauties of China. We will return there and rejoin Major Steele — surely, you will make my job easier by telling me which hospital..."

As he spoke, Colonel Goto drew a revolver and pointed it at Captain Midnight. The Secret Squadron leader raised his hands to the shoulder level, but waggled his right hand in a certain way.

A shot rang out. Colonel Goto dropped his revolver and clutched at his shoulder.

"The tables are turned, Barracuda," Captain Midnight said evenly. "One of your former prisoners, Chuck Ramsay, is up in that tower with a rifle equipped with a telescopic sight. He is an excellent shot, and I've instructed him to train his sights on your heart. One false move will be your last."

The Barracuda nodded. "The tables are indeed turned, Captain Midnight. But you are as much my prisoner as I am yours. For how do you propose leaving this island harbor without having my pilots track you down?"

Captain Midnight smiled. "I think we'll manage."

At that point the only clear victor was Cho Yuk. He had a satchel with $50,000. (All understood that in the bigger battle with Captain Midnight, The Barracuda wouldn't bother Cho Yuk about the money; that was a casualty of the struggle.)

Captain Midnight told him they would depart — with prisoners. The pirate chief was welcome to The Barracuda's airplane if his men would conceal it from sight for a few days. Then he loaded The Barracuda and Colonel Goto into the Squadron plane along with Chuck, Joyce, and Ichabod Mudd. The Secret Squadron leader took off.

He didn't fly far. As he flew, Captain Midnight scanned the area for small islands. Finding one, he landed and told The Barracuda and Colonel

Goto he was leaving them there. He pointed out that they would be picked up by their own men, albeit not for a few days.

As they took off, Chuck asked him why he marooned The Barracuda on a separate island rather than either taking him to Guam or simply leaving him at the pirate village.

"To gain time," Captain Midnight said. "If you recall, the only amphibian besides ours was his — the other planes were fighters. The island we marooned them on is too small for a land-based plane to land on. This means that they'll have to get another amphibian or rescue him by other means.

"As for Guam, the extra weight of the two prisoners was too marginal for me, given the fuel left after the water was removed. Therefore, this is our best tactic," he concluded.

The flight to Guam was otherwise uneventful.

That evening Captain Midnight conferred with the Squadron base commander. Midnight explained that he was carrying important information to the Squadron base in Hawaii. If there was no report of a safe arrival after twelve hours, the commander was to dispatch men to increase security around Major Steele and to make sure he arrived safely at Hawaii.

The base commander observed that things were getting fairly tense in that area of the Pacific. He advised Captain Midnight to fly directly to Hawaii.

With fuel available at the base, Captain Midnight could do just that.

It took some time to rescue The Barracuda and Colonel Goto. They flew back to the Chinese mainland to one of his best-equipped bases. He was angered at Captain Midnight for the loss of face he suffered. Further, the microfilm could prove a great embarrassment should it reach American hands.

It was not too late, he decided. True, Captain Midnight had a head start on him, but not as much as the Secret Squadron commander might have thought. By using an extra-fast amphibian with extended-range fuel tanks, he could catch the Secret Squadron plane before it reached Hawaii.

To think was to act. He began issuing orders.

Dawn was breaking as the Secret Squadron plane droned on over the unbroken waters of the Pacific. Captain Midnight had begun his flight well before dawn, realizing that not only was the flight long, but the flight path made them race toward sunrise. There was nothing to see ahead but water and sky, and Ichabod Mudd and Joyce took turns looking out of the amphibian's rear port, "just to play it safe."

Captain Midnight had long since shut off the radio. A storm somewhere had overloaded the set with static. From their altitude, the dawn broke clear and beautiful.

7. War Clouds Thicken

The two things that saved them were Joyce's remarkable eyesight and the fact that the sky was still darkish behind them. She detected an airplane behind them.

The Barracuda's big four-engine amphibian was gaining. Although faster, it had a shorter range; refueling at sea removed that edge for the Secret Squadron members. The Barracuda had followed the logical route to Hawaii, and his analysis proved correct. Shortly before sunrise, he was able to make out a brilliantly glowing reddish spark almost directly ahead — the gleam of the sun's rays on an aircraft.

On The Barracuda's airplane, there was satisfaction.

Colonel Goto, consulting his watch, observed, "By this time, the information on the microfilm will be of little use."

The Barracuda responded, "That is true, Goto. It is not for that reason I chase them ... now. Captain Midnight, he has thwarted me in a way that I have been dishonored."

Colonel Goto understood and sympathized. The Barracuda was spiritually an Oriental, and Captain Midnight's action had caused him shame.

And with the faster and more heavily armed aircraft, neither The Barracuda nor Colonel Goto had any doubts of the outcome. Honor would be restored.

Alerted by Joyce's warning, Captain Midnight primed everyone to be prepared for a possible air battle. He instructed Joyce to break out the binoculars to see whether she could identify the aircraft that was following them.

As the distance between the two aircraft closed, Joyce was able to report that the other airplane was a four-engine amphibian of the type The Barracuda favored.

Aboard The Barracuda's amphibian, the master criminal was satisfied. It was clear now that they were following the very Secret Squadron amphibian upon which he'd been prisoner. "Man the machine gun, Goto," he said, maneuvering his aircraft to the left of the Secret Squadron plane. "Shoot at the cockpit as we close."

As they closed, the Squadron amphibian seemed to drift to the right and rise. The stream of bullets missed, and The Barracuda tried to compensate. A dogfight ensued that pitted the speed of the larger aircraft against the maneuverability of the smaller.

In the end, Captain Midnight's superior piloting and Ichabod Mudd's marksmanship caused The Barracuda's aircraft to go down in flames. The four-engine aircraft plowed into the water and broke apart. Much of the aircraft debris sank quickly.

Captain Midnight circled the impact point. The Squadron members saw no signs of life, nor had any parachutes been seen. The engagement seemed pretty final.

The Secret Squadron leader resumed his flight to Hawaii, convinced by The Barracuda's attack that the microfilm was of tremendous importance. From the vantage point of The Barracuda plane's wreckage, the Squadron aircraft dwindled from sight; the sounds of the sea soon were the only noises that could be heard.

Then the head of The Barracuda broke the surface. He'd managed to grab a small bottle of compressed oxygen before the plane had been destroyed. And by the Devil's own luck, he'd survived. He was confident that his men would find him; and the nature of his defeat had restored his honor. He vowed that he would meet the Secret Squadron leader once more, and that their next meeting would have a different outcome.

At that, The Barracuda reflected, as he searched for a trace of Colonel Goto, that his defeat was not so much a defeat after all. He'd delayed Captain Midnight long enough. By the time he reached Pearl Harbor, it would be midmorning of December 7, 1941.

8

The War: Moves

By the time Captain Midnight reached the Hawaiian Islands, he and everybody aboard the amphibian knew of the Japanese surprise attack. The Secret Squadron leader realized even before he landed that his victory was a Pyrrhic one. Radio contact to the Secret Squadron base brought news of the bombing and strafing. That news made the meaning of the microfilm both clear and virtually useless.

The Hawaiian Secret Squadron base wasn't near Honolulu; it was semi-concealed elsewhere on the island of Oahu. Even as the military bases were pulling themselves together and preparing for any follow-up raid, Captain Midnight was meeting with the base commander. Clearly, the advent of the war would change the role of the Secret Squadron. But what that role was to be was for others to decide. It was essential that Captain Midnight reach Washington to find out.

Captain Midnight had to travel fast and light. Because speed was of the essence, he left Chuck, Joyce, and Ichabod Mudd behind, attaching them temporarily to the base at Oahu. He instructed them to help the base commander assist in the war effort. And after sending encrypted messages, he set out for Washington, D.C.

The next few days were uneventful for the island-bound Squadron members, but the same couldn't be said for Captain Midnight. Flying across the Pacific was merely tiring; flying across a suddenly war-conscious country was tense. He landed at Base 7 and obtained the fastest aircraft available. Staying just to the correct side of the tachometer's red line, Captain Midnight made only fuel stops, and "greased in" at Bowling Field.

He decided to open a direct line of communication with "Mr. Jones." While ordinarily all administration was supposed to take place through channels, Captain Midnight deemed that another line of communication, strictly for emergency situations, was necessary.

"Mr. Jones" agreed. He set up a council with communication links to himself, the War Department, and the Justice Department. Ordinarily, none of these contacts would be used, but each could supply special communications to "Mr. Jones" if needed.

At meetings precipitated by Captain Midnight, the Squadron leader asked for direction concerning the wartime mission of the Secret Squadron. Many Secret Squadron agents were crack pilots; he inquired whether they'd be transferred into the Army Air Corps.

"Jones" shook his head. "Captain Midnight," he said carefully, "I'm aware that you and your men are eager to close with the enemy. But yours has to be a special mission. Our armed forces are growing. They will be able to handle the ... *conventional* aspects of the war.

"This will not be an entirely conventional war. The degree of espionage and sabotage we experienced while still a neutral country is unprecedented. We must have a powerful and flexible force to counter the less conventional aspects of this struggle, both at home and abroad. And that is where the Secret Squadron must come in."

During the first meeting, Captain Midnight was asked to have his bases investigate local acts of sabotage while the full reorganization of the Secret Squadron was being developed. The final results of that reorganization would be classified information.

(Chuck, Joyce, and Ichabod Mudd were assigned to investigate sabotage connected with a recently launched aircraft carrier that was going on a shakedown cruise. The radio show colored the actual events by saying that the Secret Squadron was getting *its own* aircraft carrier — and that the agents, and Captain Midnight, were investigating sabotage on that carrier.)

The Secret Squadron's first wartime mission was one of the reasons the Squadron was needed for war work. Word had reached various U.S. agencies that a group of Axis sympathizers had produced something that could seriously injure the country, but nobody could get a handle on what it was. All that could be determined was that whatever it might be, it was being readied in Mexico.

There were precious few clues. An intercept or two indicated that whatever was going on seemed to be taking place at a private ranch in the Mexican state of Chihuahua, somewhere between Los Cruces and Coyame.

As a result of the meetings and secret Congressional hearings, the Secret Squadron had been given a special status: It was classified as a "limited armed force." Secret Squadron members could expect to work with and gain the cooperation of the traditional armed services, but they normally wouldn't be under the command or direction of officers or men of any armed service.

For legal reasons, all active Secret Squadron members were technically considered military personnel; field agents were informally considered the equivalent of combat troops. Each was to be trained and maintain proficiency in the use of pistol and rifle. (Captain Midnight was a superlative shot, as he demonstrated many times. The second-best of his party proved to be Joyce Ryan, whose extraordinary eyesight made other agents suggest that they should be issued telescopic sights.) Women field agents were to be as combat-ready as their male counterparts, though they weren't expected to be as physically strong.

Although Captain Midnight tactfully suggested to Joyce that she might consider transferring to base support status rather than field agent, she would hear none of it. "It's as much my war as yours," she said quietly, adding that her mother had been in Honolulu when the Japanese attacked.

Captain Midnight decided that if Joyce was to stay a field agent, she and Chuck could aid him in the Mexican matter. Since they would be going into a country that wasn't at war with the United States, they could travel in civilian dress rather than the uniforms developed for wear in war zones.

Ichabod Mudd wouldn't accompany them. Captain Midnight took his mechanic aside and gave him a special assignment. "Ikky, the Code-O-Graph you were instrumental in designing is good but, particularly in wartime, it's possible one will be captured. We need a new Code-O-Graph that can be issued if a current one is compromised. Also, we'll need an emergency cipher to take us through the transition. It will be your job to see that those vital things get done."

Reluctantly, Mudd agreed to remain behind. Although he wanted very much to accompany his friends, he knew how important the assignment was. Captain Midnight gave him the authority to convene a special cryptology section and to set up a staff that would continue development of new encrypting schemes.

Being left out of the field work, Mudd decided that, as compensation, he'd hide his "signature" in the new Code-O-Graph; a subtle form of personalization. If he just put "M," "U," and "D," in order on the dial, it would be too obvious. But if he made "M" the first letter and "U" the last, remembering that on a cipher disk the scales were circular, it would be good first step. He built up his scale from that.

During wartime, there would have to be a nontrivial reason for traveling out of the country. The region Captain Midnight would be in wasn't a lush or rich area, so there was little chance of concocting a story based on any sort of critical material.

Because nobody was sure just what was being done by the Axis sympathizers, the Secret Squadron party should have a good reason for poking around without arousing suspicions.

Captain Midnight came up with what he hoped was a credible reason. He would pose as a professor of paleontology. During his self-education phase, he'd developed some interest in the subject. He could "talk a fair game" in the field already. As a fossil-hunter, it would be logical for him and his crew to be poking around in the desert. Hunting fossils gave him even more latitude than prospecting. Paleontology was sufficiently esoteric that few, if any, would know if his fossil-hunting methods became unorthodox.

Captain Midnight would have his hair grayed by Squadron cosmeticians so that he'd appear to be too old to be called up to fight; professors were older persons anyway, in the public mind. Joyce, with just the right amount of appropriate makeup, could pose as his secretary, particularly by wearing conservative field clothes. But Chuck? How could his presence be justified with a war on?

The obvious solution: Chuck would be the party's pilot. Though a pilot, he would have to be 4-F; he couldn't qualify as an "essential" civilian function. This could be due to some condition that wouldn't prevent him flying. An appropriate restricted pilot's license and matching medical certificate were produced as well as Selective Service documents.

The airplane chosen for the expedition was a Langley Bi-Motor. The aircraft was a four-place, twin-engine airplane constructed primarily of wood. While a wooden low-wing aircraft was a little unusual, it employed "virtually no defense materials," as a description of the time put it.

The airplane was waiting for Captain Midnight and his party at a secure section of Fort Bliss, Texas, which was next to El Paso. With only three Secret Squadron members, there could have been over 200 pounds of luggage and equipment, but the craft was a bit crowded to put in much more than the essentials.

Captain Midnight arranged to hire a trustworthy local who could be interpreter, guide, and general assistant. That worthy, Pablo Velez, placed orders for equipment and supplies for "Professor Samuels" and his party. By the time the aircraft touched down on the Mexican plains, Velez had tents erected, as well as food, water, and a fairly hefty supply of aviation gasoline.

Captain Midnight decided that "Professor Samuels" should be a traditional absent-minded scholastic. Many cultures had such scholars, and Midnight hoped that a reputation for a short attention span would make people with secrets less on their guard in his presence.

As the leader of the Secret Squadron, Captain Midnight had to keep in touch with his organization. This was done by radio. Thus, even though he was investigating matters in the field, he was able to lead his worldwide organization. Save for a concealed transmitter, "Professor Samuels'" camp was exactly what one would expect of such an expedition.

The campsite was located away from anything resembling a settlement, though there were a few ranches in the region. Midnight spent a few days going over the area near the campsite, just for appearance's sake. (The Secret Squadron leader actually found a few fossil trilobites, almost to his chagrin: He was supposed to be *hunting* for fossils, not discovering any. Thus, his investigations were almost stopped to follow through with his cover story. He solved the problem by having SS-11 come down in disguise as an "assistant professor" from his college to bring back the "extraordinary" fossil find. This let Kelly brief him on many events in greater detail than practical by enciphered radio messages as well as to relieve him of the fossils. They were later quietly — and anonymously — donated to a small natural history museum.)

Captain Midnight had his airplane in the air quite frequently. Through Velez, he let it become known that the *Yanqui profesor* thought it would be easier to spot promising areas for fossils by observing topography from the air. Those locals who saw such antics weren't surprised that the *Norteamericano* should spend his time in the air looking for buried bones; it was typical of strange *Yanqui* behavior. Even in rural Mexico, they'd heard of the odd practices of college professors.

The second day aloft, Joyce spotted something interesting. A truck was traveling along a road toward a house that was separated from the surrounding ranches. Circling wide to avoid arousing suspicions, the crew was able to determine that several small crates were being unloaded and carried into the house. Perhaps they were only supplies for a long stay, but the house might bear watching.

Through Velez, the party learned that the house was owned by one Enrique Espada, who'd recently purchased it. Espada claimed to be an artist, and artist's supplies were said to be trucked to his house every few weeks.

Joyce, who had studied some art, snorted at that. After they were alone, she told Captain Midnight that the cartons she saw would have contained enough supplies to keep a colony of artists busy for months. Bringing truckloads every few weeks seemed suspicious.

Captain Midnight decided that the house required closer investigation. It was the only location in the area where any sort of out-of-the-ordinary action might be taking place. And perhaps the best "cover" was a bold approach.

Thus it was that the small twin-engine aircraft touched down close to, but not on, the Espada property. Captain Midnight, Chuck, Joyce, and Velez deplaned. The party headed to the house.

They were met about halfway there by two men — one, well but casually dressed; the other with standard ranch attire. The well-dressed man fell back slightly while the other continued forward.

The nearer man stopped and spoke in Spanish, which Velez responded to. Velez explained, "This *hombre*, servant to *Señor Espada*, asked us who we are. I explained about the work of the illustrious *Profesor* Samuels. He then asked of me why we have come here. What am I to say?"

Captain Midnight instructed Velez to say that the scientific investigation he'd been directing from the air showed signs of possible fossil finds on and near the Espada land. He was requesting that in the interest of science he could investigate the outcropping of sedimentary rock over there — and he pointed to a rocky area removed some distance from the house.

Velez relayed the information, while Captain Midnight appeared to be in deep thought, studying the rock outcropping. In reality, he was studying the reaction of the more removed man, whom he quickly realized had to be Espada.

A variety of emotions seemed concentrated in Espada's expression. Surprise, annoyance, apprehension, and exasperation seemed to flicker momentarily across his features; but almost all were suppressed quickly. Resuming something akin to a poker face, Espada said a few short words to his employee.

"*Señor* Espada regrets that such activities as the distinguished *profesor* would wish to undertake would interfere with his artistic work," Velez translated. "He does wish you good luck in your search for bones, however."

Having anticipated Espada's refusal, the Secret Squadron leader had Velez gain permission from a rancher whose land abutted Espada's to let the party do some fossil-hunting there. Since he'd told Espada already that he thought land nearby his place might contain promising fossil-bearing rocks, Captain Midnight felt reasonably certain that he wouldn't arouse too many suspicions by exploring there.

Concurrent with setting up a "dig" near the Espada land, Captain Midnight sent an enciphered message to the nearest Secret Squadron base. And one night, the Langley Bi-Motor took off, headed east for a while, then turned north. To any observer near either the Espada house or the "professor's" camp, the aircraft merely flew east.

Captain Midnight was at the controls, and he landed at a normally deserted spot where he made rendezvous with another aircraft. In addition to conferring with a contact from Washington, he helped transfer a few cases from the other plane to his Langley.

The plane returned at dawn, apparently coming from the east, and landed without incident. The cases were offloaded; one "accidentally" opened, and by the dawn's early light, it was seen to contain geological tools and fine-hair brushes useful in fossil recovery.

While it was evident to the camp personnel (and any hidden observers) that the plane had gone for new specialized tools, the "opened" case was the only one to contain such items. The other cases weren't opened until well after dark, and then only in the "professor's" tent.

The others contained electronic gear. Captain Midnight explained that, when assembled, the parts would form an experimental infrared viewing device. The viewer would enable the Secret Squadron agents to observe things in the dark. It was to be used on moonless nights. For well-lit nights, special spyglasses were included.

Several days later, after the crescent moon had set, the break came. Chuck was standing watch, and he saw something suspicious through the infrared device. A man came out of the house and caused a scrub bush to swing back, revealing a small mound with a door. The man stepped through the doorway; after he'd gone, the door closed and the plant slowly returned to its previous position.

Further observations revealed that this sort of activity happened frequently on moonless nights. An investigation was called for, and Chuck decided to go.

Although Captain Midnight warned Chuck to be careful, the youngster saw no harm in getting close to the bush. As it turned out, he was *too* close: The doorway opened and a man emerged. Although the newcomer's eyes weren't fully dark-adjusted, he managed to see Chuck. Startled, the man grappled with the youngster and dragged him below.

Instructing Joyce to stay with the night glasses and cover the area with a rifle, Captain Midnight and Velez rushed to Chuck's aid. As they approached, they heard muffled sounds of a struggle. They came across Chuck struggling with the man; nobody else was present.

Chuck had managed to grab the man so he couldn't yell. But the man was pulling free just as the reinforcements arrived. Between the three, the Espada man stood no chance. He was subdued quickly and silently.

Since things had now gone that far anyway, Captain Midnight decided to explore a bit. After a little figuring, he determined how to move the bush back into position. Then, flashlight on, he opened the door in the ramp beneath the bush.

Fortunately, the room he entered was deserted. It was a large underground chamber with a couple of printing presses in its central area.

It took no time for Captain Midnight to learn what was so secretive at the Espada property: The presses were being used to print counterfeit U.S. currency. A country, particularly one at war, could be crippled by having its currency rendered worthless through a flood of counterfeit money. Examining a sample, Captain Midnight saw that it was very good.

The Squadron party left things pretty much as they found them. They returned to their base cautiously, bringing their prisoner with them. Then Captain Midnight sent an enciphered message requesting aid and describing what they'd discovered.

The prisoner wouldn't talk. After weighing alternatives, he was drugged to simulate some sort of food poisoning. He was semi-comatose, to be found later by his mates within the Espada grounds. Before the drug could wear off, the ranch hand was whisked to a hospital where he was "put in isolation." Ironically, Espada had him driven to the hospital in the "art supplies" truck.

A message came in for Captain Midnight. Deciphered, it indicated that an agent would be dispatched to the area who could act independently of "the professor's" party. The agency dispatching the operative surmised that at least some of the bogus greenbacks were being used to finance the operation; therefore, if a federal agent "just passing through" happened to stumble on the phony money, there would be no suspicion that Captain Midnight's party was involved.

This would protect the cover of the party, since the "Professor Samuels" identity might be needed in the future.

The U.S. agent, one Harold Peters, operating on detached duty, contacted the local Mexican authorities and gave them proof that somebody was passing counterfeit American money. The Mexican forces quickly were able to determine where the money had come from, and then proceeded to arrest the whole Espada crew. They gave up without a fight.

As the case closed, Chuck observed that they were now out of a job. Joyce pointed out that until the war was won, their job was far from over.

A telegram "from the college" required the immediate return of "the professor" and his party. So, with farewells to the locals (and deep private thanks to Velez) the party departed — to return to Secret Squadron Headquarters.

Upon arrival, they learned that Ichabod Mudd wasn't there. He'd completed development of the new Code-O-Graph; and special dies for its manufacture had already been made. These were secured in the most protected area of Headquarters. In the event they were needed, they could be put into production quickly. The stamping rooms were less than 50 yards distant.

Since that job had been completed, Mudd elected to go to a Squadron base that was just set up in the Pacific. It was on an island located south of Hawaii and north of Palmyra. It was one of several offshore bases being established on "extended U.S. territory" (unclaimed islands that the U.S.

8. The War: Moves

could call its own); and it was one Captain Midnight was scheduled to visit soon.

After attending to important administrative details at Headquarters, Captain Midnight departed for the island base. He took Chuck and Joyce with him. He wanted to see how well the base had been established and to determine if there were any problems. The results would enable the base to be used as a model for any later extra-territorial bases.

The Secret Squadron had by that time developed a symbol. It was a winged clock face with the hands pointing at twelve. This highlighted the flight orientation of the organization and the man who led it. All Squadron aircraft on the island already carried the symbol, from light observation planes and fighters to the largest based there, Captain Midnight's twin-engine amphibian.

When an aircraft with United States markings (but *without* the Secret Squadron symbol) landed on the island, it was a bit of a shock. It arrived several weeks after Captain Midnight turned the island into the temporary Pacific Headquarters for the Squadron. The guards who surrounded the aircraft were even more surprised when the pilot (who, except for his parachute, was in civilian clothes) asked to see Captain Midnight.

After being escorted to Captain Midnight's office, the visitor, who carried no identifying documents, proved to the Squadron leader's complete satisfaction that he was from Washington, working in concert with U. S. Intelligence. The man never did give his name.

He had a job for the Pacific branch of the Squadron. The United States had been working on a radically new type of aircraft—the Flying Wing. Although hardly public, Captain Midnight was aware of such a project and that some Flying Wings had already flown in California.

His visitor apprised him that a second developmental phase had begun. A newer Wing, larger than the original N1M "Jeep," had been built. It had borne out earlier predictions of a stable, flight-efficient aircraft (it was part of a secret project to develop a pure–Wing bomber). One of the new models had been outfitted for a very long-range flight. The initial idea was to fly it from California to Hawaii and return, nonstop, back to California. It was hoped by this to simulate a nonstop, great-circle route to Australia. The Flying Wing was to be used as a high-altitude observation craft; a refueling stop at Hawaii was optional.

"We're not quite sure what happened, Captain," the visitor said. "Under what we thought was the greatest secrecy, the Wing landed in Hawaii at night to top off its tanks. Shortly before dawn, it took off but headed for the southwest rather than going on the assigned northeast course."

"As if the pilot decided to fly it to Australia?" said Captain Midnight.

"Yes. But it never arrived. Neither there, nor as far as we can determine, anywhere else. We radioed in code, and a destroyer on patrol here," the visitor indicated a point on a large Navy chart, "spotted it. The skipper couldn't be sure because of the altitude, but he said that it appeared as if one of its props was feathered."

Captain Midnight nodded. He suggested that perhaps the pilot had accidentally been flying a reciprocal course, and had gotten into trouble.

The visitor disagreed. "The pilot, Ted Russell, is one of the best. We know that the Wing hasn't fallen into enemy hands — yet. If it does, we'll lose a great advantage. We're beginning to suspect that despite our precautions, Russell may have been captured and substituted for by a pilot of The Barracuda...."

"The Barracuda!" said Captain Midnight. "I thought he was dead!"

"Intelligence found out otherwise," the visitor said. He went on to say that The Barracuda apparently rebuilt his organization and based it on a series of Pacific islands, not unlike the dispersal of the Secret Squadron's own forces.

Returning to the subject, the visitor indicated the last sighted position of the aircraft on a detailed navigational chart. A projection of the Wing's course would have brought it near some volcanic islands, uninhabited except for natives and visited infrequently by ships of a pearl-fishing syndicate.

If the Wing went down in the water, the flight data would be lost — to the Axis as well as to the United States. If it reached the islands, it was important for the United States to make sure that the secrets of the Flying Wing didn't fall into the hands of the enemy.

The visitor took his leave. He boarded his airplane and took off for the return trip to Hawaii. And Captain Midnight studied the navigation chart carefully.

Elsewhere, The Barracuda had been quite active. His new lieutenant, Captain Franz, and he were in conference with a sleek and well-groomed spy, Carla Rotan. The Barracuda had explained that at great risk, his agents managed to infiltrate the field at Hawaii, capture Ted Russell, and substitute one of his own pilots. (He'd totally reorganized. His pilots, for instance, had been renamed "Wolf Pilots"; wolves worked in packs, and he wanted his pilots to work closely in coordinated actions.)

The Barracuda's plan had been for his pilot to fly the Wing to one of his bases. From there, after careful examination by his own technicians, he could then negotiate with his Japanese contacts for delivery of the aircraft.

But something had gone awry. The aircraft never reached the strip prepared for it. Hence the need to call on Carla Rotan. The Barracuda was convinced that the United States would initiate a search, probably by an intelligence agency — most likely, the Secret Squadron. Carla Rotan's mission: to

8. The War: Moves

assume some sort of identity and make contact with whatever agency would be conducting the search.

If that agency could locate the Flying Wing, The Barracuda's forces could close in and capture it. Thus, The Barracuda felt, he could make his enemies work for him.

Carla Rotan chose her cover identity carefully. She wasn't entirely familiar with American ways. After some thought, she decided upon the identity of one "Mrs. F. W. Bosmouth," of Boston, Massachusetts. The patrician ways of an upper-class Bostonian, who might be a bit Europeanized, could mask cultural deficiencies. She was given a twin-engine amphibian, the services of a pilot, Jack Carstairs, and appropriate forged documents.

Interestingly, the Secret Squadron found Carla Rotan rather than vice versa. Chuck and Joyce were "trying out a new pursuit job" when they encountered the spy's plane. She'd been searching for an island when she spotted the Squadron aircraft. Seeing its American markings, she had Carstairs fly so that the other aircraft's pilot couldn't help but see the amphibian. She then had him land at a nearby island so that the Americans would be sure to follow.

Chuck landed, but wisely positioned his aircraft so that its .50 caliber guns covered the amphibian. Then, leaving Joyce to man the guns, he stepped out to talk. To say he was astonished would have been an understatement when, rather than some sinister-looking ruffian, he was greeted by a beautiful, glamorous woman.

"Mrs. Bosmouth" explained her presence to Chuck and Joyce (who'd joined Chuck after Carstairs had emerged from the amphibian and it was fairly evident that nobody else was aboard). Her story was that she was on a personal crusade to locate her long-lost brother, whose plane had gone down somewhere in the surrounding waters months before the war (her real brother was serving a life term in a Spanish prison).

Since she was in the middle of a war zone and appeared to be defenseless, the only choice that seemed open was to bring her to the Secret Squadron base. Both Joyce and Chuck agreed that, because of the situation, they would tell "Mrs. Bosmouth" as little as possible about the nature of the facility; not even that it was a Secret Squadron base.

They radioed ahead. Soon the pursuit plane, just outside the slow-flight region, led Carla Rotan's aircraft to an uneventful landing at the Squadron base.

Naturally, as Carstairs taxied over to the hangar area, Carla Rotan looked around. What she saw was many aircraft, new buildings, and activity involving many men, all in military-looking uniforms but without insignia.

Carla Rotan was far from stupid. While the winged-clock symbol wasn't known to many outside the Squadron, the large concentration of aircraft with a marking in addition to the conventional United States patterning, plus the clothing (which both the youngsters she'd spoken to also wore), made her believe that she'd stumbled onto a base of the Secret Squadron. The Barracuda had suggested that the Squadron would be a likely candidate in the search for the Flying Wing. She tried to take in every detail she could.

Captain Midnight was introduced to her only as "The Captain" in a mild attempt to hide his identity. Everybody at the base called him "Captain"; the habit was too hard to break. It was thought that the title might confuse "Mrs. Bosmouth" into thinking that the base was some sort of auxiliary Navy station.

Realizing that much was being withheld from her, and intuiting that "The Captain" might be none other than Captain Midnight, she decided to probe for the weakest link in the security chain imposed on her. In her opinion, that weak spot was Chuck Ramsay.

At the time, Chuck was just a few months shy of his eighteenth birthday. Carla Rotan reasoned that the attention of a woman, particularly one who (she was the first to admit) was beautiful, would dazzle him enough to make him a good source of information.

Her estimate was substantially correct. Although Chuck was able to keep a secret, a few little things slipped out. One was the identity of the Secret Squadron leader. One time, when he asked Chuck to tell "Mrs. Bosmouth" that it was time to eat, the youngster walked up to her and said, "Captain Midnight asked me to escort you to dinner, Mrs. Bosmouth."

Carla Rotan kept that, and other such discoveries, to herself. She reserved using the identity card until her plans were a little more settled.

"Mrs. Bosmouth's" presence was hampering Captain Midnight from starting his search for the Flying Wing, since it was a military secret. Since she was in a war zone, he could order a squadron of aircraft to escort her to United States territory. He reasoned that he could outfit his twin-engine amphibian for an extended search, and take off with the escorting aircraft; at some point he'd leave them and start his investigation.

The Barracuda had plans, too. Though he'd engaged Carla Rotan's services, he was too intelligent to put all his eggs in a single basket. He had the Flying Wing's pilot, Ted Russell, as a captive. He reasoned that whoever was conducting the investigation might think that the Wing had gone down at sea. But if he released Russell, whatever agency was conducting the investigation might be galvanized into more frenzied (and thus more easily detectable) activities in trying to locate the Wing.

Carla Rotan had become stymied. She didn't dare radio The Barracuda from the Squadron base; the transmission would have been detected imme-

8. The War: Moves

diately. When she heard about the escorted flight "back" to United States' territory, she wasn't comforted. At best, it would prove inconvenient. If she ran into the wrong people, it could be worse.

But she got lucky.

Under the careful scrutiny of the Squadron, she took off with her escort force. The aircraft formed up around her, and the flight turned toward the north. About twenty minutes' flight time later, the unexpected happened.

A formation of aircraft appeared from the west. The lead plane was The Barracuda's four-engine amphibian. Surrounding it was a number of his Wolf Pilots in fast and deadly fighters. As it happened, it was a chance meeting; but each side recognized the other as an enemy, and battle was joined.

There were aircraft all over the sky; the fighters were appreciably faster and more maneuverable than the amphibians. It took some minutes for either group to set up standard tactics; the amphibians were more or less ignored.

Eventually, it ended, and the respective sides retired. By the time everything was sorted out, the aircraft losses were four Barracuda planes and one Secret Squadron plane. Three Squadron planes were badly shot up and required major repairs upon landing.

It was just a skirmish. However, Captain Midnight, Ichabod Mudd, Chuck, and Joyce, in Captain Midnight's amphibian, heard virtually all of the battle by listening on the Squadron's radio frequency.

The one Squadron pilot who'd been shot down wasn't located, despite repeated radio calls both from the air and from the Squadron base. Joyce speculated that perhaps the pilot was wounded; possibly unconscious.

"Or he might have been captured," Captain Midnight said. "If he was, I hope he retained consciousness long enough to get rid of his Code-O-Graph." The Squadron leader realized that a captured Code-O-Graph would provide the enemies with sufficient clues so that they would be able to break messages based on field code or direct encipherment.

The Squadron fighters regrouped, then they continued on to Hawaii. Captain Midnight's aircraft turned to a heading that would bring it to the island group over which the Flying Wing would most likely have passed, according to the information given by Midnight's mysterious visitor.

The flight was uneventful. Captain Midnight found an island at the approximate location indicated on the chart. There were a few surrounding ones, but Midnight chose the largest. It had numerous areas suitable for mooring small boats or amphibians. It seemed like an excellent spot to establish an *ad hoc* field headquarters or command post.

After landing, the Squadron members discovered that the island was even better than it looked from the air. Many edible plants abounded, and the lagoon swarmed with fish. "If any of those fish are edible," Captain Midnight said, "we'll be able to stretch our supplies quite far."

"Don't worry, Cap'n," Ichabod Mudd said. "I'll find out for you." Despite his lanky frame, Mudd had a reputation of being something of a gourmand. His response provoked a laugh. But within a day, he'd determined not only which fish were edible, but which were the best-tasting!

During the first full day on the island, the Squadron members heard a droning sound which they recognized immediately as coming from an airplane. Joyce spotted the aircraft first, describing it as a twin-engine amphibian, similar to the Squadron plane. The strange airplane flew on past the island, apparently oblivious to the presence of the Squadron plane, much to everybody's relief.

Later, however, the plane returned, flying lower. The pilot obviously spotted the Squadron plane, at least on the second pass, for the amphibian banked sharply away. Joyce remarked that the aircraft was unmarked, just like "Mrs. Bosmouth's" amphibian. It flew toward the other side of the island and disappeared from view.

Chuck and Joyce decided to explore a bit of the island's jungle close to their camp. When they returned, they discovered that Captain Midnight and Ichabod Mudd weren't in the camp; but it wasn't deserted. "Mrs. Bosmouth" and her pilot were there.

The lady spy feigned surprise at meeting Chuck and Joyce again. She indicated that she was at the camp to see if anyone was there.

Joyce had been a little suspicious of her. So she asked why she was on the island at all, rather than being in Hawaii or on the mainland. Carla Rotan replied, "When I left that awful air fight, I left the company of your escorting flight. I decided I'd be as safe on my own. I don't want to cast aspersions on pilots of the Secret Squadron."

Joyce snapped, "What makes you think they were Secret Squadron pilots?"

Carla Rotan laughed. "Some nights ago, Chuck told me that Captain Midnight wanted me to know that dinner was ready. Of course, we all know what organization Captain Midnight heads."

Chuck was acutely uncomfortable, but he kept his expression neutral. After a bit of skillful verbal fencing with Joyce, Carla Rotan took her leave.

Joyce immediately checked the amphibian, and uncovered evidence that the visitors had been snooping inside the aircraft. This reinforced her suspicions of "Mrs. Bosmouth."

When Captain Midnight returned, Joyce told him of the visitation and showed him the evidence of snooping. She opined that "Mrs. Bosmouth" was working for someone.

Captain Midnight nodded. "If she's not a spy, there's certainly something very mysterious about her. When she's around, we'll all have to be on our toes." He related that while the visitors had been going through the Squadron plane, he'd been going through theirs. He added that he hadn't uncovered anything definitely suspicious.

"Her presence on this island is suspicious enough for me," Joyce said.

That noon, the Secret Squadron members tuned in to a certain wavelength to receive a general message from Pacific Headquarters. One was usually transmitted at that time; this one brought grim news. The Squadron plane that had been shot down in the recent battle had been found, and it was empty. Kelly had to assume that the missing agent's Code-O-Graph might have fallen into enemy — or at least unfriendly — hands. He therefore advised to send only routine messages using the current Code-O-Graph.

Captain Midnight realized that he'd have to take a personal hand. He ordered everyone into the amphibian. He didn't want to send messages from the island, so he flew a course that took him some 200 miles away. He decided that if anyone should triangulate his transmissions, it would be better that they come from a region of open sea.

When he reached the spot he'd chosen, he ordered the current Code-O-Graph scrapped, with an immediate shift to the emergency cipher scheme. It was sent out in Super Code 1 as the plain encipherment of a single word: "ARMAGEDDON." This alerted all agents to retire their Code-O-Graphs without immediately alerting enemy agents what was happening. He knew that within the week, the new Code-O-Graphs would be in the hands of all active agents.

"Loopin' loops, Captain," said Chuck. "We'll be the only members of the Squadron who won't have the new Code-O-Graphs. Or do you plan to have some air dropped to us?"

"No. We have to stick fairly close to the island," Captain Midnight said. "We don't want to chance having anyone tail a plane here. We'll just have to do without."

"We already have Mrs. Bosmouth around, Cap'n," Ichabod Mudd pointed out.

"That's true," the Secret Squadron leader said. "However, she seems to be acting on her own. We can handle her and her pilot ourselves. I'm concerned about The Barracuda or the Japanese. We don't want to call any more attention to this region than it already has. That's why I'm not flying to Hawaii to pick up our Code-O-Graphs, either."

Joyce then pointed out that things might not be completely lost. It was Ichabod Mudd who led the design of the new Code-O-Graph. Maybe he could reconstruct it.

"How about it, Ikky?" Captain Midnight said.

"Well, Cap'n, I'll give it a try. But if I get even one letter wrong, it might not work," Mudd said, pointing out that there were 676 ways to arrange the letters of the alphabet. (Here, Ichabod Mudd erred. There are 676 possible letter-number combinations on a cipher disk, but there are literally billions of ways to order the letters of the alphabet.)

"We all have confidence in you, particularly your memory," Captain Midnight said.

After they returned to the island, Captain Midnight kept the radio on to hear whether the order was being transmitted. It was. Just before he could turn off the radio, Captain Midnight received another message, apparently directed to him from the missing squadron agent. Deciphered, it said, "SSPFRTHRE TO CAPTN MIDNT. HAVE PICKED UP TRAIL OF FLYING WING. AWAITING ORDERS."

Chuck said, "Gee, sir, that news seems almost too good to be true."

Captain Midnight said, thoughtfully, "I'd say it *was* too good to be true. Agent SS-P43 didn't know the nature of our mission. How did he find out we were looking for a Flying Wing? And why did he send the message in a cipher he'd just been told to discard?"

After a moment, Chuck said, "Well, maybe he was afraid of losing you, since you'd be likely to turn off the radio after hearing the Headquarters message."

"The chance is slim, but I'll send another message to see whether that one was genuine," Captain Midnight said. "Since SS-P43 was probably transmitting his designator while ditching, anyone could have used it. However, the message is worth following up."

Captain Midnight told Chuck to fly the aircraft while he made up the message. "Fly 200 miles along island bearing 250, then circle." While Chuck was handling the amphibian, the Secret Squadron leader was encrypting his message, using the old Code-O-Graph, choosing his words with care.

When Chuck called back that he was at the proper spot, Midnight sent, "CAPTN MIDNT TO SSPFRTHRE. SEND POSITION AND DETAILS UNDER ARMAGEDDON CONDITIONS."

They circled for a while. The lack of response was all the proof needed that the message was a fake.

Captain Midnight took the controls and started to head the aircraft along magnetic bearing 070. Chuck asked him, "Sir, aren't you going in the wrong direction?"

When asked what he meant, Chuck said, "Well, I flew so that the island would be on a bearing of 250 from us."

Captain Midnight interrupted, apologizing. He said that what he meant to convey was that Chuck should fly along a bearing line of 250 *from* the island. They were exactly 400 miles from where the first message had been

8. The War: Moves

sent. Worse, triangulation would locate two points that, if a line were drawn between them, would run right through the island.

"Well, Chuck, let's hope that one of those two positions was *not* triangulated," Captain Midnight concluded. "But cheer up, you're not the first pilot to be done in by a reciprocal heading."

After they landed, Captain Midnight told the others he wanted to find some place inland to land the amphibian. "I'd like to find some place where I can conceal it," he said. "I want to cover the possibility that The Barracuda, or anyone else, for that matter, might follow the line between the transmission points."

Joyce said that as they were landing, she'd spotted a two-masted schooner at anchor in one of the other inlets. She asked whether Captain Midnight thought it could have anything to do with someone having his signal traced.

"It's doubtful, Joyce," Captain Midnight said. "The schooner would have to be very close to the island to get here in time to drop anchor before we returned. But it does suggest that this island seems to attract people. Perhaps one of them will have seen the Flying Wing, though we'll have to be careful how we ask them."

Chuck and Joyce decided to explore inland for a clearing to land the amphibian. This couldn't be done by air, because what might look like a promising clearing from the air could have holes, stumps, or other obstacles that could damage a landing aircraft, especially an amphibian. Each took a .45 caliber automatic, so Captain Midnight worried that they'd run into more than they could handle. He wasn't concerned that they'd get lost. Although the trees didn't grow moss, Chuck had a ruggedized compass with him.

Captain Midnight's chief immediate concern was whether Ichabod Mudd could reconstruct the new Code-O-Graph. The Squadron's Chief Mechanic was seated at the navigation table with several sheets in front of him. Midnight asked how he was progressing.

"I'm not sure, Cap'n. When you assigned me to design the Code-O-Graph, I thought I'd have a little fun by … well, kinda personalizing it. I took the letters 'I,' 'M,' 'U,' and 'D,' and scattered them around the dial. I put 'M' in the first position, and worked counterclockwise. The next letter was 'U,' of course. Then, because 'D' appears twice in my last name, I stepped off eleven more spaces, since eleven times 'D' would be 'DD.' And since 'Ichabod' has seven letters in it, I dropped 'I' in the seventh spot on the dial, but to keep it out of the last name, I started working clockwise. Then I noticed that the only two letters together were 'UM.' Since you used to kid me about chewing gum, I put 'G' in front of it, to make it 'GUM,' and then, because I had a hankering for some soup at the time, I added 'BO' to it to turn it into 'GUMBO.' Then it gets a bit harder. I remember adding a 'Q' to the 'BO' because when we visited that Army flying field, we were housed in the Bachelor Officer Quarters. I remember a clockwise 'NYC' for 'New York City,' which I put in because I like the New York Yankees, and I couldn't use the 'Y' twice. Then I wanted to use the word 'play,' on accounta' doing what I was doing was fun; and because I already used the 'Y,' I spelled it 'PLAE,' which I also set clockwise. From there on, it gets harder."

"Keep at it, Ikky. You've got more than half the letters already," said Captain Midnight. "With that much accomplished, I'm sure you can reconstruct the rest."

"I'll do my best, Cap'n."

The Barracuda hadn't heard from Carla Rotan for some time. He speculated that Carla Rotan's reputation might have been overblown, or she might betray him for a higher bidder. Whichever, it was without her help that he secured a Code-O-Graph; and through an assistant who was expert in codes and ciphers, he found out how to operate it. Through a careful message, he was able to determine that Captain Midnight was leading the search for the Flying Wing. And through triangulation, he established a line that should bring him to Captain Midnight.

The Barracuda was no coward. He realized that there was no way that Captain Midnight could conduct a secret investigation with a small fleet of aircraft; he'd use only one or two. Therefore, he had no qualms about doing some "singlehanded" investigation of his own. His new four-engine amphibian had been engineered for speed and maneuverability, and Captain Franz was a skilled pilot.

The Barracuda left instructions at his island base for his lieutenants to monitor a certain radio frequency. If he were to call them on that wavelength, they were to be in the air within 20 minutes. Then he departed to track down Captain Midnight, and perhaps the Flying Wing as well.

The expedition mounted by Chuck and Joyce bore fruit. They had worked their way to the center of the island and found a small lake and a natural clearing that was as smooth as if the land had been bulldozed. It was a perfect spot to relocate the amphibian.

Just before they left the clearing, Joyce noticed something. Some trees at the edge of the clearing showed signs of damage. After studying them closely, she and Chuck came to the conclusion that they'd been broken as the result of some sort of air crash. Her excitement rose momentarily as she speculated that perhaps the two of them found the location of the downed Flying Wing; but only momentarily. It took little study, even from a distance, to see whatever accident befell the trees took place years ago.

Captain Franz was a very skilled pilot. After locating one of the triangulated transmission points, he flew unerringly along the line connecting that point to the other located by The Barracuda's radiomen. In due time, an island was spotted dead ahead, visible for many miles in the clear air. Captain Franz noted that the island was almost exactly midway between the two triangulated points.

The Barracuda surmised that it was the island where Captain Midnight had to be. He ordered Captain Franz to lose altitude in hopes of catching his enemy before being spotted. The pilot complied.

Close to the island as air travel goes, The Barracuda spied an amphibian aircraft dead in the water near a beach, to all appearances tied or at anchor. Suspecting the aircraft might belong to Captain Midnight, he had Captain Franz land with as much speed as he could consistent with safety and spray a stream of machine-gun fire across the bow of the other aircraft to prevent it from making any sudden moves.

There were none. Eventually, from the other aircraft, Carla Rotan emerged. She was as annoyed with The Barracuda as he was with her. Because she hadn't communicated, The Barracuda told her, he suspected her of double-dealing, and he wanted an explanation.

She in turn snapped at him that it was hard enough for her to learn what she already had without his barging in and nearly spoiling everything. Hadn't she trailed Captain Midnight to this very island? And was she not on the verge of getting a key to the Secret Squadron "code"? She resented his lack of trust, and said they could still work together — but only if he wouldn't try to hamstring her or insist upon looking over her shoulder as she worked.

Approving her efforts to obtain information on the "code," The Barracuda directed Carla Rotan to observe the Squadron agents closely. As soon as they located the Flying Wing, she could call the Wolf Pilots through him, and the Wing could be recovered — with Captain Midnight probably destroyed in the bargain. The Barracuda would be elsewhere, but close enough so that even a very weak signal on a specified frequency could reach him and his forces.

The meeting ended, and The Barracuda's plane took to the air. It landed further along the periphery of the island, in a sheltered inlet, where it would be very hard to spot from the air, particularly with camouflage markings spread across its wings. Despite his assurances to her, The Barracuda still didn't entirely trust Carla Rotan.

The lady spy returned to the site of the Secret Squadron's lagoon camp and found it deserted. During the time she'd been fencing with The Barracuda, Captain Midnight's party had loaded their equipment, boarded their amphibian, and flown off.

Captain Midnight landed the amphibian at the surprisingly smooth clearing and taxied it under cover. From the air, the plane couldn't be seen, but it could take off easily should the situation arise.

At the new campsite, Ichabod Mudd put the finishing touches on his "homebrew" Code-O-Graph. Nobody in the Squadron party had the slightest desire to interrupt his work. They all realized that if he couldn't reconstruct the cipher alphabet, they would have to compromise their security by either flying for one or having a Squadron plane fly some down. Captain Midnight thought the security was shaky enough already; however, the leader of the Secret Squadron *had* to be able to communicate with his organization.

Chuck and Joyce spent the afternoon exploring the area at the clearing's edge. There Chuck examined a peculiarly shaped piece of wood that Joyce had happened upon. Chuck recognized it as a piece of a tail skid from an old-fashioned airplane. He became convinced that there once had been an air accident in the clearing, though years ago.

The two youngsters took their find to Captain Midnight. He said that the information was interesting, but that it would have to wait. The Squadron had distributed the new Code-O-Graph more rapidly than originally scheduled, and the new cryptological scheme would go into effect the next day! Given the criticality of Mudd's work, thoughts of the air crash were dismissed for a while.

The following morning, the first message in the new cipher was transmitted by Kelly to Captain Midnight. The "homebrew" Code-O-Graph worked perfectly, to everybody's relief. Midnight ordered the amphibian made ready for a reply. He and Mudd took off.

Contact was established with Pacific Headquarters; and with it came startling news. Ted Russell, pilot of the lost Flying Wing, had been recovered. Details followed: Russell had been released rather than escaping, and his captor was The Barracuda.

It was obvious to him that Russell had been released to goad the Squadron into intensifying its search for the Flying Wing. That told him that the Flying Wing was not in the hands of the enemy, and that his party was being watched constantly. This further dispelled any doubts about "Mrs. Bosmouth." There was no question that the sleek and glamorous lady could be nothing other than a spy.

The entire Squadron party went on a search mission. Returning late, they decided not to land at their new camp, and instead landed in the inlet abandoned the other day and tied up near Carla Rotan's aircraft.

While they were landing, Joyce spotted a fire inland, the sort of glow that might have come from a campfire. Captain Midnight speculated that it might have been lit by natives, who were notoriously shy on such islands. He added that it was also possible that it might have been lit by someone

8. The War: Moves

from the schooner that Joyce spotted the other day. But he kept his speculation to himself and to the Secret Squadron members, and used the appearance of the fire as an excuse for revisiting the lagoon, asking "Mrs. Bosmouth" whether she had any idea about it.

The Squadron members, Carla Rotan, and Jack Carstairs spent a little time in social chit-chat. The lady spy indicated that she had no idea what the fire could represent, and voiced doubt that it was anything significant, probably natives. The rest of the conversation had no more depth than discussing the weather.

Shortly, the Squadron members excused themselves, mentioning the need of rest after a hard day. Naturally, the Squadron members took turns keeping watch that night.

The next morning, Carla Rotan spied Chuck Ramsay and approached him with a request. She knew that the Secret Squadron could send out messages in code. Her radio was out of commission, and she had a message for her "poor, dear mother" with confidential information in it. Batting her eyelashes at Chuck, she asked him if he would prevail on Captain Midnight to send the message in code on his obviously powerful radio.

Chuck, flustered, said he'd see what he could do.

After scanning the message, Captain Midnight realized immediately what "Mrs. Bosmouth's" scheme was. She obviously kept a copy of the message. It was reasonably long, and some of the words were chosen to provide character-sequence recognition. These two things would give her a key to the basic code scheme. But he said with a smile, "We don't want Mrs. Bosmouth to think we suspect her of being a spy, do we?" and agreed to send her message.

He sent it out, but using the retired Code-O-Graph, which was compromised. He sent it out as a simple cipher, with no second-level encryption. He sent it in the Super Code 4 key: the Super Code designator immediately alerted the Squadron listener that the message was spurious. There were no Super Code designators on the new Code-O-Graph.

After breakfast with the "Bosmouth" party, the Squadron plane took off and headed to the clearing by a circuitous route. The landing was uneventful, and the aircraft was soon concealed and oriented for an easy takeoff.

At the clearing, Captain Midnight said there was no doubt that "Mrs. Bosmouth" was some sort of spy. He agreed that the damaged trees were evidence of some sort of aircraft accident. Although they were probably ancient history, for safety's sake, they should be investigated. Similarly, the mysterious fire she'd spotted while they were landing was worth some study. Therefore, Captain Midnight divided the Squadron party in two. Chuck and Joyce would investigate the broken-tree area. Perhaps between the two groups, they might come up with some clue on the whereabouts and disposition of the Flying Wing.

They did, but only in the most roundabout way.

While Captain Midnight and Ichabod Mudd worked their way south, Chuck and Joyce returned to the area where they found the tail skid. By casting about just a bit more, they found parts of a rudder, which Chuck tentatively identified as coming from an early Fokker cabin plane. He also found a rusted lump of what once was an aircraft engine (which could have been one of a pair; he couldn't be sure). And Joyce found the bulk of the fuselage.

They approached it carefully, in case there was someone in it. It was deserted. The interior had been converted from a cockpit-and-cabin area to rough living quarters. Evidence within suggested that its occupant had been living on the island for many years.

The youngsters instantly realized what had happened. An early aviator had been forced down on the island and effectively had been a castaway ever since. But considering the many people now visiting the island, that seemed a bit strange.

As they were discussing their find, they heard in the distance first one, then the other of the Secret Squadron amphibian's engines cough into life. The awkwardness of the startup alerted the youngsters that an inexperienced hand was at the controls.

Breaking into a run, they arrived at the clearing just as the amphibian was beginning an awkward takeoff roll. However, whoever was trying to get away with the amphibian was sufficiently inexpert that the aircraft never became truly airborne, and it cracked up. (In the radio sequence, the crackup was supposedly abetted by Joyce clambering onto the empennage. Actually, the pilot realized he'd never clear the trees and tried to abort, too late. Although not as dramatic as the radio version, the effect was the same.)

When the youngsters reached the damaged amphibian, the sight that greeted them was picturesque. The pilot, who'd been knocked out, was a tanned, scraggly-bearded individual dressed only in a breechcloth that appeared to have been made out of parachute silk.

Captain Midnight and Ichabod Mudd ran up, inquiring what had happened. Chuck and Joyce briefed them, adding that the stranger could be none other than the missing pilot.

The Secret Squadron leader investigated, finding a mildewed old briefcase. Besides some trinkets, the briefcase contained the remnants of a wallet with a pilot's license issued in 1927 to one William S. Madison.

Captain Midnight nodded. "So that's what happened to him," he said. He explained that years ago Madison had been reported to be going on some

8. The War: Moves

sort of Pacific treasure hunt and had simply disappeared. He added, "Such disappearances were common in those days."

Madison was transported to the Squadron tent. He was placed on a cot. Ichabod Mudd left to investigate the condition of the plane. He returned shortly, with the gloomy news that he couldn't be sure whether the amphibian could even be repaired.

This news was made doubly frustrating a few minutes later. Madison awoke, and anxiously looked around for some way of escape. Despite reassurances from the Squadron members that they were friendly, he was still uneasy. He asked them if they were connected with a Captain Peter Burley, and was relieved to find out they weren't. Then he confided that he was getting worried about his exile; his prolonged near-isolation, he feared, was beginning to affect his mind. Only a week or so ago, he reported, he'd seen a *thing* flying in the sky. Something impossible: like part of an aircraft without the rest.

"The Flying Wing!" the Secret Squadron party said almost in unison.

Captain Midnight told Madison not to worry about his mental condition. He pointed out that the isolation had deprived him of more than a decade of aeronautical knowledge. He explained in broad (unclassified) terms what the Wing was, and that it was important for his party to find it.

Madison was perfectly willing to talk about the Wing, having been assured that it wasn't a hallucination. He said that one of its engines seemed inoperative. It had passed over the clearing, then headed in the direction of another island, flying low. He added that when he'd had his accident, he had tried the other island first and found the place not suitable to land. With the Flying Wing in trouble, the only possible deduction was that it crashed either on the other island or in the sea nearby.

As Captain Midnight started speculating on the chances of how best to follow up given the loss of his amphibian, there was an interruption. A gruff voice called from the edge of the clearing, inquiring whether anyone was in the camp.

The sound of the voice terrified Madison. He identified the caller as Captain Burley and begged the Squadron members not to turn him over to the gruff-voiced man. Assuring Madison that he'd be protected, Captain Midnight, Chuck, and Joyce went to meet the newcomer.

Burley was patently a seafarer, and his appearance matched his name. Peter Burley was a powerful, almost gorilla-shaped man, with a whisker-stubbled face and an aggressive attitude. He made no bones about his mission: He came to find Bill Madison and would tolerate no interference.

The Secret Squadron leader indicated that if Madison wanted to see Burley, it was between the two of them. But not in his camp.

Since Captain Midnight confronted Burley with a drawn automatic, and since he was backed up by Chuck and Ichabod Mudd, the fact that Burley had several of his own men with him didn't matter. It was a standoff. Burley departed, suggesting that Captain Midnight and crew quit the island quickly — if they knew what was good for them. He didn't say he'd be back, but the implied threat was understood by all.

As Captain Midnight walked back to the tent, he reflected that, given the clue just supplied by Madison, he'd be more than happy to oblige the sea captain. However, whether he'd be able to do so would depend upon the skill of his Chief Mechanic, and perhaps a bit of luck.

Joyce ran out to meet the others with disturbing news: She'd left the tent where she'd been watching Madison to get an idea of what was going on. She left for only a few moments; when she returned, Madison was gone.

Captain Midnight shrugged. "Probably it was his fear of Burley. Too bad he didn't trust us, but he did give us the clue we needed."

While Mudd worked on the amphibian, Captain Midnight studied the navigation charts. He was checking to see whether there was something he might have overlooked to help him travel between the islands, should the amphibian prove unflyable.

Unfortunately, the charts helped little. The island group wasn't charted in detail; it wasn't quite "uncharted," but the islands' fine details were absent. The only one who could probably give him useful information might be Captain Burley, who hardly could be considered an ally.

He was reaching to roll up the charts when Ichabod Mudd entered the tent carrying the limp body of Bill Madison. He explained that while he was working on the aircraft, someone scrambled aboard. Mudd couldn't see who it was, as the brighter light from outside showed the intruder only in silhouette, and thought it might be one of Burley's men. Mudd knocked him out before his eyes could adjust to the dimmer light of the cabin. It was then that he discovered it was Madison.

"Poor devil," Captain Midnight said. He added that it seemed curious that Madison would return to an obviously wrecked aircraft.

"Oh, I found out why, Cap'n," Mudd said. He reached into a pocket and withdrew a rude pouch made of parachute silk. "Look inside."

The pouch contained pearls, big ones and perfect. The fortune they represented explained a lot, including the behavior of Captain Burley. If Burley knew of Madison's pearls, then he would naturally try to get his hands on them.

Madison regained consciousness, saw the others looking at his pearls, and moaned. Captain Midnight gathered them up, replaced them in the pouch, and handed them to him. He told the castaway not to worry; if he or Mudd had wanted his pearls, they could have hidden them before he came to.

8. The War: Moves

A warning shout brought the Squadron members outside. Burley and his men were back, and they were approaching the wreck of the amphibian. They were armed. Captain Midnight, Chuck, and Joyce raced into the clearing. Mudd disappeared into the tent for a few moments, then brought up the rear, carrying a bulky object wrapped in cloth.

Captain Midnight ordered Burley to stop. When that worthy didn't do so, the Secret Squadron leader fired a warning shot. This brought everybody to a halt, but the situation was still volatile.

Burley demanded that Madison — or at least the pearls he had — be surrendered immediately. Captain Midnight replied that it was up to Madison, but that he would permit them to meet, face to face, alone.

"Sure," Burley said with a sneer. "Separate me from my men so one of you can stick a knife in my back."

Captain Midnight frowned and commented that he didn't play by such rules; though, he added, those who normally associated with Burley seemed to.

Ichabod Mudd broke the impasse by unwrapping and quickly setting up a machine gun, taken from the amphibian. Burley knew then that, despite his numerical superiority, his men had little chance of capturing Madison. He left, promising that things would be different next time.

After Burley and his men had departed, Captain Midnight congratulated the Chief Mechanic. "That was quick thinking, Ikky. That jury-rigged machine gun saved us from a messy battle."

"I'm glad of that," Mudd confessed. "You see, Cap'n, it was a bluff. The machine gun was broken in the crash. I brought it into the tent to see if I could fix it."

Carla Rotan tuned into his encrypted broadcast and copied down the message carefully. Her message was quite long, since she incorporated every letter of the alphabet and set up several double-letter pairs to help her analysis. Thus, it was not surprising that she was able to "crack" the Squadron cipher. She felt very smug about her accomplishment, and awaited her next meeting with The Barracuda in pleasant anticipation.

With tranquility returning to the Secret Squadron camp, Madison said he'd point out which island the Wing flew toward. Captain Midnight directed Chuck and Joyce to go with him. He made sure that each had an automatic and two extra clips of ammunition. He and Mudd would remain in camp: Mudd to see if there was *any* way to fix the amphibian; Captain Midnight to guard the operation and take care of a few details.

Madison took the youngsters along a faint trail through the tropical growth, saying that the island's natives showed it to him. He explained that when he crashed, the natives held him in awe, possibly thinking that by coming to the island by air made him something supernatural. They gave him food and the run of the island, treating him reverentially over the years. Recently, they presented him with a fistful of pearls, he supposed to maintain his friendship or to ward off curses; he couldn't figure which.

When the youngsters expressed surprise that there were natives on the island, Madison said they were very shy. They had little to do with outsiders other than trading for basic supplies. It was no wonder they weren't seen.

During his explanation, they reached the top of a rise, the highest point on the island. The lagoon where "Mrs. Bosmouth's" amphibian was still anchored was visible almost directly in front of them. Just to the limit of the horizon, a dark strip was visible. Madison indicated that it was the other island. The Wing had circled his island once and then headed for the other.

As Madison was speaking, Chuck grabbed Joyce's arm and pointed. There, beneath them, another amphibian was flying toward the bay where "Mrs. Bosmouth" was moored. And Joyce, with her incredibly acute eyesight, was able to identify at once the new craft as the type favored by The Barracuda.

Neither The Barracuda nor Carla Rotan could see the watchers on the island summit, but the lady spy was quite agitated about her visitor arriving so openly. But her agitation paled beside the annoyance of The Barracuda. He let her tell him that she had cracked the Secret Squadron's "code." Then he informed her that he'd deciphered the message himself, quoting the opening lines to prove his point.

He then told her that Captain Midnight used the discarded "code" to send the message, and that it was because of The Barracuda's forces that the change had been made. He directed her to work more closely with him in the future. In the meantime she should resist any impulses to take initiatives without checking with him first.

He left Carla Rotan fuming. She stared as his plane taxied away; and she cursed fate. It would make her job just that much harder.

Her musings were interrupted by the foghorn voice of Captain Peter Burley hailing the amphibian. Startled, she had Carstairs hide out of sight with a submachine gun. Then she invited Burley aboard.

The sight of a beautiful woman startled Burley, but a short conversation convinced the sea captain that Carla Rotan could take care of herself and was hard as nails. He explained that he was trying to get his hands on some pearls, and that a party ashore was preventing him from doing so. He added that if she helped him, he'd divide the proceeds.

Carla Rotan, as "Mrs. Bosmouth," identified the leader ashore as Captain Midnight and her just-departed visitor as The Barracuda. She explained that for the moment, she had to appear on good terms with Midnight, but in due course she'd be delighted to help Burley.

Burley was startled by the identity of both leaders, observing that he'd

8. The War: Moves

heard of both. Under his breath, he observed that he'd apparently stumbled into something big.

Shortly, he departed from Carla Rotan. He observed to one of his men that something told him not to trust her. He decided to seek out The Barracuda, to whom he'd make the same proposition.

The Barracuda received the sea captain and listened to his story. He indicated that he might have use for Burley's crew — if the sailors were up to a bit of fighting. The Barracuda explained that he had important business to settle with Captain Midnight, and that one of them was not likely to leave the island alive. "If we join forces, you may keep all the pearls for your help," he said.

Burley left to think things over.

From the rise, Chuck, Joyce, and Bill Madison traced the actions of the sea captain. It seemed evident that Burley was soliciting aid from "Mrs. Bosmouth" and The Barracuda. The only obvious reason was to obtain their aid in wresting the pearls from Bill Madison.

As they watched Burley's motorboat travel toward the schooner, Joyce exclaimed, "Of course! Why didn't I think of that before?" She spun around to Chuck and excitedly told him to get Captain Midnight and bring him to the clearing below, at the inlet where the schooner was tied up. Then, without another word, she drew her automatic and dashed into the tropical growth leading to the inlet.

Madison was aghast. He suggested that they follow the girl before she could come to harm. Chuck had shared enough previous adventures with Joyce Ryan to trust her instincts. "Joyce can take care of herself. Let's get to Captain Midnight *fast*. This has got to be very important."

Joyce found the clearing and decided that the only way to get Peter Burley where she wanted him would be to decoy him to the beach. She reasoned that anything suspicious-looking might attract the sea captain; she judged that he wouldn't delegate any investigation. At the very inner edge of the clearing, she started a small fire, garnished with green leaves to produce copious amounts of smoke. She retired to the undergrowth and waited for Burley as patiently as a cat waits beside a mouse hole, ready for instant action.

Burley took the bait. After calling to the beach from the schooner and getting no response, the sea captain and two of his men clambered into their motorboat and came ashore. The three of them approached the smoldering fire site with caution, and started to search inland. Joyce had left faint traces of her movements to prevent the party from fanning out. Then she doubled back. All three men were following her trail cautiously when she stepped out from behind them, automatic drawn. She told them to drop their weapons.

The weapons were dropped with alacrity. Joyce told them to turn around, slowly and carefully, and then to take two steps forward. As they turned, they were surprised to see that their captor was the young woman they'd seen in Captain Midnight's party. They also noted with respect the thoroughly professional way she held her automatic on them.

Joyce got right to the point. "What claim do you have on Bill Madison's pearls?"

Burley spluttered. "*Madison's* pearls? They're *mine!*" He went on to explain that the pearls were gathered by the natives for him as payment for trade goods, as had been the case for years. But a short time ago, the natives withheld a large cache of pearls. They claimed that they gave them to a strange man who manifested much *mana* (a common native term representing supernatural force). It took some time for Burley to learn that the person was Madison; and the direct demand for the pearls caused Madison to flee and hide (the natives treated him with deference, but mostly left him alone). Apparently, some sky manifestation, conceivably even the Flying Wing itself, spooked the natives. Since they knew Madison came from the sky, they gave him an offering so that he would ward off any bad luck. Burley said that in his eyes, Madison had stolen his pearls, and that nobody could do *that* to Pete Burley and get away with it.

Joyce suggested that since Madison had received the pearls in good faith, being unaware of the arrangement between Burley and the natives, that it would be just to compensate him in some way if he were to turn the pearls over to the sea captain.

Burley expressed some doubt that Madison would agree to such an arrangement.

The sea captain explained that he'd asked both parties for help in recovering the pearls, and that The Barracuda came up with the better deal. He noted that The Barracuda said he could keep the pearls if he and his crew would help against Captain Midnight's party.

"And you accepted?" Joyce asked.

Burley nodded, saying, "And since you daren't shoot me..."

The automatic barked in Joyce's hand, and the sea captain's cap flew off his head and into the undergrowth. "I could just have easily aimed two inches lower," Joyce said calmly, not adding that she was one of the finest shots in the Secret Squadron; it was obvious that the cap's removal wasn't accidental.

"Cripes! I didn't mean it, lady," Burley said. His hands went up a few inches higher.

When one of the sailors on the schooner called out to see if anything was wrong, Joyce instructed Burley to reply that he'd discharged his pistol by accident. He did so with alacrity. Then Joyce asked him why he thought The Barracuda wanted to have Captain Midnight's party attacked.

8. The War: Moves

"It's something personal, I guess," Burley ventured.

"Then you don't know that there's a war? And that you, an American, are dealing with an agent of Japan? And that by opposing an official government investigation, you might be shot as a traitor or a spy?"

All the members of Burley's party were shocked to learn of the war. They pressed her for details. For the last year their seafaring activities had kept them isolated from news. They were all Americans and, given the facts, wanted to become Captain Midnight's allies.

By the time Captain Midnight arrived, the situation had clarified considerably. Joyce pointed out that, throughout the entire affair, Burley hadn't acted as if he were trying to steal the pearls but rather to regain something that belonged to him. Madison, hearing for the first time the story behind the pearls, said that, under the circumstances, the sea captain was entitled to them. Burley gruffly told Madison to keep half for himself — the usual finders' share, and what he'd promised "Mrs. Bosmouth" for her help.

Turning to Captain Midnight, Burley pointed out that, with the amphibian wrecked, his chance of reaching the neighboring island was slight. He volunteered the use of his schooner, the *Flossie*. When Captain Midnight pointed out that the sea captain could well lose his ship in the forthcoming encounter, Burley said that with the share of pearls he received from Madison he could buy several boats like the *Flossie*.

Captain Midnight smiled and extended his hand. "I really misjudged you, Captain Burley." His offer of the *Flossie* was a good option. Not counting The Barracuda's amphibian, the only flyable aircraft at the island was "Mrs. Bosmouth's." Even if the Squadron leader could get to and capture it, it was so overmatched by The Barracuda's plane that it would be a sitting duck. And it would surely tell The Barracuda where to send his forces if he should see that airplane heading for the nearby island. Even with the *Flossie*, Midnight realized, he'd have to make certain preparations before making any moves.

Before departing, the augmented party returned to the Squadron campsite. Captain Midnight excused himself to prepare an enciphered message; and Chuck, Joyce, and Bill Madison filled Ichabod Mudd in on all the details. The mechanic was relieved to learn that the party now had allies, not just foes.

Captain Midnight emerged shortly with an enciphered message. He transmitted carefully; since the aircraft was grounded permanently, the batteries had become weak. His message identified the island upon which the Flying Wing surely must have landed or crashed (unless it fell close by in the sea) and ordered an appearance in force the following morning. It was no time for finesse.

There was almost no time for anything. When the transmissions

The Northrop N9M Flying Wing. A modified version of this experimental aircraft was involved in the adventure Captain Midnight had with The Barracuda in the South Pacific. The Northrop progam culminated in the YB-49 Air Force bomber and the B-2 Stealth bomber. (Photograph: *Northrop Grumman.*)

started, The Barracuda ordered Captain Franz to get his aircraft into the air so he could at last find the Secret Squadron camp. Just as the message finished, he found it.

There was little warning until the aircraft strafed the clearing, narrowly missing the Squadron members and Burley's party. Everybody beat a hasty retreat into the jungly undergrowth.

The "Mrs. Bosmouth" matter was settled by a sudden turn of events: She and her pilot got the drop on the party. The female spy, having seen Captain Burley go ashore, correctly surmised that he and Captain Midnight had come to some sort of accord. Having captured them, she indicated that she'd get rid of all of them except for Captain Midnight, who would be rendered helpless and brought to her master, so that he'd give her a special reward.

"Do you mean The Barracuda?" Captain Midnight asked quietly.

"No, you fool. Ivan Shark!" she snapped. "Did you think that The Barracuda is the only one who's known about the Flying Wing experiments? He will accept Axis gold as easily as The Barracuda, and..."

8. The War: Moves 121

In her frenzy, bordering on the fanatical, her expression and mode of speech caused Captain Midnight to recall a photograph and a description. "Of course," he said. "Carla Rotan!"

She acknowledged her identity, adding that its discovery would do the party little good, since they were about to die. Joyce, however, created a diversion; a rapid scuffle ensued, and Carla Rotan and her pilot became prisoners.

A quick inspection revealed that Carstairs removed a few critical engine parts to make Carla Rotan's amphibian unusable. Midnight, realizing that neither the pilot nor Carla Rotan would reveal where the hidden parts were located, ordered Mudd to remove additional parts to make sure the plane couldn't fly in their absence. He also had the Chief Mechanic disable the radio.

It was up to Burley, then. The sea captain suggested that they get under way after dark and move slowly over the waters for the distant island. "It'll take near all night, but that way, we can get over there without bein' seen," he said. Moving too fast in the waters usually resulted in leaving a phosphorescent wake. He added that if they moved without running lights, The Barracuda might not be aware of their departure until the following dawn.

Having loaded the two prisoners aboard the schooner, the party lapsed into a rest period, waiting for sunset.

Darkness came with the typical suddenness of the tropics. After twilight deepened into early night, Burley made his move. The schooner eased from the harbor, slowly and quietly. The waters were calm, and Burley chanced running without navigation lights. The trip to the neighboring island was quiet and uneventful, thanks to the skill of the sea captain. It also took the whole of the night.

Everything happened at dawn. The Barracuda, rising early, noticed immediately that the schooner was gone. He surmised that somehow Captain Midnight had gained control of the vessel. Together with the Secret Squadron leader's radio message (in that damned new code), it meant that he couldn't delay.

Shortly, The Barracuda's amphibian was aloft, spiraling outward from the island in the most efficient type of search pattern, on the lookout for the schooner. During his search for the ship, The Barracuda radioed his Wolf Pilots to rendezvous over a nearby island.

On the deck of the schooner, Joyce spotted a telltale pattern in the trees of the island ahead. The tops of the trees were damaged in a pattern that spelled "aircraft crash." The Flying Wing's location had been found.

But so had the *Flossie*. From the great four-engine amphibian, The Barracuda had spotted the lumbering schooner. Immediately, he grabbed a microphone and called for the Wolf Pilots to speed to his location. After a noticeably unsuccessful strafing run on the *Flossie*, The Barracuda decided to leave such actions to those aircraft best designed for it.

The Wolf Pilots arrived, but they didn't arrive alone. In response to Captain Midnight's enciphered message, a sizable group of Squadron fighters reached the island at about the same time, and all Hell broke loose. A really vicious dogfight spread airplanes all over the sky.

Burley looked at the Secret Squadron leader with respect. "You sure don't do things by half, Captain Midnight."

Seeing his fighters engaged, The Barracuda ordered Captain Franz to try another run on the *Flossie*. This proved his undoing, because a Squadron plane that had just finished off a Wolf-Piloted fighter got on the tail of the amphibian. When it became clear that the four-engine amphibian was attacking a helpless schooner, he guessed who was onboard the sea craft and shot up the amphibian. It crashed spectacularly on the island.

Seeing the destruction of their leader, the Wolf Pilots broke off the engagement. The Squadron fighters orbited the island, forming protective cover, while Captain Midnight went ashore.

A short time later, dense smoke from the island's interior signaled that Captain Midnight had found the Flying Wing and had rendered it useless to the enemy. When he emerged from the jungle-like growth, the Secret Squadron leader said he found the corpse of The Barracuda's pilot, who had died in the crash. He'd also recovered the flight log written by Ted Russell, so much of the important flight data was recovered.

The Flying Wing was shattered, but there was sufficient fuel remaining so that igniting it destroyed the Wing's remains sufficiently to prevent an enemy gaining any useful data from it. American defense information was secure once more. (In the radio version, the Wing supposedly landed with little or no damage and was intercepted and destroyed while attempting to take off. The dramatization was added to confuse enemy agents who knew part of the story.)

(Flying Wing research continued into the 1950s, with the last plane of the series the U.S. Air Force YB-49. A newer Flying Wing was developed later, the supersonic B-2 Stealth Bomber.)

An amphibian was dispatched to bring Captain Midnight back to the Pacific Headquarters. Once there, he reviewed the operations performed in his absence and determined that the Pacific base was well established. Captain Peter Burley was recruited as an observer for the Squadron; while not a full Squadron agent, Burley proved brave and valuable during the entire Pacific campaign. (He eventually retired and settled in California.)

Captain Midnight's party returned to Secret Squadron Headquarters near Grant City. His work at Headquarters was administrative, yet he knew that soon he'd have to work in the field again.

9

The War: Countermoves

Captain Midnight took several weeks devoted entirely to the administrative functions of the Secret Squadron. Ichabod Mudd spent several days with the Crypto Group on the development of a newer code/cipher scheme, in the event the just-issued Code-O-Graph was compromised. Captain Midnight, Chuck, and Joyce were issued regulation Code-O-Graphs. Captain Midnight already expressed concern about a proper method of identification for Squadron members when dealing with Allied military forces. The matter had to be handled through channels, so he sent appropriate memoranda, and waited.

Word came that Captain Midnight should attend a secret meeting in Washington, D.C. Thus it was that the Secret Squadron leader clambered into one of the new Merlin-engine P-51 fighters and roared into the sky — destination: Bowling Field.

Major Steele met Captain Midnight, who'd arrived at night. The two were taken to a conference room in a high-security building. There they met with the head of a scientific department, who explained the reason for the meeting.

A scientific expedition in South America had discovered a high concentration of an ore that contained a metallic component with what appeared to be revolutionary properties. This new ore's component promised the development of alloys that could be used to good advantage in the next generation of aircraft. "The reporting scientist, Dr. Barbados, is a trustworthy and competent researcher," he explained. "But his instruments for field work are quite primitive. He didn't dare send out an ore sample for fear it might be intercepted."

Captain Midnight inquired as to the expedition's location.

"Chile, well south of Lake Titicaca," the department head said. "In the Andes, really, near an Inca ruin. The land hasn't been explored thoroughly; the Chilean government reported some indication of local tribes, but little about them is known."

Further details followed, including the approximate location of Barbados' camp. Because of the importance of the mission, Captain Midnight could make any reasonable request concerning equipment and supplies, and his request would be filled within a week.

After the meeting, Captain Midnight discussed details of the mission with Major Steele. The mission would be done under cover. Midnight indicated that the best aircraft for the mission would be a Lockheed 14 transport with Cyclone engines. "With Ikky tuning them up, I'll be able to get sufficient climb for good flying in the Andes," he said, smiling.

Steele smiled back. Though not a pilot, he knew enough about aircraft to realize the choice was good. But the reference to Ichabod Mudd was an oblique way to tell him that Captain Midnight intended to bring him along.

Captain Midnight decided to adopt the name "Red Roberts" once more and have himself listed as a mining engineer. Boning up for the part of "Professor Samuels" had given him enough practical knowledge to pull it off. As for his presence in the area, Dr. Barbados had indicated that the region had interesting geology. Midnight requested that Steele have the proper credentials prepared for him, for Chuck and Joyce (as "his children"), and for Ichabod Mudd (as "Bill Gold"). The names Charles and Joyce were common enough to require no change.

At sunrise a refreshed Captain Midnight climbed into his Mustang and took off for Grant City. While en route, he alerted Ichabod Mudd, Chuck, and Joyce to prepare for a trip. He didn't say where they were going.

The next week made their destination clear, including several new sets of shots, much to the youngsters' disgust (nor was it greeted with relish by their elders). Mudd commented that their global troubleshooting made them more susceptible to shots than combat troops. Captain Midnight pointed out that if he was really bothered by the shots, he didn't have to take any. Of course, then he couldn't go on the mission.

A few selected people located along the proposed route were alerted, in only the broadest terms, that somebody was coming. In several Central American countries and Mexico, Axis agents were stationed; so it would be best to avoid contacting the en route people except *in extremis*. The Secret Squadron leader chose a route that would avoid major population areas where Axis agents would more likely be found.

Soon a Lockheed 14 arrived, stocked with the provisions. The tents were not Army Regulation, nor was the food patently Government Issue.

9. The War: Countermoves

The North American P-51 fighter, arguably the finest fighter aircraft in World War II. The Secret Squadron was issued a few of these, and Captain Midnight used one frequently for high-speed trips to Washington, D.C. After the fighters were deactivated, one was presented to Captain Midnight for his personal aircraft collection. (Photograph: *National Air and Space Museum, Smithsonian Institution*, SI Neg. No. A 42335 G.)

Automatics and rifles had no Government markings; ammunition, too, was in unmarked cases.

Just before their departure, they were told that their Chilean contact would be a Colonel Valdiva. He was to meet them at the small township of Cocos. Chile still had diplomatic relations with the Axis powers, though it seemed evident that the relations might be broken soon. For the sake of relations between Chile and the United States, it was vital to conduct the mission as unobtrusively as possible.

Weather was excellent, clear with unlimited visibility, when the Squadron aircraft took off just before dawn. Captain Midnight pointed the nose of the Lockheed transport nearly due south, and headed for a refueling stop almost 2,000 miles away, on the other side of the Gulf of Mexico. For the Lockheed 14, even such a long trip was easy to do with plenty of reserve fuel.

The trip was mostly uneventful. Their last refueling stop, in Peru, however, *was* eventful. They landed after dark on what they thought to be their rendezvous field — and were arrested! They'd inadvertently landed in an area prohibited to foreign aircraft.

Although he hated to do it, Captain Midnight was forced to call the American military aviation attaché for help. Once the Peruvians were convinced it was all an honest mistake, they even permitted the aircraft to be refueled at the field; the plane was then cleared to continue its flight.

One of the workers at the field, placed in a menial job, had several contacts; in particular, Magnus von Grift. Despite the name, von Grift wasn't a German national, though he was from Bavarian stock. Von Grift was an agent of Ivan Shark, who had recently engineered a successful prison escape. Von Grift was instrumental in recruiting Carla Rotan and insinuating her into The Barracuda's camp. When he received the worker's report of the incident, he considered the information important enough to forward to Shark.

Shark, upon receiving the report, couldn't relate it to any of his activities. But he decided to take certain defensive measures, just in case.

Cocos was the rendezvous point for a simple reason: It was the only area thereabouts that could safely accommodate the Squadron aircraft. Close to the mountains, Cocos had a flat area outside of the town proper that proved an excellent landing site.

A large, swarthy man with a thick black mustache and a brilliant smile greeted the plane. He introduced himself as Colonel Valdiva and authenticated his identity by a series of signs and countersigns. Captain Midnight in turn introduced his party and soon got down to business.

Valdiva, after being assured that the Squadron plane had more than ample fuel, suggested they go aloft so that he could show them the region. "I regret that this plain is the only area where you can land this fine *aeroplano*," the colonel said. "But a view from above can tell you much about the land to which we will be going, *sí?*"

Captain Midnight took the Lockheed to several thousand feet above ground level, then followed Valdiva's guidance. The routing brought them over relatively sparse but rugged terrain, leading gradually toward the mountains. As they approached the first real mountains, Joyce exclaimed, "Geemanee! Captain Midnight, look."

Trusting Joyce's eyesight, he swung the nose of the Lockheed in the direction she indicated. Shortly, they found themselves over an ancient Inca city. The buildings, squatting near the top of the peak, were massive. They suggested strange and ancient mysteries beyond the ken of the 20th Century.

"*La Ciudad de Los Espectros*," said Colonel Valdiva. "The ... the Phantom City, you might say in English. It is near here that Doctor Barbados has his camp." He gestured toward the ruins.

The Secret Squadron leader circled the Inca city once, then returned the way he'd come. It was clear to his trained eye that there was no place to

9. The War: Countermoves

set down any aircraft with a landing roll greater than an autogiro. They would trek in the hard way.

When they landed, Valdiva promised to obtain a few trustworthy guides to help them get to the Barbados camp. He would follow within a day with a *Señor* Taggert, a mining engineer who could be a valuable resource for the mission.

After they returned to the Cocos area, Valdiva arranged what was necessary, while the Squadron members refreshed themselves. Ichabod Mudd took personal charge of a package that had been included at the insistence of the Washington science bureau chief. Although Valdiva made arrangements to make sure that nobody would bother the aircraft save for the Secret Squadron party, Mudd hid a few small but vital components to make certain the plane would be there upon their return.

The trek into the Andean foothills was uneventful. It took them several days to reach the vicinity of Barbados' camp.

Shortly before they reached the camp though, the guides entered a clearing and stopped suddenly. As Captain Midnight caught up with them, he saw that they stood transfixed, staring at a pile of rocks. Atop the pile was a large red feather.

"What is it?" Captain Midnight said to one of the locals who could speak a smattering of English.

"*La Pluma Carmesi*," said the guide. "I am sorry, *Señor*. We go back." With a word to the others, he placed his share of the load on the ground; the others followed suit.

When Captain Midnight found he couldn't persuade the locals even to remain, he paid them their wages to that point. He requested that they contact Colonel Valdiva and inform him of the situation and location.

The rest of the day was uneventful. A campsite was established; tents were set up. Even with the enigmatic red feather sign — patently a warning — in sight, there were no signs of anybody lurking in the area. Nor, though the Squadron members took turn standing watch, were there any skulkers detected around the campsite that night.

During the next morning, Joyce remarked to Captain Midnight that while she couldn't be positive, she believed that the campsite was in the valley she'd spotted from the air. The one with the ancient Inca city. In fact, they might be fairly close to it.

"If that's the case," responded Captain Midnight, "there's something really curious about that mysterious city. Given the barrenness of the region, that red-feather 'warning' could have come only from there. And that 'warning' can't be more than a day or two old."

"Gee-manee," Joyce said. "It's almost if they knew we were coming."

"That's right. Whoever 'they' might be, they've got my curiosity up.

How did they know we were coming? I, for one, don't believe in magic and witch doctors, or whatever the Inca equivalents of them are."

It was close to noon when Colonel Valdiva arrived. He'd encountered the returning guides on the trail and got the story from them. He then had Captain Midnight show him the "warning."

"*La Pluma Carmesi,*" he said. "In English, the ruby ... no, better would be the Crimson Feather." He said that he'd heard of the Society of the Crimson Feather. The society was a secret organization that traced its beginnings to the sun-worshiping priestly caste of the ancient Incas. The wilder tribes of the local Indians had also heard of the people of the Crimson Feather, as had some of the town workers. All gave them a wide berth.

"Most interesting," said Captain Midnight. "For some reason, the Crimson Feather people decide to set up fresh warnings timed to coincide with our arrival. Why should they care if we meet Dr. Barbados' party? If *he'd* received any Crimson Feather warnings, I'm sure he'd have mentioned it in his report."

"I will be glad to help you find any relationship between the events," Colonel Valdiva said.

Taggert, the mining engineer, arrived in camp shortly, accompanied by another man. Taggert was a crusty older man, slender and wiry, who was white of both hair and mustache. With him was an even thinner, somewhat younger, clean-shaven, and bespectacled man who Captain Midnight deduced as being Dr. Barbados, even before introductions were made. Taggert, who turned out to be more of a prospector than a mining engineer, and Dr. Barbados, had both heard of the Secret Squadron leader. Dr. Barbados was happy that someone of his caliber had been sent to check on his report.

"I have found an ore here," Barbados explained, "that seems to hold promise for superior alloys in the future. Far superior, with strengths whose orders of magnitude are greater than those of high-grade steel alloys. I had never seen the like of this form of ore before. It was only with the greatest difficulty that I've been able to separate a small piece. I've named it 'Juvarium' in memory of my first guide, Ernesto Juvarra, who perished in a landslide." Although he'd found only a small pocket of the ore, he suspected that there was a major vein of Juvarium not too far distant. The mountains, he pointed out, were volcanic locally, and the Juvarium vein was probably pushed up from the earth's interior.

Ichabod Mudd was introduced. He excused himself momentarily, then returned, lugging a case. This he presented to Dr. Barbados.

The box proved to contain a compact but surprisingly complete chemical laboratory. Dr. Barbados noted that with the laboratory, he might be able to determine a few facts about Juvarium, other than that it was an extremely strong material.

9. The War: Countermoves

Captain Midnight asked whether Dr. Barbados had encountered any Crimson Feather warnings. When the scientist told him he hadn't, it confirmed the Secret Squadron leader's suspicions that the warnings were directed toward him and his expedition.

Dr. Barbados pointed out that he'd not explored the region where the Squadron members set up camp; the scientist's camp was located somewhat to the south. In fact, the only one who had even a smattering of knowledge about the area was Colonel Valdiva. Even to the colonel, much of the area had only been observed from a distance.

Captain Midnight observed that it seemed clear that someone was interested in what they were doing. Therefore, it seemed important to do a bit of scouting around. All agreed, but Dr. Barbados suggested that he help in the initial round of scouting, since the last few weeks had given him some understanding of the region.

So it was done, and the group split into several parties. These went off into different directions, to see what could be seen.

Chuck and Dr. Barbados made the important discovery of the day. They'd started down from a ravine near the foot of the peak upon which the Phantom City squatted. Turning past a bend, they came across a portal of some sort in the side of the mountain. Further investigations revealed several more.

Neither could explore what lay beyond the portals, for they hadn't brought flashlights with them. A few feet inside, and the passageways became velvet black, forcing an investigator to go on by feel.

They returned to camp with their news. Dr. Barbados speculated that the portals probably represented entrances to a labyrinth beneath the Inca city. From carvings on the portals, the doorways definitely had an Inca-like "flavor."

While others discussed the implications of the portals they'd discovered, Dr. Barbados excused himself. He retired to a tent, then emerged to drag in his newly acquired laboratory. The others supposed he was beginning his research on Juvarium.

They were wrong. Much later, Dr. Barbados emerged holding some dampish paper, which he spread on a large, flat rock to dry. He explained that he'd developed something that would help them explore the labyrinth in relative safety, and he would show them later how it worked.

That evening, he did. Dr. Barbados pointed out that they had only so many flashlights among them, and a limited supply of batteries. In exploring the labyrinth, there had to be a means of retracing one's steps should a flashlight malfunction. The inky blackness gave him an idea. Using a bit of chemistry, Dr. Barbados created a solution.

Asking the rest of the party to follow him, he brought them from the campfire to a dark area behind one of the tents. There he withdrew a glowing rectangle of some sort of material from an opaque envelope. He explained that with his new laboratory, he'd created a luminous compound, with which he'd impregnated some paper. Such paper could be used as place markers in total darkness. If one of the flashlights was damaged or a battery failed, it would still be possible to retrace one's steps safely.

Captain Midnight was impressed. Not only could this be applied to their current mission, but to wartime activities in Squadron bases and Squadron members' homes, particularly during blackouts. Since blackout drills had been common since the war started, he congratulated Dr. Barbados in making a contribution to the war effort. He passed the idea along via an enciphered message. Shortly, kits of luminous paper sheets were made available to Squadron members.

The members of the party believed that what lay beyond the portals should be investigated. The following morning, two parties started out. Joyce and Colonel Valdiva were in one; Ichabod Mudd and Taggert comprised the other. Chuck and Captain Midnight scouted for any signs of observers. Dr. Barbados began investigating his chunk of Juvarium using the new laboratory equipment.

Shortly after noon, Captain Midnight found a Crimson Feather marker. Concerned, he returned and called in Chuck. He speculated that in light of this second warning, the exploring parties might be heading for trouble. He suggested that they should go to the labyrinth entrances. Dr. Barbados excused himself for a few minutes; then the three of them started for the portals.

They arrived just in time to see a disheveled Ichabod Mudd emerge from one of the entrances. They rushed up to him, and then heard his story.

It transpired that the two parties entered different portals but ran into each other inside the labyrinth. They discovered that the various portals all led to a passageway. This led to a set of steps that spiraled up into the darkness. They climbed the steps, which neither branched nor had any exits. As they neared the top, a glow from above gave sufficient illumination so that they could turn off their flashlights.

They emerged in a hallway made of polished rock. It was obviously in the Inca city, in a central area. To their left was a large portal at the end of the corridor. Curiosity made them check on it.

Beyond the portal was a huge chamber whose purpose wasn't immediately evident. As they began to inspect it, an Indian in a simple costume entered. He raised a cry of alarm.

The party fled, and Indians followed them. After a brief but intense struggle, Joyce, Colonel Valdiva, and Taggert were captured. Mudd barely got away.

9. The War: Countermoves

When he determined he'd escaped cleanly, the Chief Mechanic retraced his steps carefully and followed as closely as he dared to see where the others were being held. He couldn't find out — the captives were taken through a chamber so large that it afforded no cover. He returned cautiously to the stairway, then to the labyrinth. He emerged to get help when he spotted Captain Midnight, Dr. Barbados, and Chuck.

All three were willing to start right out. Dr. Barbados wanted to know how much help the luminous paper had been and was gratified when Mudd said that without the paper, he'd never have been able to make it to the portals. Dr. Barbados confessed that he'd brought along a small jar of a luminous paint he'd concocted, in case the pieces of paper had scattered. Mudd assured him that there were no drafts strong enough to disturb the trail of paper scraps.

Cautiously, the four of them entered the labyrinth, Mudd taking the lead. He took them along the glowing trail of paper scraps to the stairs. They climbed in total darkness, after being assured that the stairs were both even and solid.

After what seemed to be an interminable climb, the darkness began to lighten. Eventually they emerged at the portal that led to the chamber where the others had been captured. Mudd paused, and whispered that to reach the region where the natives led the prisoners, they'd have to go through the chamber unobserved.

Ordering the others to remain behind, Captain Midnight stole silently to the chamber and scouted around. Finding nobody inside, he motioned for the others to join him. They did so, stealthily.

The chamber proved to have significance in Inca or quasi–Inca religion. The room was large and almost bare, save for a dark, rectangular slab of rock with cunning designs carved on its periphery. It was clearly an altar, doubtless of the sacrificial variety. But the attention grabber wasn't the altar, it was a stylistic representation of the solar disk in a wall directly over the altar. At its center was a great blazing jewel of some sort.

Light streamed forth from the gem. Dr. Barbados determined that what was making the jewel shine so brilliantly was sunlight, which was directed by a cunning arrangement of mirrors. Somehow the jewel was made to shine from sunrise to sunset, though the feature wasn't evident at the moment. (An optical engineer with interest in ancient cultures later indicated that this was probably done with a series of mirrors so oriented that as the solar rays reflected by one would leave the jewel, the rays from another would fall on it. A series of baffles would prevent unwanted beams from striking the wall beyond the jewel's edges. Pre-Columbian Incas had little to control light but mirrors and light masks.)

They wasted little time in the room, but stole carefully through the chamber, then along the route Mudd had seen the captured party taken. Somewhere along this route they made their most useful discovery. The noise of some approaching natives caused the rescue party to duck into a recess, out of sight. There they heard the voice of Joyce Ryan!

As it turned out, they were not close to the prisoners. They had stumbled upon an acoustic freak, like the "whisper galleries" found in some buildings. In such arrangements, sound waves from a person speaking in one location are reflected somehow so that a person in another, usually distant, position can hear them as if they were standing right next to the listener. These have been found in some structures and caverns. Such spots are isolated and enable two-way communication, while those in between can't hear a thing.

Captain Midnight once demonstrated such a phenomenon to Chuck on a Washington, D.C. visit, and within a minute or two understood what was happening. He established communication with her.

After assuring Joyce she wasn't "hearing things," a conference between the two groups followed. Colonel Valdiva was able to understand some of what the Indians were saying after they'd been captured; they spoke a dialect very similar to those he already knew.

What he heard wasn't very promising. It seemed, as best as he could make out, that at sunset the three of them would be sacrificed to the sun god, Onti. Captain Midnight checked the time and realized sunset was no more than two hours away.

A rescue would be tricky. There were only four in the party, and only three were armed. A direct assault against an indeterminate, but probably large, number of Indians was out of the question. The obvious place to stage a rescue would be at the chamber with the shining jewel, since the exit to the labyrinth was close. The key, though, was to find some way of maximizing their chances.

Ichabod Mudd came up with a brainstorm. He asked Dr. Barbados whether the luminous paint he'd brought along could be painted on a smooth, nonporous surface. When the scientist said it could, Mudd suggested that they should paint the rear of the jewel in the center of the solar disk. The glowing of their jewel after the sun disappeared should spook the natives.

This idea was passed along on the "whisper line." Captain Midnight, thinking fast, expanded on it. He suggested that Colonel Valdiva coach Joyce to say certain words that the Indians could understand, and that Joyce should act regally. Midnight explained that it was doubtful that many, if any, of the natives had seen a woman with blonde hair before; this might suggest that she might have supernatural powers. Since sunlight was golden, her golden hair might suggest some kinship to Onti. She could announce that she would

9. The War: Countermoves

call upon the sun to show some sort of manifestation. The effect of the still-shining jewel, it was reasoned, should confuse the natives.

Colonel Valdiva understood and started coaching Joyce on what to say. The rescue party worked its way back to the chamber, dodging parties of Indians, until they were able to conceal themselves behind the altar. It took three tries to detach the stone, while praying that nobody would come across them while they were working. Doctoring the backside was done quickly, and restoring the gem to its place was easy. When it was back in place, its luster was scarcely diminished.

The rescue party hid behind pillars along the wall. Late afternoon sunlight was concentrated in the great gem, casting shadows that helped conceal them. By the sunset procession, the color of the gem became a baleful near-crimson.

Joyce carried it off well. Though flanked by Indians, Joyce managed to act sufficiently aloof that they didn't touch her. When she arrived at the middle of the chamber, she stopped, and made a peculiar gesture at the image of the solar disk. She barked out a few words in the native tongue.

The Indians looked at her in surprise. They hesitated. She turned to the group of Indians, perhaps fifty, and said something else in the native dialect.

A robed Indian stepped forward and said something. Colonel Valdiva barked two words. The other Indians looked back and forth between Joyce and the robed one. There seemed to be some sort of impasse.

Then, sunset. The chamber was plunged into gloom as the jewel's red glow died. Yet a new, soft, blue-white glow remained. In the flickering light of torches, the Indians could be seen reacting with wonder and fear. The robed one, infuriated, snatched something from within his robes and cried out a few words. He dashed the object on the floor, and the chamber was quickly filled with thick, billowing smoke.

Captain Midnight kept calm and ran to where he remembered the prisoners to be. Quickly, he located them. With a few whispered words, he had them retreat with him until they reached the portal to the labyrinth. Before they entered the stairwell, Joyce cried out to them in the dialect. They encountered no Indians on the way out.

As they traversed the labyrinth, they picked up their pieces of glowing paper. If the Indians didn't know how they found their way through the darkness, so much the better.

When they returned to camp, Colonel Valdiva explained what had happened. Joyce had claimed to be daughter to Onti. She then told the Indians that, through her, Onti would manifest a sign in the sacred gem. As a sign of her coming among them, its light would persist after the sun had set.

The robed Indian, who was called Lutro, claimed that Joyce wasn't speaking truthfully. He demanded her immediate sacrifice. Colonel Valdiva called Lutro a false priest, and there the matter sat for a few moments. The gem's afterglow created by the luminous paint tipped the scales toward Joyce. Then Lutro cried out that the glow would not last, and he threw the smoke bomb, which allowed the party to escape. As she left, Joyce called out, repeating that she was a daughter of Onti.

"That Lutro is more than he seems," Captain Midnight said. "The smoke bomb used modern chemicals; you could tell by the odor. It's highly unlikely that their medicine man, or whatever he's called, would have such devices. He's the one we'll have to watch out for."

Once they got to camp, Dr. Barbados developed a few effective native-scarers, mostly using mercury fulminate fuses, to chase them away. After a few encounters with these devices, the Indians left them alone. They were convinced that the battle between Lutro and Joyce and those with her was strictly supernatural, and none of their business.

So it was that a few days later Lutro appeared, carrying a flag of truce. He asked, in English, to speak to Captain Midnight. If the Secret Squadron leader was surprised that Lutro knew who he was, he didn't remain so for long. Lutro identified himself as an agent of Ivan Shark's, with whom he was in contact by radio.

He had a message. Shark was aware that some sort of important discovery had been made. He proposed that they share the discovery, if Midnight threw in with him. Otherwise, he and "the other group" would surely get it anyway. By cooperating, a lot of strife could be avoided. Shark wanted a response to his proposal.

The Secret Squadron leader refused. Only with greatest reluctance did he permit Lutro to leave the camp; he'd have preferred to take him prisoner. He wondered how and why somebody like Lutro, a part of, or at least closely associated with, a Quasi-Inca tribe of natives in a remote Andean area, would be part of Ivan Shark's gang.

The link was Magnus von Grift. The Shark operative was one who kept his finger on the pulse of unusual activities, and when a hint of something important was transmitted from Chile, he contacted Shark. Shark instructed von Grift to establish a contact in the region. Some careful probing found him Lutro, who was a local criminal and who'd drifted to Cocos from the tribe of Inca-like natives. He'd already used a few modern devices, such as smoke bombs and fireworks, to set himself up as someone with supernatural powers.

He'd hardly set himself up for the program when he received a radio message from von Grift reporting the landing of an aircraft in a restricted area and ordering Lutro to keep strangers away from the area. Lutro made local inquiries and learned that a Colonel Valdiva had arrived in Cocos,

9. The War: Countermoves 135

expecting visitors. Lutro had some of the Indians scout the area toward Cocos, and through them he learned of the approaching party.

That is what prompted the Crimson Feather warnings, and what followed.

After Lutro departed the encampment, Captain Midnight mulled over what he'd learned. If his cover identity was blown, and if two separate enemy groups were after the Juvarium (even if they had no idea what it was), then it was time to withdraw to Cocos.

Fortunately, Dr. Barbados had eliminated all traces of his stay at his previous campsite. He realized the potential value of Juvarium and was doing everything he could to keep it from falling into the wrong hands.

They made their move after dark. With utmost stealth, the party broke camp and, with Colonel Valdiva leading them, headed back toward the Lockheed. Since Lutro already knew the location of their camp, they didn't bother obliterating evidence of their stay.

As a precaution, before they left, Captain Midnight transmitted an enciphered message to Squadron Headquarters directing them to send down fighters to act as an escort for the Lockheed. "Why not?" he asked wryly. "Everybody in the enemy camp seems to know who I am. What's the sense of remaining Red Roberts?"

During the trek back to Cocos, there was evidence that they were being shadowed. There was one attempt to abduct a party member — Taggert — but the Squadron members acted too quickly. The closest thing to a clue was the finding of a scrap of paper with a star printed on it in purple ink. Captain Midnight wondered whether this was "the other group" that Lutro had mentioned.

When Lutro mentioned "the other group," he didn't have the slightest idea of any such thing. He'd thought it merely a bluff that Shark was running in order to put his enemy off-guard. So it was that when one of the Indians came back from scouting around with an envelope he'd found, Lutro was a bit surprised to see it was a proposal of aid from an unknown party, who suggested a meeting at a site not too far from the Phantom City.

With sufficient precautions, Lutro arrived at the site, where he met someone dressed in civilian clothes who was obviously an Oriental. The newcomer identified himself as Captain Yoshita, who headed an organization called the Purple Star. The captain politely pointed out that both Lutro and he were trying to obtain whatever it was that Dr. Barbados had discovered. It was obviously important. He suggested an alliance.

Captain Yoshita observed that the Crimson Feather had manpower, but their resources in other respects were sufficiently restricted that they'd been unable to determine the nature of the discovery. The Purple Star had modern weapons and other resources but was limited by its relatively small numbers. Together, each group would supply resources that the other lacked.

It was a deal that Ivan Shark would never have agreed to. The Purple Star (or any such organization) might be a potential customer. Magnus von Grift would have at the least contacted Shark before agreeing to any such proposal.

But Lutro, who was only on the fringe of the Shark organization, bought in. His pride had been injured by the diminished influence with the Indians, brought about by his run-in with the "daughter of Onti." The glowing of the jewel was considered a genuine miracle by the Indians. Though Lutro realized that the trick had to have been accomplished by some sort of chemical, he dared not try to remove it. A success through Captain Yoshita's group would help him.

Back at Cocos, Dr. Barbados suggested that, with all having reached the aircraft safely, the best move would be to take off immediately and head for the United States. Neither Taggert nor Colonel Valdiva disagreed with the idea.

Captain Midnight admitted that flight to the United States was a very good idea but wasn't so sure that an immediate takeoff would be good. He pointed out that the Lockheed wasn't an armed aircraft. Several fighters were en route; by waiting a day they could fly back under protection.

Colonel Valdiva made a suggestion. If they could obtain a high-resolution camera, they could fly past the region of the Phantom City and take pictures of the area. Dr. Barbados could point out the precise area where his camp had been located. Then, he could carry on his work in a laboratory while others came to work his Juvarium deposit.

Dr. Barbados agreed. He'd worked with aerial photographs before. He was delighted to learn that Captain Midnight had experience with aerial photography, both during and after the previous war.

Fortunately, a suitable camera and film were found. The camera was entrusted to Ichabod Mudd, who'd handled cameras for Captain Midnight before. With a little effort, Mudd rigged a steady-camera mount for the flight.

By the time all the equipment had been found and paid for, then installed and tested, the fighter escort had arrived. There were three identical fighters, Republic P-43 "Lancers," manned by Secret Squadron pilots. Unlike the Lockheed, the fighters were clearly marked as Squadron planes. It was hoped that a show of force would scare away — or at least discourage — attempts on the twin-engine aircraft.

Although the Purple Star was a small group, it kept careful watch on the comings and goings of Secret Squadron members in town. When the camera and film were found, it didn't take long for word to get back to Captain Yoshita.

The head of the Purple Star digested the news and became convinced that the camera would be used for aerial shots. He guessed correctly that the region around the Phantom City would be photographed. Such photographs wouldn't be in the best interests of his country.

The Japanese officer played what he thought was a trump card. He'd recently brought several Nakajima Ki-27 fighters into the country and had them concealed. Ki-27s acquitted themselves well against Russian fighters, and two of them would be more than sufficient against an unarmed transport. He didn't learn, until too late, of the recently arrived Squadron fighters.

Dr. Barbados and the Squadron party bade farewell to Colonel Valdiva. Captain Midnight indicated that he'd try to keep in touch. Everybody expressed effusive thanks to the Peruvian. Ichabod Mudd pointed out that without him they would never have rescued Joyce, Taggert, and Dr. Barbados. Taggert remained behind; he'd direct the mining operations whenever they started.

The photographic plans had changed. With a fighter escort, the Lockheed would take two passes over the region, which would supply them with enough photographs. Then they would turn north and start the trip back to the United States.

The aircraft met near the Phantom City. The Secret Squadron fighters were told to fly high, at a considerable altitude above the Lockheed. Two Purple Star aircraft were a little higher than the Lockheed when Joyce spotted them. As they started their attack, Chuck radioed the Squadron planes. And suddenly, the attackers became the prey.

Light and maneuverable as the Ki-27s were, they were outclassed. The dogfight had barely begun before the two Japanese aircraft fell out of the sky, streaming smoke. Both pilots bailed out, and their planes, unattended missiles, fell crushingly to the ground.

What followed may or may not have had any connection. One of the two aircraft fell in an almost vertical dive near the peak of the mountain where the Phantom City was located. The smoke from the wreckage didn't diminish but began to thicken and change color. Dr. Barbados, who'd been watching, called to Captain Midnight to gain altitude fast. Unhesitatingly, the Secret Squadron leader began a full-throttle climb and alerted his fighter escort to do likewise. As the aircraft ascended, Joyce exclaimed that the smoke was continuing to thicken and spread.

Dr. Barbados explained. Whether by coincidence or by being triggered somehow by the airplane crash, the mountain was beginning a volcanic eruption. The volcano had been dormant for thousands of years, but now was becoming active. Whether a transient or more permanent phase of the mountain's life cycle, the region would be inhospitable for a while.

Captain Midnight turned his plane north.

There was a disappointing footnote to the story. Under the more rigorous testing conditions available in a major laboratory, more things were discovered about Juvarium. The Juvarium chunk showed a natural alloy of metals that gave the appearance of great strength — but also great brittleness when treated alone (the brittleness was masked in the raw ore). The mineral seemed a fluke. Nor was it possible to determine whether the "vein" of Juvarium varied, if a vein even existed. The volcanic activity was slight, as such things go, but it utterly destroyed the Phantom City and its inhabitants, as well as Dr. Barbados' campsite, which was buried in extensive ash and lava deposits. The Juvarium may still be there, for all anybody knows.

Of the Crimson Feather and the Purple Star, there were no traces, and neither were ever heard from again. Perhaps Lutro and Captain Yoshita saw the dogfight from the Phantom City, but it's doubtful that such will ever be determined, since all the clues are buried under uncounted tons of volcanic residue.

For the next few months, Captain Midnight was absorbed in purely administrative duties. It's worth stressing that, despite his many individual feats, Captain Midnight was the leader of a large organization. Many hundreds of dedicated field agents performed heroically before, during, and after the United States' entry into World War II. There are literally hundreds of stories that could be told of their exploits. Someday, they may be.

The next event that required Captain Midnight's personal services started in Washington. It ended on a lonely Pacific island, much closer to Tokyo than the Squadron's Pacific Headquarters (or even the island group where the Squadron leader confronted The Barracuda for the last time).

The message requesting Captain Midnight's presence in Washington, D.C. was short. Its source implied a very high priority: It was direct from "Mr. Jones."

Captain Midnight flew his Mustang to Washington because of its range and speed. Since it was a single-place aircraft, he went alone. He touched down at Bowling Field, practically at sunrise, and was able to find showering and shaving facilities as well as a place to have breakfast before meeting his superior.

The rest of the day was occupied with work. Chief among the items covered was the formation of a command general staff to operate at Squadron Headquarters in Captain Midnight's absence. The delegation of authority "by direction" would leave the Secret Squadron leader freer for long, drawn-out assignments.

Once that was settled, Captain Midnight was given such an assignment.

He was told that a great deal of experimental work had been done on both sides of the Atlantic on instrument guidance of aircraft and on radar detection. Midnight knew something of radar because of previous briefings.

A major in the U. S. Army Signal Corps was the briefer of the moment. "Some of our electronics wizards are attempting to couple radar to antiaircraft guns to knock out enemy aircraft, even when they can't be seen by the naked eye." He added that the results were as yet "strictly laboratory stuff," but it had been decided to set up a unit in a war zone.

Puzzled, Captain Midnight asked why.

"Because, unfinished as it is, it might afford protection to another experimental effort being mounted by our chemical experts," the briefer said. He expanded, explaining that a research group was developing what they hoped would be an answer to the vulnerability of bombers on the ground at forward bases, particularly in the Pacific Theater.

Colonel Delacroix, an Air Corps liaison officer, said, "Things are rough on Pacific islands. A bomber field in a forward area can be hit, hard. Our fighters are good, but an island is awfully vulnerable. A high-flying bomber traversing the island can damage any installation just by dropping a few bombs in the vicinity of the airstrips. Something's bound to be hit, and it could be the fuel supply."

The briefer picked it up from there. "We've taken what we hope will be a first step in protecting our bombers. In an area of the Arizona desert, away from any real habitation, we've been conducting research on a variety of smoke screen that we believe will enable us to blanket an island from enemy eyes.

"With such a screen we hope to keep the enemy guessing where our installations are. By making the island invisible from the air, they won't know where to place their bombs."

"One minute," Captain Midnight said. "With such a smoke screen, we won't know where to place the aircraft when we try to land. Under those conditions, landing would be suicide."

The major nodded. "So it would — if the smoke screen extended down to the surface. But a brilliant chemist, Dr. Wilkins, has developed a formulation that becomes smoke only after reaching a certain altitude. I'm not privy on how it works, but on clear days, returning aircraft should have a 1200-foot ceiling after breaking through a periphery of conventional smoke.

"Your assignment is to help Dr. Wilkins establish an experimental setup on an island here," and the briefer indicated the location on a chart of the Pacific. The island's operation would be nominally under the command of Dr. Wilkins, but he was to defer to Captain Midnight on matters involving the island's security. In addition to a small Secret Squadron force, the main island defenses would be supplied by a squadron of Marine Corps aviators.

Once everything was set up, a contingent of Army Air Corps bombers would join them.

After the briefing, Major Steele amplified a bit on mission details. Captain Midnight would be given a lot of leeway on how the mission was to be run. However, he first was to travel to Arizona to coordinate with Dr. Wilkins. Major Steele also pointed out that the Marines would be flying Grumman torpedo bombers, and that it might be a good idea to become familiar with them.

Captain Midnight replied that he intended to familiarize his whole party with the plane. It was no surprise to Major Steele when he learned that, in addition to Midnight, the primary Squadron party would consist of Chuck Ramsay, Joyce Ryan, and Ichabod Mudd. While Mudd wasn't a pilot, the Secret Squadron leader was sure that by the time they arrived on the island, he would know the plane inside and out.

Captain Midnight returned to Squadron Headquarters, where he arranged for Chuck and Joyce to get training on the Grumman Avengers they might have to fly. He obtained a pilot's manual on the Avenger and, still using the Mustang, flew out to Arizona.

Well south of the Grand Canyon, in an area of Arizona removed from settlements, was a military installation known only as K-14. Captain Midnight had been given its coordinates, and he flew out there directly via a great-circle route. As he approached, he studied the base spread out below him.

Besides the inevitable barracks and the long X of a pair of runways, the facility had what looked like four large storage tanks, placed in a rough square surrounding the base. They looked like water towers, and seemed a bit out of place in the remote setting. Captain Midnight suspected the tanks had something to do with his mission.

After landing, Captain Midnight was taken to see Dr. Wilkins. The scientist was a thin, middle-aged individual with a surprisingly firm grip. He radiated a level of enthusiasm that the Secret Squadron leader had found in few individuals.

Wilkins explained the overall mechanics of his smoke screen. He'd developed two types of chemical which were dispersed into the air via heated elements. Each was invisible and nontoxic; when the two mixed at the appropriate altitude, they combined to make a cloud- or smoke-like cover. This cover was quite thick. Combined with a more orthodox smoke screen around the periphery, the K-14 development could blanket an island.

Dr. Wilkins' assignment was to set up an experimental base on a Pacific island. Located in the western Pacific, this site, designated "X Island," was sufficiently large to support a reasonable air base. It was hoped that if the experiment proved successful, the island could be used as a base for long-range bombing missions, perhaps to the islands of Japan.

At the time, the island was effectively uninhabited and seemed, in conventional terms, to be of little strategic importance. This made it a good place to stage an experiment, and it could probably be settled before the enemy could react.

Initial plans called for a small occupying force of U.S. Marines to land and secure the island. They would be followed by Navy Seabees, who would construct the base and runways. Then the smokescreen generators would be installed; at the same time, a radiodirectional beacon would be put in place. When personnel were to be moved onto the base, the secret, radar-directed experimental guns would be emplaced as a defense measure.

Since the island had a mountain area, it was possible to establish hangars and living quarters beneath the surface. The smokescreen towers, however, would have to be above ground and at some distance from the base, nearly at the shores of the island. An inland harbor, which would be covered by the smoke screen, could, with but little modification, be used for submarine pens.

Captain Midnight was given a solid briefing on the operation of both the smoke screen generator and the radar-directed gun arrangement. He was also checked out in a Grumman Avenger.

Since they were going into a war zone, Captain Midnight left instructions that Chuck Ramsay would "succeed as the leader of the Secret Squadron mission" should anything happen to him. This led to some misunderstanding, with word going around among outsiders that Chuck was to be made leader of the *entire* Secret Squadron. Captain Midnight didn't expect the youngster to do any such thing; while Chuck had plenty of experience near the center of Squadron activities, he'd yet to gain the mature perspective necessary to run so complex an organization. However, Captain Midnight had high confidence in the youngster's ability to handle himself in the field, so there was no reason Chuck shouldn't be able to lead the X Island mission.

Both Captain Midnight and Ichabod Mudd departed for X Island first. Chuck and Joyce would follow after receiving special briefings. Midnight flew via the Squadron's Pacific Headquarters, where he was able to obtain local intelligence, then to New Guinea, which was the jumping-off point to X Island.

At a large New Guinea airfield they met Lt. Colonel Hugh McDonnell, U.S. Army Air Corps. He was flight commander for a group of B-17 Flying Fortresses, and was among the few who had some inkling of the X Island project. Should the "smoke" prove effective, his bombers would be moved to the island for possible strikes against Japanese-held territories and maybe even Japan itself. He also had several aircraft set aside for the Secret Squadron.

After conferring some time with Colonel McDonnell, Captain Midnight took one of the single-engine planes, a Bell P-39 Airacobra, on a scouting flight to X island. Surveying it as he arrived, he felt that the place seemed almost perfect for the job.

There were no nearby islands. There was no reason the actual project shouldn't begin. Captain Midnight returned to the New Guinea airfield and began sending special encrypted messages that would start the operation.

Shortly thereafter, a battalion of Seabees landed and began construction. In record time the installation was complete, except for the personnel. And the Seabees departed as suddenly as they had arrived. Captain Midnight hardly got to meet any of them.

First to arrive as "permanent residents" was a flight of 24 Avenger fighter-bombers. These were commanded by Major Davis Preston, USMC. One of his officers, Lieutenant Mark Cross, USMC, was to act as personal liaison to the Secret Squadron.

Finally, since the island was in waters with a strong level of enemy control, it was decided that as soon as the island was up and running, vital supplies would be shipped in by submarine. Commander Craig MacDonough, USN, would be in charge of the logistics. Whenever the base completed the experimental phase and became militarily operational, the naval officer would become its commanding officer.

As the final touches were being put on the base, Captain Midnight was informed that Dr. Wilkins, Chuck, and Joyce had arrived in New Guinea. He and Lieutenant Cross flew there in an Avenger to see that everybody met everybody else.

Amazingly, everything had come through at once. Both the chemical tanks and the radar unit came on the same transport with the two Squadron agents and the scientists. This meant that the two experiments could be set up in parallel, saving valuable time.

Captain Midnight personally flew the precious cargo plane to its destination. Upon deplaning, Dr. Wilkins assumed command (calling it "directorship," maintaining that "command" was a completely military term, and he was an experimenter). Work progressed smoothly, since all those on the island had an idea of what a successful experiment would mean.

Then, near-disaster struck. The island was spotted by a Japanese aircraft.

It was later determined that the pilot of the aircraft was on a long-range practice mission over what he assumed were "safe" waters when he overflew the island at some altitude. It happened that Captain Midnight, Joyce, and Chuck were in what in later times would be known as the "radar

9. The War: Countermoves

Grumman "Avenger" fighter-bombers. The Marine contingent on X Island used these as all-around defensive aircraft while the X Island base was being established. (Photograph: *National Air and Space Museum, Smithsonian Institution*, SI Neg. No. 78-14827.)

shack" when the lone aircraft approached. The plane appeared as a spot of light on the display (which was referred to as the "luminous screen" back then). After the radar specialist told them its range and bearing, the Secret Squadron members went outside to spot it.

Through binoculars, Captain Midnight verified that it was an enemy aircraft. He sprinted to the Airacobra and got it ready for flight. He completed the checklist just as the other aircraft overflew the island.

As he departed, the Secret Squadron leader radioed Chuck that he might be delayed coming back, depending upon where he caught up to the other plane.

The other plane was a Mitsubishi A6M (or "Zero"), and closing with it took some time. The Airacobra was a little faster, but the Zero had quite a lead by the time Captain Midnight reached altitude. This was further complicated by deteriorating weather west of their location, and the Zero was flying west.

Just as Captain Midnight was finally closing, the Japanese pilot maneuvered so he happened to spot the overtaking aircraft. The Zero's pilot didn't hesitate, but joined battle at once. An intense dogfight ensued.

The Japanese fighter was good, and he was flying a highly responsive aircraft. The Airacobra was much less maneuverable, but Captain Midnight had superlative skill. By using virtually every maneuver he'd ever learned, the Secret Squadron leader finished off the other aircraft. But as the Zero spun down, trailing smoke, Captain Midnight realized he wasn't in much better shape.

His Airacobra had been seriously damaged in the engagement. Captain Midnight realized he'd have next to no chance if he ditched in enemy-controlled waters. From his position, he was much closer to the Philippines than to X Island or any other land. The Philippines, however, were still occupied by the Japanese.

The Filipinos hated the Japanese. If he could make it to the islands and could avoid capture, the natives should help him.

It was a gamble to head there, but he had to chance it.

Luck was with him. He brought his aircraft down in the water near some island at dusk. He ditched near what proved to be a fishing boat crewed by Filipinos. One of the fishermen understood a little English and indicated a hatred of the Japanese. He indicated that he would hide Captain Midnight and shortly would "bring to Manuel."

It took the better part of the night. First the fisher-folk had to smuggle him from the dock area. Then they had to arrange transportation — devilishly difficult to do, for the Japanese even overstamped their occupation currency to make sure people didn't travel between provinces. Yet it was done, and in due course Captain Midnight was brought to Manuel.

Manuel was a leader in the Philippine underground. Some of the people associated with the fisher-folk explained to him how Captain Midnight happened to be found. This, along with a description of the aircraft he was flying, helped establish his *bona fides*— at least to the extent of being an enemy of Japan. But Captain Midnight wasn't wearing a uniform of the conventional American armed forces, but the khaki clothing without insignia that was standard for the Squadron. So the Filipino wasn't sure about his guest's status.

Captain Midnight took a calculated risk. He identified himself. He explained who he was (even here in the Philippines, the Secret Squadron was known), and verified it by disengaging a special catch in the heel of one shoe and withdrawing his Code-O-Graph from the reinforced hollow. The current model was designed to show a picture of the person to whom it was issued, and Manuel was convinced.

After Captain Midnight returned his Code-O-Graph to its hiding place, Manuel assured him that he would be hidden and assisted "until the Americans returned."

Aghast, the Secret Squadron leader explained that he was

The Secret Squadron Code-O-Graph that saw service during the wartime years. To increase its usefulness as a personalized identifier, this unit had an insertion area for the member's photograph. It was designed as one of the thinnest units ever issued, and could be concealed in the hollow heel of an agent's shoe during covert operations. (Photograph: *Stephen Kallis, Jr.*)

involved in a highly important mission that should bring the war to the Japanese. He pointed out that he had to make every attempt to get back.

Manuel, reasonably, asked Captain Midnight how he proposed to return. "We would certainly like to help you, most certainly," he said. "But alas, we have no means of getting you there."

"I'm not asking you for the impossible," Captain Midnight replied. "You're doing valuable work in the war effort. But I'm hopeful that you can help me find the way to return."

He explained that he'd previously tangled with the Japanese — even before the attack on Pearl Harbor — and that on at least one occasion, he'd managed to capture a Japanese aircraft to help him complete his mission. His hope was that he'd be able to do something like that again.

Manuel smiled. "You are a brave man," he said. "Your goal is a worthy one. We can offer but little help, but we will see what we can do." He added that he'd pass word to other members of the underground — without revealing precisely who Captain Midnight was.

The Secret Squadron leader expressed his thanks. At Manuel's suggestion, he ate a small meal and took some rest.

Captain Midnight was in luck. Several things were happening that would make it possible for him to leave the Philippines in short order. Most of them derived from Japan's worsening position in the war.

The famous admiral, Isoroku Yamamoto, predicted prior to Japan's entry into World War II that a prolonged war against the United States would be one Japan would be unlikely to win. He predicted early Japanese victories and suggested that a quick and decisive war would be Japan's best hope for triumph. He observed that the United States' industrial potential would alter the balance should the war be drawn out.

After the Battle of Midway, some professional military men in the Japanese armed forces began to see how prophetic Admiral Yamamoto's words were.

There were, however, diehards who insisted that Japan would triumph militarily. One of these was Rear Admiral Ito Himakito. Admiral Himakito knew of many of the troubles facing Japan, including a lack of fighters and properly trained pilots to man them. He felt he had an answer that would turn the tide of the war. He would establish a naval aviation group trained to his exacting specifications and details. He would establish a reserve location in a Japanese-controlled section of China to manufacture weapons and spare parts for his forces.

As it happened, Admiral Himakito was in the Philippines, overseeing a phase of his program, when Captain Midnight arrived. At the time, every command was sorely in need of aircraft. Admiral Himakito, feeling that the plan would go through only with his personal supervision, had established a small and isolated airfield from which to launch those Zeroes that were to go to his forces.

The Filipino underground knew of the field, and even planned to raid it as part of the sabotage effort. While it was well guarded, the natives had painfully established a tunnel through a hill that gave them access to the field. It was shortly after Captain Midnight arrived at Manuel's headquarters that news came of the tunnel's completion.

Recalling Captain Midnight's words, Manuel faced a dilemma. Ideally, he'd have directed his forces to inflict maximum damage to whatever aircraft and supplies were present. Yet, since the famous Captain Midnight mentioned having previously made off with a Japanese airplane, perhaps the tunnel might provide a means of escape for the renowned aviator. He would ask.

When Captain Midnight awakened, Manuel explained the situation.

9. The War: Countermoves

He asked whether the Secret Squadron leader would wish to try to "liberate" an aircraft. Given the importance of Captain Midnight's mission, the underground would be willing to help if he thought it wise.

Captain Midnight asked what types of aircraft were kept at the field.

Manuel reported that almost all of the aircraft at the field were Zeroes. He asked, "Do you know how to fly them?"

The Secret Squadron leader nodded, saying that during the Aleutian campaign, the Japanese lost a Zero, almost intact. It had been transported to the mainland United States, where it had been put in working order and tested exhaustively. From this, the Army Air Corps had been able to determine the strengths and weaknesses of the plane. Captain Midnight had been able to try it out on a secret visit to the test field. He added that without his knowledge of how Zeroes flew, he would never have been able to defeat one while flying an Airacobra, observing that, "...an Airacobra is the favorite target of Japanese fighter pilots."

Late that night — or, more precisely, early the next morning before sunup — a party of the Filipino underground, with Captain Midnight, made its way carefully through the tunnel leading to the hidden airfield. Although the Filipinos weren't aware of the airfield's exact purpose, that it was Japanese and that it was heavily guarded made it a prime target.

At the tunnel's end, they paused, easing back the camouflage to take stock. Even at that late (or extremely early) hour, there was some activity. From the distance, the roar of an aircraft engine indicated that some testing was going on. The field was mostly dark, but in the dim glow the silhouettes of two Zeroes could be made out.

In hushed whispers, Captain Midnight pointed out that if the two Zeroes were fueled, he could make off with one easily. Manuel nodded, and added that he and his men could create a diversion that would give the Secret Squadron leader time to get airborne (as well as being very satisfying to the Filipinos).

As they emerged from the tunnel, they practically ran headlong into two men, indistinct in the dark, but doubtless Japanese. Instinctively, Captain Midnight swung a fist at one before he could cry out, flattening him with one blow. The other man collapsed with a low moan as Manuel smashed him with the butt of a pistol.

Manuel unsheathed a knife to dispatch the two, but Captain Midnight stopped him. "Let's see if they can give us any information about this field," he said. So, reluctantly, Manuel's men dragged the unconscious men to the tunnel, which they sealed sufficiently to prevent any stray light from escaping.

The two were tied and gagged. When they recovered, Captain Midnight asked them whether they understood English. Both nodded.

Although Manuel wanted to torture the information out of them, Captain Midnight discouraged him, pointing out that the two were prisoners of war and had to be treated accordingly. He then told the two prisoners that to make any loud sounds, such as a shout, would bring their instant death, and no aid. Then Captain Midnight had their gags removed.

The older of the two immediately demanded under what authority the two had become prisoners of war. Before the Secret Squadron leader could stop him, Manuel identified him as "the famous Captain Midnight of the American Secret Squadron."

Sighing, Captain Midnight told Manuel to replace the gags. "That sort of information will just make them refuse to talk," he said. He added that, under the circumstances, they might have to work fast.

Manuel agreed, saying his people could rig explosive charges that would create a diversion for Captain Midnight's escape. And since he promised that he wouldn't harm the "prisoners of war," he wouldn't. But he and his men would position them on the hill so that they could see the "famous Captain Midnight" steal one of their aircraft and watch the base be destroyed. Perhaps even though Manuel and his men wouldn't kill them, they might prefer to do the job themselves, ceremonially.

Indeed, the two Japanese were the only eyewitnesses to the operation that then took place. Manuel's men fanned out carefully, each carrying a small parcel. Shortly, they returned, even as Captain Midnight stole toward the Zeroes. Discovering one was fully fueled, he signaled Manuel, climbed in silently, and waited.

Then, as Manuel's men withdrew into the tunnel, all Hell broke loose. Several explosions rocked the area, one after another, and at least two fires sprang up simultaneously. As the troops raced to the area, Captain Midnight started the Zero.

Fortunately for the Secret Squadron leader, there was so much confusion and noise that nobody noticed his actions until well after the Zero he'd appropriated began to roll. By that time, it was too late. He vanished into the predawn light, flying east without navigation lights.

And the two bound and gagged men near the tunnel, Rear Admiral Ito Himakito and his aide, Lieutenant Taru Ichi, had to sit and watch the whole thing. Admiral Himakito vowed that he would never forget Captain Midnight. If the two of them should ever cross paths again, he would make the Secret Squadron leader pay for the shame he'd brought.

Once well away from the Philippines, Captain Midnight "leaned out" his engine as much as possible to gain as much fuel as he could. Then he laid in a course that he estimated would bring him fairly close to X Island.

On X Island, a radioman was brought to full wakefulness by a message coming in on the island's assigned frequency. It started off: "Master Code 6.

9. The War: Countermoves

1-21-23-8-14 24-21-15 26-15-6-18-8..." The radioman copied down every symbol. Then he called Chuck Ramsay at the officer quarters.

Chuck, who'd been increasingly worried about Captain Midnight, had been sleeping uneasily. When he heard of the incoming message, he was galvanized into action, pulling on his uniform in record time. He raced to the radio shack, and in a trice was deciphering the message.

It read: ARVNG FRM LUZON IN JP ZERO HV CHK ND LT CROSS RNDZVZ FTFY MLS WST F X LND IN WN HR TO SCRT ME IN SSWN. Chuck was elated and ran to awaken Lieutenant Cross.

The lieutenant was a bit groggy, but when Chuck explained that Captain Midnight was returning in a Zero and needed an escort, he became quite alert. As he dressed, he said, "He'll sure have a story to tell. How do you suppose he did it?"

"He almost never goes into details," Chuck said ruefully. "Normally, Ikky, Joyce, or I are along to find out how it was done."

Shortly, two Avengers took off and flew west. Over the open sea, they spotted a Zero that proved to be the one Captain Midnight liberated. The flight back was uneventful.

Dr. Wilkins had made a great deal of progress since Captain Midnight's departure. Within a week of his return, the first tests of the "smoke" screen took place. It was eerie to see a manifestation like a cloud deck appear from four corners and spread out to blot out most of the overhead sky.

Concurrent with the deployment of the "smoke" generators was the installation of a radio beacon. The beacon was an essential ingredient in making the "smoke" screen work, since it guided aircraft through the smoke at the critical point in the flight path. Without it, incoming aircraft might smash into the mountain.

Shortly after the radio beacon was installed and its operation checked out, Captain Midnight took an Avenger and flew out from the island to inspect the screen. He flew out some distance and was bemused by the effect, which looked like a clump of white cloud squatting on the ocean's surface. In a lifetime of flying, he'd never seen anything like it.

Returning, he orbited the screen and noticed that, intermittently, a few glimpses of the island's edge could be seen. He flew out to intercept the radio beacon so he could land and provide data to Dr. Wilkins.

Within a day of Captain Midnight's observations, adjustments were made so the island was completely cloaked.

While Dr. Wilkins and his associates were laboring to complete the experimental station, Admiral Himakito wasn't idle. More than 200 Zeroes had been transferred to the admiral's special force. He was in command of two light aircraft carriers, one cruiser, and four destroyers. The admiral wanted, and got, the most devoted and hard-line men available. He directed that all of his pilots be trained, almost mercilessly, over and over to perfect their skills.

It was evident to Admiral Himakito that his greatest requirement would be for pilots. All too frequently, pilots who were shot down weren't rescued, and that was Japan's greatest loss. He was aware that the Americans spent a great deal of effort rescuing their downed fliers, and he was willing to emulate them in that. Therefore, he ordered that special rescue teams be organized and trained.

By the time Captain Midnight made his getaway from the Philippines, the admiral's program was near completion. Even the underground's raid on his field destroyed only half the remaining planes. As he joined his forces at sea, Admiral Himakito was confident that he would be able to reverse the trend of battle in the Pacific, despite such naval foes as Admirals Halsey and Spruance, and special operatives such as Captain Midnight.

During the next few weeks at X Island, Dr. Wilkins declared the experimental station operational. After briefing his technicians thoroughly, he left to return to his laboratories in the United States. It seemed that one of the two "smoke" screen components, compound Y-24, was being used in higher proportion than the original experiments had indicated (the reason being, in part, that the higher-humidity air surrounding the island resulted in increased consumption of the one compound). It would have to be replenished soon.

Once having established the screen, the station personnel were obliged to keep it up. And while Commander MacDonough established a tenuous supply line via submarine, he had no reserves of compound Y-24 to send over.

Periodically, the Marine pilots and the Squadron agents would fly the Avengers, both to maintain proficiency and to perfect the technique of landing through the screen. With the limited amount of aviation fuel available, no aircraft flew too far from the island. So it was that one day when Chuck Ramsay and Lieutenant Cross were flying for practice, they were discovered by a couple of Zero pilots.

Fortunately, Chuck spotted them first. It was sheer luck. The young Squadron agent happened to look in the right direction after completing a maneuver. He radioed the information to Lieutenant Cross, who advised him to fly evasively, but to head for the island immediately. A Zero was more maneuverable and could easily outrun an Avenger. Since it was a close-in practice flight, neither pilot had brought along gunners.

The factors that saved them were that they'd spotted the Zeroes first, and the Japanese planes weren't directly behind them. Both American pilots gave their aircraft full throttle and dove to gain speed. Chuck called ahead to alert the island; both lined up on the radio beam.

9. The War: Countermoves

They began to slow at the outer fringes of the screen, which they entered just as the Zeroes approached. By the time they entered the clear area, at an altitude of 900 feet, they'd slowed sufficiently to begin using flaps. The rest of each landing was routine.

The Zero pilots circled the screen several times, suspecting that the American aircraft had taken temporary refuge in some sort of natural phenomenon — perhaps a forming volcano. But when neither aircraft emerged, they began to speculate that perhaps the screen was a trick of "the devil Americans."

Noting the location of the mysterious cloudlike manifestation, they flew back to report to their superiors. Word reached the admiral himself, who decided that it would be worth investigating. He ordered his force to steam in the direction of the screen.

Since the screen had been extended well beyond the shores of the island, nobody viewing the screen from the outside could know the exact location of what it concealed. But the "smoke" screen towered several thousand feet and was highly visible in the clear air of the Pacific. As Admiral Himakito's fleet approached, locating the general position of the island was merely a matter of steering towards the "smoke."

Those on X Island were aware that something was happening, but the radar unit could tell them only so much. Therefore, Captain Midnight decided to take a look.

He took an Avenger and took Ichabod Mudd along to act as gunner. He took off, banked away from the mountains' direction, and began to circle when the screen began to thin before him. Maintaining a position just inside the screen, he continued to spiral upwards until he broke out of it at the top.

What they saw was Admiral Himakito's force, located at some distance from the island but clearly visible from the Avenger's altitude. They could see two carriers and at least two destroyers. They might have taken a more thorough inventory but, suddenly, Captain Midnight spotted a Zero.

Periodically, a plane from Admiral Himakito's force was assigned to orbit the screen. It was obvious from the pilot's actions that he hadn't spotted the Avenger. Midnight thought it would be prudent to withdraw.

Although he emerged from the top of the screen, the Secret Squadron leader couldn't safely reenter that way to land. So, waiting for the opportune moment, he flew out in a direction that would enable him to intercept the radio beacon. However, because he was forced to fly out some distance, the Zero spotted him.

The Zero closed with the Avenger. Captain Midnight used the interphone to Mudd. "Ikky, no matter what I do, keep your sights on that Zero." And Ichabod Mudd complied.

The fight was a tough one for Captain Midnight. The Japanese pilot had the superior fighter. But Captain Midnight was unquestionably the finest aviator of his era. After the battle, Ichabod Mudd noted, "I couldn't tell you all Cap'n Midnight did. He told me to take a fix on that Jap, and I did. But leapin' sawfish! We were all over the sky! Finally, though, the Zero got in range ... again ... for the last time, and I polished him off."

No other aircraft could be launched in time to prevent Captain Midnight from reentering the screen. On final approach, knowing that no other friendly aircraft were aloft, he ordered the radio beacon turned off, as a precaution.

It was well he did. Captain Midnight's actions made it clear to the Japanese that he was using a radio beacon as a landing aid. One of the radiomen on the flagship managed to discover the frequency, getting a Morse "N," before the beacon ceased transmitting.

Admiral Himakito could afford to wait. Having found an American installation, he could have his radiomen monitor the frequency while a flight of Zeroes stood ready. When the radio beacon was next turned on, Japanese aircraft would fly along it. They would bring death and destruction to enemies of the Empire.

So, there was a stalemate. The Japanese forces couldn't mount an effective air attack against X Island. Because of the heavy Japanese numerical superiority, any American air attack against them would be suicidal. In short, neither could make an effective move against the other.

But the advantage lay with the Japanese. The dwindling supply of compound Y-24 meant that unless some replacements could be supplied soon, the island would be laid bare for Japanese attack.

Captain Midnight ordered that the ratio of compound Y-24 to compound Y-14 (the other component) be reduced to the minimum acceptable thickness of the "smoke" screen. Then he radioed New Guinea in a service cipher to explain his situation.

He received encouraging news. At the staging airfield, a fresh supply of the two compounds had been delivered from Dr. Wilkins, with a high proportion being the sorely needed compound Y-24. Since the "smoke" screen had proven successful, Colonel McDonnell would fly up a number of B-17s. Among the bombers were several with the new screen compounds as cargo. He would then commence operations from X Island.

Captain Midnight sent his thanks. He explained that because of the presence of the Japanese fleet, he wouldn't broadcast the radio beacon continuously. He'd have the beacon transmit on a schedule that was irregular, so the Japanese would have trouble taking advantage of it. He said that when they determined the bombers were close enough, he'd have the beacon broadcast continuously.

9. The War: Countermoves

Aichi "Val" dive bomber. There were many of these attached to Admiral Himakito's command. Some of these were shot down by radar-coupled antiaircraft guns while "blind bombing" X Island. (Photograph: *National Air and Space Museum, Smithsonian Institution*, SI Neg. No. 78-3680.)

Colonel McDonnell was satisfied with the arrangement and indicated that he'd fly his bombers up the next day. Fully 25 Flying Fortresses would fly to X Island, nearly half loaded with the screen compounds. Additional supplies would be shipped in by U-boat: Commander MacDonough, who had come to X Island by submarine to be briefed on the project's progress, made that clear. The compounds from the Fortresses would give the island more than two weeks' worth of maximum cover.

In addition to about 200 Zeroes under his command, Admiral Himakito had 25 Nakajima B5N attack aircraft, known to the American forces as "Kates." These could be employed as light bombers. The admiral decided that though the island was shrouded in the smoke, even blind bombing would have some effect. Even if nothing were hit, the bombing should motivate some American pilots to come out from the screen to engage the bombers. Then his Zeroes could home in on the radio beacon.

When the Kates were launched, they were picked up on radar, their presence shown on the screen. Captain Midnight, who happened to be close to the radar shack, was called in for consultation.

It was evident to Midnight that the approaching aircraft had to be on a bombing mission. He pointed out to the technicians that this was a golden opportunity to try out their radar-coupled antiaircraft equipment.

The B-17 "Flying Fortress" bomber was famous throughout most of World War II. Although these aircraft normally were used in bombing missions, they were also used to ferry some emergency amounts of the vital Y-24 compound for the smokescreened X Island. (Photograph: *Boeing.*)

As the technicians raced to ensure that their connections were activated, Captain Midnight directed that X Island personnel be alerted to seek cover because of a possible bombing attack. He requested that Chuck Ramsay and Commander MacDonough join him at the radar shack.

The Kates overflew the island's screen in tight formation so that as they dropped their bombs, they'd be most likely to do significant damage. It made the bombers easy prey for the radar-coupled guns, which performed flawlessly. Fully half of them were destroyed.

Admiral Himakito monitored the radio traffic between the Kates, hoping to hear reports of explosive flashes seen through the smoke. What he heard was something else, with pilot after pilot reporting that his aircraft had been hit. As the surviving Kates returned, the admiral took stock of his losses and decided he wouldn't try that tactic again — the costs were too high. Whatever sort of weapons system the Americans had, he realized, they needn't bother sending out aircraft.

The American warplanes weren't damaged by the bombs. The hangar

9. The War: Countermoves

area was built into the side of a mountain. There were several such cavernous areas, built to house the Flying Fortresses to be assigned to the island. Several of the X Island personnel used one of these as a bomb shelter. Captain Midnight, Joyce, Chuck, and Commander MacDonough observed the action of the radar-coupled guns directly; no bombs came close enough to do them any harm.

Several X Island personnel were injured in the attack, mostly due to bad luck. These included three pilots from Major Preston's squadron. Although none was critically injured, each would be out of action for a week or so.

Early the following morning, a fleet of B-17 bombers took off from New Guinea, heading straight for X Island along a great circle route. As they climbed for altitude, they were spotted by a Japanese spy boat, which radioed the information to its command. The report was forwarded to Admiral Himakito. He suspected that the flight's destination might be the smoke-shrouded island that had frustrated him so far.

The admiral called a meeting of his senior staff officers and outlined the situation. He explained it was his belief that the B-17 bombers would arrive on the island to press the war closer to Japan's shores. "This must not happen," he said, "even if it means taking extraordinary measures." He developed a plan: If the bombers should arrive, the fleet's Zeroes should overfly them and dive, four abreast, on individual B-17s. Escorting fighters should be ignored, and the Zeroes should not turn aside; if bullets from the fighters didn't destroy the bombers, the pilots should set the planes to ram them, waiting until the last possible moment before bailing out.

On the island, it was decided to have Major Preston's Avenger squadron escort the bombers when they approached. Although the bombers were well armed, and the Avengers were only secondarily fighters, every gun aloft would help insure the survival of X Island.

When the radio beacon on X Island was turned on for short, preplanned intervals for the approaching bombers, never exceeding two minutes, the action confirmed Admiral Himakito's suspicions. He was certain beyond any doubt that the bombers were headed for the island. Consequently, he called in the chief of his rescue forces and told them that he expected great loss of aircraft in the upcoming encounter. The admiral directed that extra care be taken to retrieve downed Japanese pilots. He then added, "The American pilots should not be rescued. See that not one you find be taken from the water alive."

His administrative aide, Captain Kaga, who was to direct much of the rescue effort, took that to mean that the rescue parties should make certain that every American who was still alive should not just be left in the water, but should be executed. Whether this is what Admiral Himakito really meant is open to debate, but that is how the subordinates interpreted it.

As the time neared for the bombers to arrive, the Marine squadron took off, led by Major Preston. With three Marine pilots injured, the Secret Squadron members took two of the Avengers to support the action. Captain Midnight took Ichabod Mudd to act as tail gunner; Chuck took Joyce for the same function. Joyce Ryan was known to be the second-best shot in the entire Secret Squadron.

The battle was joined southeast of X Island and was almost indescribable. Zeroes in groups of four dove toward and into the formation of Fortresses. Many Zeroes simply disintegrated under the combined firepower of the bombers and the Avengers, but even some falling pieces of the destroyed Zeroes damaged the bombers as they plummeted through the formation.

A few Japanese pilots engaged the Avengers. Joyce shot down a couple of them, and Captain Midnight got one. During the battle, Captain Midnight's plane and a Zero collided, shearing off more than half the Avenger's left wing. Both Captain Midnight and Ichabod Mudd bailed out.

They hit the water close together. In the jump or the landing, Mudd managed to wrench his right shoulder, making it difficult to swim. Captain Midnight swam over to him and started towing him toward the island. They were sufficiently far out that they expected that they would be rescued before they reached shore. And they hoped that they wouldn't be "rescued" by the Japanese.

Chuck and Joyce had seen Captain Midnight's plane go down. Though shocked, they couldn't break off from the battle to go to his aid. They vowed that if they survived the battle, they would try to find their downed comrades. (And although they almost ran out of fuel trying, they didn't find them.)

The Japanese found them. As a Japanese motor launch approached, Captain Midnight and Ichabod Mudd stopped swimming and tried to float on their backs, as if dead. They were able to see out of the corners of their eyes that the Japanese sailors were machine-gunning American pilots in the water. The Japanese were using spotlights to identify who was floating in the water. Captain Midnight whispered a plan to Ichabod Mudd in case the spotlight found them. The spotlight did give them a few seconds' warning; when the two were bathed in light, they dived, coming up along the motor launch.

Captain Kaga was on the launch. When Captain Midnight's head broke the surface, he told his men to hold their fire, drawing his pistol to administer the *coup de grace* himself. But then he saw Captain Midnight's face. He held his fire and ordered both the Secret Squadron leader and Ichabod Mudd into the boat.

9. The War: Countermoves

It happened that Captain Kaga had heard of the incident in the Philippines. He'd looked up intelligence reports on Captain Midnight. Recognizing the Squadron leader from a photograph in the reports, he thought that it would be only fitting that he be brought to Admiral Himakito.

The admiral was in his office, fuming at the reports he'd been receiving. Most of the Fortresses got through, and his forces had lost 74 aircraft. He was in something approaching a rage when Captain Kaga entered.

"Where have you been?"

"I have been rescuing many Japanese pilots," Captain Kaga replied, unaccountably in English, which he knew the admiral understood. "And I have been making sure American pilots have not been rescued. Except for two, which I have brought to you."

Startled, Admiral Himakito snapped, in Japanese, "*What?* I told you to bring back no live prisoners! Bring them to me ... and I ... I will kill them myself!"

"I am so sorry," said Captain Kaga, still in English. "I have disobeyed your orders." Then, in Japanese, "Bring in the American dogs."

As Captain Midnight and Ichabod Mudd were brought in, Captain Kaga continued in English, "I am sorry to have disobeyed your order. If you wish, I will kill them now..."

He was interrupted by the nearly hysterical laughter of Admiral Himakito. The admiral shifted to English, saying, "You have disobeyed my order, yes. Ordinarily, I would have you court-martialed. But this time, I will give you a medal! You have captured Captain Midnight!"

The Secret Squadron leader started. Belatedly, he recognized the small man in the admiral's uniform as one of the two he'd jumped in the Philippines. He began to wonder whether it might not have been better to face a clean death in the water.

Admiral Himakito ordered Captain Midnight and Ichabod Mudd taken away. He told Captain Kaga that on the following day, the American would pay for the humiliation he heaped upon the admiral. "Several hours of concern will make his suffering that much more exquisite," he said with satisfaction.

Had Admiral Himakito known what was transpiring on X Island, he wouldn't have hesitated to take his revenge immediately. The arrival of the B-17s had consolidated the position of the island. It could be used as a permanent base. The majority of the Flying Fortresses had gotten through, 18 in flyable condition. The supplies of Y-14 and Y-24 assured them a nearly three-week supply. Commander MacDonough, who had two submarines in the island's pens, was able to take command of the base and was ready to take action.

Chuck Ramsay, as "Captain Midnight's successor," was brought into a three-way conference with Commander MacDonough and Colonel McDonnell. The commander proposed a massive strike against the Japanese early in the morning. Both air and naval forces would be employed.

As dawn broke, Captain Midnight and Ichabod Mudd were taken to the flight deck of the flagship carrier. Admiral Himakito had let them know that the special ceremonial preparations he had ordered for them would begin at sunrise — symbolizing the Rising Sun of Japan.

Whatever was going to happen — and both men knew that it would be slow, painful, and merciless — was to be a show. The ship's complement, save for a skeleton crew, was assembled on the deck in dress uniform. Admiral Himakito began to address his men, but he had barely begun speaking before he was interrupted.

Coming upon the carrier from out of the glare of the rising sun was a flight of American Avengers, flying at nearly flight-deck height, machine guns blazing. It was the first wave of the offensive from X Island. The planes had flown at almost wave height so as not to be spotted until they reached Admiral Himakito's naval force. After overflying the first carrier, they headed for one of the destroyers and strafed it.

Admiral Himakito spoke to the two Americans in English. "So, Captain Midnight. Your allies would attack us. I have ordered my men to bind you and leave you and your companion on this flight deck, exposed to the bullets of your friends." He laughed harshly. "It would be a most fitting end for you to die at their hands ... as good as anything I had planned. And if, somehow, you survive this attack, I believe we can find something else that would be satisfactory." After barking another order to the sailors, he turned and left the prisoners.

Captain Midnight and Ichabod Mudd were bound hand and foot. They were dumped roughly on the flight deck. The sailors then joined the others in war activities. The Americans were left in an exposed position to face the battle alone.

The way the two fell, their heads were fairly close together. Captain Midnight thus was able to speak to the Chief Mechanic without raising his voice. "Listen, Ikky. We may have a chance. As they were binding me, I tensed my muscles as hard as I could, and I believe that I can get my hands free with a little work. Try to keep a lookout while I work on the ropes." In a short time, the Squadron leader made progress, even with bullets whizzing past the two of them.

The Japanese were indeed busy. Avenger after Avenger flew over the ships, guns chattering, pinning down the Japanese sailors. This prevented them from making their best countermove: launching their Zeroes. From the belly of one Avenger came a torpedo that smacked into the water and headed for one of the destroyers, missing it narrowly. And after the last

9. The War: Countermoves

Avenger overflew the ships, the first Avenger, which had circled, began the second pass.

After freeing his hands, Captain Midnight rolled closer to Mudd and untied his bonds. Then he freed his own feet. He told Mudd to follow him, and sped to the rope locker, where the two of them grabbed several coils.

Crouching low, the two Secret Squadron members ran until they reached the edge of the flight deck. By using ropes, they could lower themselves to the water safely. This would give them a chance of getting away. It was certainly a better risk than staying on the carrier.

They reached the water and began to swim as rapidly as they could from the flagship. Although Ichabod Mudd's arm was still bothering him, he managed a crude side-stroke that, while tiring, was enabling him to progress without being too great a burden to Captain Midnight.

The two Americans had managed to get about 200 yards from the carrier when the two sailors who had bound them discovered they were gone. The sailors spotted the former prisoners in the water, and sent a volley of shots after them. Nothing came close.

While the sailors were standing at the edge of the flight deck, shooting at the escapees, one of the Avengers swooped down and strafed them. Thus it was that Admiral Himakito didn't find out about the escape while the battle raged.

In one of the Avengers were Chuck and Joyce. Against all logic, Joyce had insisted that instead of a torpedo, the crew place a large, inflatable life raft in the plane. "Just in case," as she put it. And it was by virtue of her superb eyesight that she spied the two figures in the water as Chuck overflew the carrier.

She contacted Chuck on the interphone, reporting what she'd seen. She wasn't sure that the two in the water were Captain Midnight and Ichabod Mudd, but the men were swimming away from the carrier, toward open sea. And who but an escaping prisoner would do that?

Chuck radioed Major Preston and received permission to return to the area where the swimmers were seen after he completed his pass over the ships. He returned, and as he circled the area, Joyce cried out excitedly that the two in the water were indeed Captain Midnight and Ichabod Mudd.

Chuck broke from orbit and, flying as low and slowly as was safe, passed over the area while Joyce released the doors and dropped the life raft. Young Ramsay orbited once more, rocking his wings, before returning to the attack.

Gratefully, Captain Midnight swam up to the raft and pulled the ring to inflate it fully. He clambered aboard and pulled Mudd from the water. He found paddles and began to put greater distance between himself and the battle.

As he rowed, he remarked to Mudd that he couldn't understand the tactics of the attackers. They were pinning down the Japanese, true. But it was only a matter of time before the Japanese would be able to reach the ships' guns and drive off the Avengers. Captain Midnight mused that there had to be some factor that he didn't understand.

The answer to his implied question was quick in coming.

Near where they were floating, a shape hurtled by, a little below the surface of the water. It was a torpedo, running straight and true toward the carrier. It detonated amidship, and it was evident that the flagship had been hurt. A second torpedo, impacting somewhat aft, compounded the blow.

Other torpedo explosions were heard, and Captain Midnight understood. The Avengers were sent to keep the Japanese busy so that the submarines could get into perfect position. The menace of Admiral Himakito's force was virtually at an end.

Aboard the carrier, Admiral Himakito realized what was happening after the impact of the first torpedo. The explosion of the second told him the ship was done. He directed the ship's skipper to order all hands to abandon ship.

With the torpedo explosions on all ships, the Avengers banked away and headed for X Island. Smoke rose from every Japanese vessel, and the submarines surfaced. One was close enough to the raft to pick up Captain Midnight and Ichabod Mudd.

As flames swept the carrier, Admiral Himakito, mindful of Japan's desperate need for aircraft and trained pilots, ordered all pilots to their planes. He told them to fly where he directed. With sincere regret that the ordinary sailors had to take to life rafts instead of being evacuated by air, he climbed into a gunner position in a Kate and told the pilot to take off. Soon the few Kates and escort Zeroes took off from the carriers and flew off to the west.

Although he'd suffered defeat, Admiral Himakito realized that the war was far from over. He still had his area in China from which he could work to destroy the cursed Americans.

The reunion on X Island was joyous. Major Steele, upon hearing the news, sent special congratulations for a job "very well done" to all concerned. The Squadron's work was finished, and X Island would become an operational base for the B-17s. In due course, the Avengers would be supplemented with some F4U Corsair fighters.

While the Secret Squadron's work was completed on X Island, it wasn't finished in the Pacific. During his stay on the island, Captain Midnight had kept in touch with Squadron Headquarters and thus became aware of certain critical information.

Intelligence reports from China indicated massive Japanese activity near a valley in an occupied province. Just what this activity was couldn't be determined because of the heavy security. The natives were so impressed by the intensity of the security that they named the area the "Hidden Valley." It was a wry joke among the locals that the Japanese would even shoot unfriendly clouds that might drift over the region.

Since the "first team" was already in the western Pacific, they went back to New Guinea and retrieved the Squadron amphibian. Then they made contact with a French operative, Captain Boudreau, who had his own connections within Japanese-controlled areas of China. Boudreau was to help them reach the area of the Hidden Valley, with help from friendly Chinese, both civilian and, if possible, military.

Even though the Hidden Valley wasn't too far from an area controlled by free Chinese, the armaments mounted by the Japanese in the valley were sufficiently powerful that no concerted attack had been attempted. The Japanese air defenses were so strong that Captain Midnight's party couldn't risk flying to the nearby free area.

Captain Boudreau pointed out that even the most practical way to reach the region was highly dangerous. The party would have to travel through Japanese-held areas by land. Such an undertaking virtually mandated that they'd have to travel in disguise. If discovered and captured, they'd be treated as spies.

Captain Midnight mulled the idea over, then agreed to it. Following instructions from Boudreau, the Secret Squadron leader flew his amphibian to a small Chinese fishing village and landed it at a specified inlet. He taxied it up to the head of that body of water.

The village was considered so unimportant by the Japanese that, though within their sphere of occupation, few troops were stationed in the immediate area. Coolies brought out coverings that camouflaged the plane. Captain Boudreau assured the Secret Squadron leader the amphibian would be safe until his return.

The Frenchman led the Squadron party to the top of a hill where an ancient Chinese temple was situated. He told them to follow him inside. When they reached an antechamber, Boudreau told them to stop.

As far as the Squadron members could see, the temple was deserted. There appeared to be no internal lighting — no lamps, candles, or even torches. The only light came from behind them, spilling in from the entranceway.

Taking a flashlight from his jacket, Boudreau directed its beam through the semi-gloom to a wall, where it illuminated a stylistic design of a dragon. "Regard that symbol, my friends," he said. "Although appearing to be very ancient, the design is quite new. It represents an association of Chinese patriots acting much the same way as the Underground in Europe. They call themselves the Secret Dragon Society, and it is through their help that we will get you to your destination."

Then Captain Boudreau took them through the main part of the temple, cautioning them to walk quietly and speak softly, if at all. To the Squadron members' surprise, the faint tinkling of a temple bell could be heard, and a sweetish odor, doubtless some form of incense, was present. Although these phenomena indicated that the temple wasn't deserted, none of the party ever met the priests of the temple.

At the rear of the building they came across another wall with the same Secret Dragon Society figure inscribed. Without saying a word, Boudreau motioned the others to stand still. Then he pressed the image with his open palm.

A section of the wall slid back, revealing a chamber. The Frenchman indicated they were to enter. Once they were inside, Boudreau moved the wall back to its original position, leaving them in near darkness. Resorting to his flashlight once again, he led the others to stairs that brought them to a large underground room.

Several members of the Secret Dragon Society were already present. Through carefully established clandestine message routes, they'd received information about Captain Midnight's mission to China. All were willing to help.

After Captain Midnight relayed what he'd heard about the Hidden Valley, and pointed out that the only way his party could obtain the necessary information would be to go there, he said, "It's clear that the only way to approach the Hidden Valley is in disguise. But we don't know the conditions at the region, and we'd welcome any suggestions on how to proceed."

One of the Chinese nodded gravely. He identified himself as Lieutenant Fan. He was a member of a guerilla army that was a wing of the Secret Dragon Society. The lieutenant was an aide to General Chu of this army, and was stationed at the temple as liaison to friendly forces helping China's cause. He suggested that the party dress as coolies. "There are so many of such folk in my land that the addition of a few more will attract no notice," he said with a friendly smile.

The lieutenant spoke briefly in Chinese, and a youngster who Captain Midnight judged to be about 16 years old stepped forward. The youngster was introduced as Ah Ting. The boy would act as guide and aide to them. The lieutenant explained that Ah Ting could speak perfect English and thus could ease the way for Captain Midnight's party, which he suspected couldn't speak Chinese.

Ah Ting proved to be a remarkably nice youngster. He procured appropriate clothing for the Secret Squadron party. He also found some dye to darken the skins of the Americans so that they'd be less conspicuous.

The Squadron members and Captain Boudreau made their way toward Shanghai, though the Frenchman went by a separate route. As coolies, the

9. The War: Countermoves

Secret Squadron members had to walk to the city. Ah Ting spent much of the walk tutoring them on the proper behavior of coolies.

They reached Shanghai without serious difficulty.

Shanghai was to be the jumping-off point to the Hidden Valley. The Squadron members met Captain Boudreau in hidden underground chambers controlled by the Secret Dragon Society.

Their meeting was interrupted by the arrival of a Dragon Society member who brought interesting news. Periodically, the Japanese required supplies be shipped to the Hidden Valley. For security, the supplies were usually shipped upriver by a barge or barge train manned by an all-Japanese crew. However, a shortage of available workmen developed; the next barge to go upriver would be manned by Chinese coolies.

Captain Midnight realized that the news could be a big break for the Squadron party. If they could somehow be integrated into the barge's work force, the elaborate plans they'd been working on would be unnecessary. They would be able to go directly upstream, bypassing many of the dangers that any overland route would bring.

The Secret Dragon Society helped. Precisely how they did it was unclear to the Squadron members, but Captain Midnight, Ichabod Mudd, Chuck Ramsay, and Joyce Ryan (all in disguise) soon found themselves mingling with a large number of coolies. Shortly, they were aboard one of the supply barges.

A train of three barges was to be pulled upstream by a tugboat, Ah Ting informed them. When they neared the area of the Hidden Valley, the barges were to be diverted to a canal. There, further towing would be by land vehicles. At that point, the coolies would be used to help pole the barges away from the canal's banks. Japanese personnel, of course, would man the vehicles.

After boarding, Ah Ting maneuvered his charges to a relatively obscured section of the second barge. He instructed the four of them to squat down and tilt their pointed hats to obscure their faces. They all stayed in that position for some time.

Ah Ting left for a little while and circulated among the other coolies. Returning, he urged the four to follow him. He'd learned that the Japanese were going to check all Chinese personnel aboard each barge.

Captain Midnight asked Ah Ting in low tones whether there was a way to get below decks. He explained that perhaps they might be able to hide somewhere, if there was sufficient cargo. Staying above decks would undoubtedly mean their eventual capture.

Ah Ting checked and found a hatchway toward the rear of the barge, which, like many Chinese boats, rode fairly high in the water. Captain Midnight suggested that the best time to try to go below decks would be when the Japanese boat approached. The coolies would then be paying more attention to the Japanese than to other coolies.

Shortly, the Japanese boat came toward the barge. Ah Ting and Captain Midnight silently raised the hatch. They went below, easing the hatch closed very quietly.

The cargo areas were very crowded; the whole party had to crawl almost snake-like away from the hatch. They worked toward the front of the barge. Although stifling and sufficiently dusty so that it was all they could do to keep from sneezing, they were soon out of direct sight of the hatch.

Ichabod Mudd found a slight horizontal crack in the hull, above the water line. It was long enough so that all five could look out of it. And although the field of view was restricted, it enabled fresh air to circulate, easing everybody's distress.

Mudd pointed out that all of them could stretch out by the crack and, as he put it, "take it easy all the way to the Hidden Valley." Smiling, Captain Midnight agreed that it was an excellent strategy.

The Japanese inspectors did open the hatch and glance down at the cargo, but no thorough inspection was made. With one barge behind them and still another to do, they figured a cursory glance was all that was needed.

The trip upriver was slow, but for the Squadron members, it was also scenic. Away from the port city, the land reverted to the timeless state it had remained in since the time of the great emperors. Once in a while, a reminder of modern times would intrude, such as when a Japanese military vehicle could be seen driving along the nearby roadway, but after it had passed, the feeling of timelessness would return.

After dark, the barges slowed and eventually stopped. Captain Midnight asked Ah Ting if he could find out why. The Chinese boy said he would try, and left.

Ah Ting learned that the barges were near the entrance to the canal, and the tug had stopped. Apparently, the Japanese decided to wait until morning before connecting the barges to land vehicles for the canal transit. Each barge was anchored for the night.

A couple of hours later, three Japanese soldiers boarded the barge. They were security guards for the trip up the canal. The guards' uniforms and insignia told Captain Midnight that they were among the lowest ranks of Japanese troops. Having them onboard complicated matters.

Ichabod Mudd suggested that under cover of darkness—particularly since there were now "unwanted guests" aboard—it might be wise to venture out on deck and see if there were some way they could abandon the vessel. If they weren't too far removed from shore, they might be able to slip unobserved over the side and quietly swim ashore.

After much consideration, Captain Midnight reluctantly agreed that

Mudd should try. The mechanic emerged carefully from the hold — and almost straight into the arms of one of the Japanese guards. Mudd reacted more swiftly and leaped at the soldier. After a fierce, but mostly silent, struggle, both toppled into the river with a resounding splash.

Captain Midnight and Ah Ting came above deck, but neither could spot either the soldier or Ichabod Mudd. The Secret Squadron leader realized that the remaining Japanese aboard the barge would have to be dealt with quickly. He didn't dare call out to Mudd, or all remaining aboard the barge would be captured.

Quickly he whispered for Chuck to join him. He passed Chuck a crude belaying pin, taking one for himself. Then he told Ah Ting to go forward and tell the other two soldiers to come aft, explaining that their comrade had fallen overboard.

Captain Midnight and Chuck hid in the shadows. As the Japanese soldiers passed them, the two Squadron members struck, clubbing them unconscious. They dragged the victims below deck and closed the hatchway.

Since Ah Ting seemed to be able to circulate among the coolies freely, Captain Midnight asked him whether it would be in keeping if he passed word unobtrusively that the soldiers decided to take some rest at the rear of the barge and didn't want to be disturbed.

Ah Ting smiled and said it could work. He left to spread the word, discreetly.

After some thought, Captain Midnight decided that he and Chuck should strip the uniforms off the soldiers before they regained consciousness, then tie and gag them. Fortunately, both soldiers were rather large, so that the two Squadron agents would probably be able to fit into their uniforms.

Once the guards were bound, Captain Midnight went to one of the packing cases and opened it cautiously. He was hoping that it might contain some cushioning material he could use like a drop cloth to cover the soldiers in case they tried to thrash around after they came to. A drop cloth would cushion them sufficiently to muffle any noises they'd otherwise make.

The first case contained metal parts. A second case yielded a cloth of sufficient size to wrap around the guards.

After attending to that, Captain Midnight turned his attention to what he found in the first case. It appeared to be airframe parts. Yet something about them bothered him. In some way, his aviator's sense said the parts seemed a bit *alien*, though he couldn't put his finger on just why. While he couldn't ascertain their exact purpose, he suspected that somehow they were tied to important activities in the Hidden Valley.

Captain Midnight's hunch was correct. Even as he was resealing the cases, a meeting was taking place. It was being held in an isolated office, guarded by the highest level of security found outside of the Japanese home islands themselves. Behind a large but functional desk, Admiral Himakito sat. A stranger, European by dress, had just been ushered into the admiral's sanctum. He was introduced as Mr. Rolf von Falz.

Neither man spoke the other's native tongue. Ironically, the only language they shared in common was English, the language of their enemies. Both commented upon this awkward point as the meeting commenced.

Admiral Himakito cut through the preliminaries and indicated that the parts required by von Falz were either en route to the Hidden Valley or were already in place. He added that he had several hundred skilled workers who could be relied upon to follow the instructions his visitor would give.

"That is good," said von Falz. "The cursed Allies are pressing us hard. But we can hold Europe as we prepare these new weapons to turn the tide. From our instructions, you will be able to do likewise in this theater."

Admiral Himakito bowed his head in assent. "We can head to the Hidden Valley at once."

"I have been without rest for some time," said von Falz. "We can wait until morning."

And so it was arranged.

By dawn, the barges were under way. The coolies knew their jobs, and if the guards chose to remain out of sight, so much the better: The coolies suffered less grief that way. Thus it was that Captain Midnight, Chuck, Joyce, and Ah Ting traveled with confidence in their privacy as the barges proceeded up the canal.

From their improvised observation port, the party could see details of the Hidden Valley as the barges moved into the secure area. It was extensive. Several large-scale wooden buildings were evident. There were large numbers of Japanese troops, and, under camouflage cloths, a few aircraft were visible.

Eventually the barges stopped. They could see that there was only one pier, so the barges would have to be offloaded one by one. The barge ahead of theirs was maneuvered to the pier. Shortly, offloading activities commenced.

Captain Midnight realized he'd have to do something soon, or the whole party would be discovered and captured. The Secret Squadron leader noticed that occasionally the Japanese soldiers would accompany coolies who were carrying certain objects. The soldiers appeared to direct them to distant objectives. After a while they'd return. It became evident that the laborers had a certain amount of range from the pier area, if under the soldiers' direction.

Captain Midnight asked Ah Ting whether he knew any Japanese. The youngster said he could speak a little. "Good," said the Secret Squadron

9. The War: Countermoves

leader. "Then you and I can pose as guards. Chuck and Joyce will carry special equipment away from the barge after we tie up. And we'll just keep going."

"Ah. Very good," said Ah Ting. "Do you speak any Japanese?"

"No," said Captain Midnight. "You'll have to speak for both of us if we're stopped. It's a long shot, but it's better than just being caught."

The Chinese boy thought for a short interval. Then he said, "Can you say '*nodo no itami*'?

"Yes. *Nodo no itami*. What does it mean?"

Ah Ting smiled. "It means 'a sore throat.' If you say it with a hoarse sound in your voice, it will explain your lack of speech. Perhaps."

By the time the barge with the Squadron party had been tied up, Captain Midnight and Ah Ting were dressed in the Japanese soldiers' uniforms; Captain Midnight's being a bit tight and Ah Ting's being a bit loose. They waited until there was much activity above decks and the coolies had started to offload the cargo tied to the decks.

The Squadron leader edged the hatch cover up a crack and looked out. When nobody was in the area of the hatch, the party stepped up and out. Chuck and Joyce, faces obscured by coolie hats, each carried a box; and Captain Midnight and Ah Ting, as their "guards," seemed to urge them forward.

Ah Ting cried, "*Kori wa chuui shite atusukatte*" (meaning, "Handle this very carefully") and "*Hyaku*" (meaning, "Faster"). And the four of them plowed through the other coolies and trotted off, away from the pier area.

Luck was with them, and they got away cleanly. When they had put enough distance between themselves and the barges, Chuck and Joyce ditched their loads, hiding them among some bushes. As they did so, Captain Midnight said to Ah Ting, "There's no sense staying here any more. We've seen enough, and soon they're bound to find the barge guards." He outlined a plan to get them away from the valley.

The burden had to fall to Ah Ting, since he was the only one of the quartet who could speak Japanese. In time, they approached a sentry area near the edge of the Hidden Valley. Captain Midnight, acting as though he were guarding "the coolies" like prisoners, stood back as Ah Ting approached the sentry.

Ah Ting told the guard that the two coolies had mentioned a secret entrance to the valley near the sentry post. Since the area was near where the rebel Chinese army was known to be active, it had to be checked out. He'd taken another soldier along to make sure the coolies weren't leading him into a trap.

The guard said it was a bit irregular, but let the party pass. Once out of sight of the sentry, the party headed toward the region commanded by

General Chu. The sentry was on the alert for people trying to infiltrate the Hidden Valley, not for soldiers trying to leave.

That both Ah Ting and Captain Midnight were wearing their liberated Japanese uniforms was a mixed blessing. It would keep any other Japanese soldiers from investigating them too closely. But the uniforms made it difficult when they approached the area of the guerillas.

Eventually they reached what could be called a haven, though the Japanese uniforms almost got them shot dead. The youngster, who was as eloquent as he'd ever been in his short life, managed, just barely, to convince the Chinese guerillas that they were indeed friends.

After the misunderstanding was cleared up and (to minimize complications) fresh clothing was found for Ah Ting and Captain Midnight, they were taken to General Chu. The general, acting as commander of a guerilla group, was using his troops for harassing tactics at the periphery of the Hidden Valley. His forces weren't numerous enough to mount a strategic attack on the valley.

General Chu seemed to be a throwback to an earlier China. His basic loyalty was to the land, and his soldiers' loyalty was to him. Perhaps because of this, he seemed more formidable than the average soldier.

Captain Midnight conferred with him at length. The general had accumulated a lot of data regarding the Hidden Valley, but he hadn't been able to make much sense of it. He realized that the Secret Squadron leader, as one used to much of the modern world, might be able to use the data, along with whatever he'd observed during his brief visit to the valley, to determine just what was going on.

General Chu's data was hard won. It was clear at the outset that some sort of feverish activity was ongoing; this was connected with some massive form of manufacturing enterprise. During the early stages of the Hidden Valley activities, many coolies had been drafted and enslaved. Some coolies who were getting progressively weaker as they worked feigned death. Since corpses were routinely pitched into the river, these coolies hoped to float downstream to freedom. However, many of the floating "corpses" were shot at by Japanese soldiers looking for amusement. Some died of these gunshot wounds. Some drowned. A few survived and brought to General Chu what information they had.

According to these reports, an extremely large complex was being built at one end of the Hidden Valley. The location was the most defensible site in the valley. Machinery, power generating plants, and even vast quantities of fuel were being stored there, but to what end wasn't clear. After a certain point in the construction process, the Chinese were moved out. A few coolies were used to help move large crates into a storage area, but whatever was in those crates was not for Chinese eyes.

9. The War: Countermoves

Captain Midnight told the general about the strange metal parts he'd discovered in one of the crates on the barge. He pointed out that the parts he'd found were akin to aircraft components, but were somehow different. The Squadron leader said that while he hadn't been able to learn their purpose, in light of the data General Chu provided, they doubtless were key to the Japanese activities.

As they were discussing the matters, an aide knocked softly and, at a word from General Chu, entered the conference area. Bowing low, he and the general conversed in the singsong dialect of the region. The aide was then dismissed.

The general turned toward Captain Midnight again. He said, "News has come of a white man who was fished from the river near the entrance to the Hidden Valley. We believe he is the one you have reported losing on your journey here. We are bringing him to you."

Captain Midnight said that it was wonderful news. He requested that he be excused so that he could give the rest of the party the news.

The next morning General Chu took Captain Midnight on a tour of the area. While traversing an open area, both men suddenly found themselves under attack by a lone Zero. It had been cruising high, and dove upon them with a retarded throttle to minimize the noise as it approached. Both men dove for cover; however, it was a one-pass strafing. Neither man was injured seriously, but General Chu was wounded in the leg.

He took it philosophically. "This is the reason we are mostly hidden underground, my friend. We have no antiaircraft guns."

When it was clearly safe to do so, Captain Midnight brought General Chu back to his headquarters area. Despite some first aid that the Squadron leader had administered, General Chu had lost a goodly amount of blood. All agreed he'd be out of action for at least a week as he recuperated. His deputy, Colonel Chon, would act in his stead for any field activities.

The next day Ichabod Mudd arrived. With him was another man, also an American.

Mudd explained that after falling into the river, he'd been pulled unconscious from the water and revived in a nearby temple.

He noticed a Secret Dragon Society symbol on the temple wall. Pointing at it, he mumbled "General Chu" before relapsing into a stupor.

When he next regained consciousness, he found himself in the hands of the Secret Dragon Society. A young man there named Lee could speak English well enough so that Ichabod Mudd could communicate. The mechanic conferred with him, and Lee said that he'd be smuggled past the Japanese in a manner that wouldn't arouse their suspicions.

Ichabod Mudd soon found himself in a large and ornate casket that was transported in a large and showy Chinese funeral. And though (as was often the case) the "funeral" was quite noisy, it was "inconspicuous" in Japanese eyes. He found out later the cover story was that he (as the corpse) died far from his home village and was being returned there.

They found the second American in an area so sparsely settled that it was deemed safe for the "corpse" to stretch his legs. By wearing a spare white robe, Mudd would be inconspicuous to a casual observer at a distance.

An odd, European-looking twin-engine aircraft with Japanese markings was lumbering slowly overhead. It was a Hiro G2H1, a relative aeronautical rarity. Most of them had been previously destroyed by fire on an island base.

It started to lose altitude while circling.

The pilot landed it wheels up in one of the many rice fields, causing a little damage. Upon emerging, the pilot was seen to be a westerner. Once he realized the "funeral party" was composed of Chinese, he asked for help.

The pilot was Spike Randall, who'd been caught in China as the war escalated. His original intent had been to join the Flying Tigers, but he was unable to make contact in time. He'd been "on the dodge" for so long, he'd been kept effectively isolated as the war expanded. Finally, he spotted an aircraft he'd once flown, the Hiro G2H1, at a small and secondary air base.

As Randall put it, "After I took off in the thing, I decided I'd made a mistake. I could barely fly the beast, but it was all I had." He added that he'd flown next to a valley ringed with antiaircraft, and was just praying that nobody there knew about the theft or attempted to radio him.

That sounded like the Hidden Valley. Possibly, some aerial observations could help Captain Midnight in trying to piece together information about the place. And Mudd was certain that the Secret Squadron leader had reached General Chu.

So the party acquired another "mourner." It made its way to the vicinity of the guerilla camp without further incident.

Captain Midnight questioned Spike Randall closely and became convinced that it was the Hidden Valley he'd flown close to. The man knew his airplanes, and his observations from nearly overflying the valley seemed to fill in the blanks that the guerillas and the Secret Squadron leader hadn't been able to.

(For dramatic reasons, the story was altered for the radio program. Spike Randall was portrayed as an ex-Flying Tiger rather than a potential recruit.)

The next few weeks were very slow, at least for the Secret Squadron members. As Captain Midnight put it, "We have all the pieces of a giant jigsaw puzzle, except for the key piece. We know that something very big is going on ... something we must stop. But we still don't know what we're up against."

9. The War: Countermoves

The burden of finding out was primarily thrust upon the guerillas. After the escape of Captain Midnight's party and the discovery of the trussed-up guards, security reached near paranoid proportions. There were still Chinese slave workers at the valley, but these were rigidly scrutinized; and there were no new workers taken into the area.

At one point, Ichabod Mudd suggested that perhaps the bomber that Spike Randall had deadsticked into the rice paddy could be repaired. With its Japanese markings, it might be able to fly close enough to the Hidden Valley so that a few oblique photographs could be taken. Given the slowness of the infiltration effort, Captain Midnight agreed to let the Chief Mechanic have a look at the aircraft—if it was still there.

The airplane was still there, possibly because the downed aircraft was in a sparsely settled area. The farmers were no friends of the Japanese. None of them was likely to tell the Japanese about what looked like a mishap among their forces.

Ichabod Mudd clambered through the aircraft and emerged, shaking his head. "Nothin' like my idea of an airplane," he said. "It'd take a lot to get it flying. But ... leapin' sawfish! Maybe we could do something with it if we make the effort."

General Chu's agents managed to slip into the Hidden Valley, at extreme risk. They managed to attach themselves to the underside of one of the increasingly rare supply barges. By using breathing tubes, they had been able to remain submerged for extended periods of time. When the barge was docked, they were able to slip beneath the pier.

They stayed there until well after dark. When they deemed it safe, they swam up the canal until they were away from the major area of activity. They intercepted a slave whom they were able to question. Having gathered the data they needed, they waited until dark, silently made their way back along the canal, and then entered the river.

They almost got caught in antipersonnel nets at the mouth of the canal. However, they were able to wriggle through. They went downriver, drifting with the current much of the time. When safe, they swam to shore. They headed to the guerilla camp, which took them days.

They learned that the manufacturing complex was somehow involved with a new and terrible weapon to be launched against the Allies. Other than the fact that the weapon was connected to a German named von Falz, they could learn nothing much of it.

Captain Midnight could make a few guesses about the nature of the weapon. Recalling the case of parts he'd opened, he knew that the weapon was somehow aviation related. Captain Midnight recalled that the parts looked like airframe components, but were *different*. They seemed *cruder* than an aviator would expect of an airplane.

Mudd then reported about his expedition. He pointed out that the airplane Spike Randall abandoned might be put into flyable condition without too much effort.

Captain Midnight said, "I don't understand. Why would you want to bother with an aircraft that's both old and tricky to fly?"

"I'd rather not say at this point, Cap'n," Mudd replied. "But I've got me an idea. And if my hunch is right, it could be something important."

Realizing that the master mechanic had time on his hands, Captain Midnight nodded. "All right, Ikky. Go see what you can do." He had to smile at the enthusiasm Mudd showed at receiving permission.

After weighing all the factors, the Secret Squadron leader decided that the only way he could get at the heart of the matter was to penetrate the Hidden Valley himself. He now had sufficient information about the overall layout of the place so that, unlike his last effort, he'd be able to work effectively.

General Chu tried to dissuade him. He pointed out that the odds against success must be greater than 100 to one.

"I've faced those odds before," Captain Midnight said with a smile.

Although it was dangerous, Midnight's proposed venture wasn't foolhardy. Rather than going in alone, he assembled a team: Chuck Ramsay and Lieutenant Lee. Chuck, because he was a skilled pilot; Lieutenant Lee because he was a good fighter who was an Oriental and spoke both English and Japanese. (In the radio dramatization, they had been joined by Captain Boudreau rather then Lieutenant Lee; Boudreau would have added nothing to the party, since he was neither the appropriate ethnicity nor able to speak Japanese.)

Infiltration was a slow process. It employed the barge-and-breathing-tube method. (For dramatic effect, the radio show presented the team parachuting in. Given the temper of the guarding forces at the time, any parachutists would have been machine-gunned before they reached the ground, no matter how dark the night.) It consumed a lot of time. It was very taxing. But it worked.

The first night after penetrating the defenses of the Hidden Valley great care was used to locate a safe place to hide out. Captain Midnight was aware they needed rest before they could attempt anything. All three had brought rations for several days.

They found their spot. After dawn, the three took turns snoozing and keeping watch. They spent the daylight hours resting up, because after dark, they'd have to act.

The hideout, though some distance from the large manufacturing facility, was close enough so that they could make useful observations. They could see the massive building, and determined that roof camouflage had been added since its completion. It was now hidden from view aloft, but from the hideout it was imposing. Before it lay a pair of runways, diverging at an angle of about 45 degrees. Captain Midnight remarked that the two runways formed an almost perfect arrowhead pointing at the building.

"They can't disguise their landing strips," the Squadron leader said. "Their pilots have to see them to land. So, though the building may be almost impossible to see from the air, we'll be able to locate it by following the direction of the 'arrowhead.'"

During the afternoon, an airplane landed. Captain Midnight recognized it as an early model of the Mitsubishi Ki-21, or "Sally." It had been converted into a military transport. The two pilots of the party studied it carefully as it landed, trying to gage as much as they could of its characteristics; under desperate circumstances, it might have to serve as an emergency means of escape.

Midnight was curious about who was getting off the Sally. While Captain Midnight couldn't see him clearly, the deplaning passenger was von Falz. The German was paying one of his periodic visits to Admiral Himakito. He wanted to see about the progress being made, and to offer whatever advice seemed appropriate.

Admiral Himakito's office was in the middle of the complex. Von Falz was able to see plenty as he was escorted there. Both men were pleased with the facility's progress. The admiral announced proudly that a preliminary assembly area had been set up and was proving successful. Within a couple of weeks, full-scale production could start.

Von Falz pointed out that he was familiar with production methods in Germany, and he might be able to offer hints and shortcuts if he saw the preliminary setup. Admiral Himakito smiled. "Later this evening, we can use the transport to go to a regional military base where I have a special security area so you can send protected messages to Germany. In the meantime, you can view the work that will sweep the accursed Allied forces to their well deserved doom."

After nightfall, Captain Midnight studied the security around the complex and found it fairly light. Soon he'd determined the deployment of guards around the building, and the frequency of the guards' movements.

Midnight decided that the easiest way to reach the complex was via the attached hangar. The airfield side of the building was relatively unguarded—the area was flat and extensively lighted. However, the Squadron leader was able to see an area of shadow. It was thin, but stretched so that it would cover most of their way toward the hangar. So, at the most appropriate point of the guards' rounds, they made their move.

As they were traversing the shadowed area, Chuck spotted a trip wire that was doubtless connected to an alarm. It became clear why the guard population was low: it was augmented by mechanical devices.

Now sensitized, the three realized they had to be on the lookout for more trip wires. They found and avoided several others while en route to the hangar.

The Sally wasn't the only aircraft in the hangar. There were also a couple of half-assembled fighters, undergoing overhaul. Engine cranes and other tools were also present.

The three infiltrators stole to the back of the hangar. They found several doors there. Captain Midnight eased each open a crack to see what lay beyond.

Most led to well-lighted areas that provided no cover. However, one opened on a dimly lit region which turned out to be the building's maintenance area. It was the best possible entrance.

In the maintenance room they found a high-velocity blower connected to a large-diameter air duct. Everybody understood that the system was used to pump fresh air to inner areas of the complex. It was big enough to navigate by crawling.

Captain Midnight decided to use the ductwork to explore the complex. Leaving Lieutenant Lee and Chuck behind, he entered it. After a dozen yards, he came to a grated opening; he stopped to peer out. There he discovered the secret of the Hidden Valley.

He saw part of a production line. He could see enough to make out several objects that looked something like airplanes. However, they were too small, had no propellers, and had no cockpits. On their tops were structures that looked like some sort of tube. Perhaps rocket tubes.

Captain Midnight had no way of knowing that he was seeing a pilot production line for the V-1 "buzz bombs," shortly to be made infamous by their use against England, particularly London. It dovetailed neatly with the vague reports he'd heard. It further explained what the "airplane parts" he'd found on the barge were for.

Captain Midnight retraced his steps and emerged from the duct. He conferred briefly with Chuck and Lieutenant Lee, telling them what he'd seen. Although he wasn't sure exactly how the devices would be used, they represented a real menace to the Allies.

The three started to steal back to their hideout, but they were thwarted at the hangar door. Chuck spied a squad of Japanese workers heading directly toward them.

Captain Midnight suggested that they take temporary shelter in the Sally. "One of them might go into the maintenance area, and we can't trust the other doors," he said.

The three clambered quickly and silently into the Sally. Chuck, who

9. The War: Countermoves

The German V-1 "Buzz Bomb" pilotless aerial torpedo. Components to manufacture these were shipped to Admiral Himakito's facility in China to help start the manufacture of Asian-based robot bombs. (Photograph: *National Air and Space Museum, Smithsonian Institution*, SI Neg. No. 78-14828.)

was first aboard, noticed a door to a rear compartment. He whispered that it might be a good idea to hide there, "just in case somebody should look into the passenger area."

And none too soon — the crew came over to the Sally and began to fuel it. They were preparing it for flight. All three realized that if they were caught, it would mean a quick and brutal death. In the preflight preparations, none of the crew checked the rear compartment.

As the line personnel left, others entered. From what Lieutenant Lee could overhear, the pilot and two passengers had boarded; a flight was to commence in minutes.

Thoughts racing, Captain Midnight said that if they were undiscovered prior to takeoff, the turn of events was a lucky break. They could leave the Hidden Valley. Once in the air, it would be three against three, with the pilot being at least somewhat occupied.

And so it came to pass. Under instructions from Captain Midnight, Lieutenant Lee listened to the radio technique of the pilot, so that he could communicate with the Hidden Valley after the takeover to tell them all was well with the flight, should that be necessary.

When Captain Midnight's air sense told him it was the proper time, he started the action. With drawn automatic, he sprang through the door from the rear compartment, followed by his companions. The Chinese guerilla cried out for everyone to hold still.

Nonetheless, the two passengers stood up. Captain Midnight was thunderstruck to recognize Admiral Himakito. While the admiral was as stupefied to recognize Captain Midnight, his anger made him dive and draw his gun.

The German, for his companion was von Falz, followed suit. A brief gun battle took place. Given the circumstances, Captain Midnight could take no chances; and thus both the admiral and the German were killed quickly. Captain Midnight regretted this deeply. He'd have preferred to capture and question the two.

The pilot, who had little chance to act during the exchange of gunfire, reached for his microphone. He was shot in the shoulder, fortunately without damaging the instrument panel. He slumped forward, and Captain Midnight pulled him away from the controls.

Chuck dragged the pilot further back as Captain Midnight took over flying the plane. He had Lieutenant Lee call the Hidden Valley and tell them that the flight was going normally, but that the radio seemed to be malfunctioning. During the transmission, the transmit key was released momentarily a few times to simulate a failing radio. Captain Midnight hoped this would forestall problems that might arise from any standard broadcast that might have been scheduled.

Captain Midnight "felt out" the airplane. Thus it was that the Secret Squadron leader was able to land at a flat area not too far from the guerilla base.

(In the radio version, things were more flamboyant. In that drama, Admiral Himakito hid in the rear compartment of the converted bomber while Captain Midnight stole the aircraft. This *was* dramatic, but silly. With the full force of the Hidden Valley's personnel at his disposal, he would have been able to checkmate Captain Midnight's party without having to fire a shot.)

After returning to General Chu's headquarters, Captain Midnight reported all that had happened. It appeared that the development of a "rocket bomb" was just about complete. The facility was a full-blown manufacturing enterprise. Somehow, the whole complex had to be eliminated.

It was Ichabod Mudd who pointed out that the base was quite vulnerable. He had no idea why the base was laid out the way it was, but both explosives and fuel were stored centrally. If one of those two detonated, the explosion would level the whole complex.

General Chu explained that there were sound reasons behind the

9. The War: Countermoves

layout, based upon the idea that the camouflage would be effective (which it was). He was excited at the idea of destroying the base with a single blow. He added that a mission to do so would be suicidal.

Mudd disagreed. The mechanic said that he'd been working on a little "secret weapon" of his own. If he could borrow Lieutenant Lee, he believed he could manage something. He added that he'd have to "borrow" some high explosives too.

The following day, around midmorning, observers at Hidden Valley outposts heard the sound of an airplane. As the drone grew louder, the controller at the Hidden Valley's field was asked for landing data. The voice over the radio explained that the incoming aircraft was bringing the German subordinate of von Falz, who came to get documents.

The antiaircraft gunners at the defense perimeter relaxed as the controller gave instructions, and the plane banked into the traffic pattern for the appropriate runway. The plane was well along its final approach when the controller suggested that the plane should throttle back or go around for another pass. Yet despite assurances that the pilot would comply, the airplane droned on.

As the controller yelled frantically, the Hiro G2H1 dove into the building, smashing spectacularly into the complex before exploding. The shock was enough to set off the stored fuel and explosives. The resulting detonation could be felt back at the guerilla camp. The Hidden Valley menace was no more.

Ichabod Mudd explained that he rigged up Spike Randall's stolen airplane as a form of large flying bomb. He operated it by remote control. "I loaded it with explosives having an impact-delay fuze. After Spike briefed me, we got it airborne. Lieutenant Lee, who knew how to talk to the controller, tuned another transmitter to their frequency. While he made 'em think it was just another landing, Spike Randall and I flew it right into 'em." Since the enemy was making a flying bomb, it was merely a case of fighting fire with fire.

The Secret Squadron members retrieved their amphibian. They also brought back reports of the new robot bomb. By the time they regained contact with the Squadron's communication network, V-1 bombs were already falling on London. They had scored a brilliant victory by denying the Axis what would have been many thousands of robot bombs.

The Squadron members made their way to Secret Squadron Headquarters at Grant City. Captain Midnight resumed directorship of the Squadron, and was briefed on many of the latest intelligence aspects of the war.

The next Secret Squadron operation involving Captain Midnight's direct participation, as well as that of Chuck Ramsay, Joyce Ryan, and

Ichabod Mudd, began with a refugee boy in his mid-teens. The boy, Henri Brouvard, had come from France. He wished to stay in his native country and help his people in their struggle against the Nazis. However, he'd been sent to the United States to live with a distant relative.

Maurice Brouvard, Henri's American relative, was a production foreman at one of the aircraft manufacturing plants at Grant City. He was an excellent supervisor, and his workers consistently produced aircraft parts ahead of schedule and well above minimum specifications. In his way, Maurice Brouvard was an outstandingly valuable employee at his plant.

Young Henri was scheduled to arrive on the train from New York the evening it happened. So far as anyone could tell, Maurice Brouvard didn't have a care in the world that morning. Nor would he ever have a care again; on the way to work, a stone from the roof of an abandoned building fell and struck him, killing him instantly.

Because he was engaged in war-critical work, the police took exceptional care examining the area. On the roof, near where the stone that killed Brouvard "worked loose," they found a cigarette butt. It was fresh and showed no signs of weathering.

With the Secret Squadron Headquarters so close, the police requested their assistance. Because of the defense-related nature of Brouvard's work, it was given freely. Several Squadron teams scoured the area for additional clues.

When Henri Brouvard arrived, he didn't know a soul in Grant City. Maurice Brouvard was a widower with no children. There were no other relatives in the United States to whom Henri could turn.

Chuck and Joyce learned of his plight. The two youngsters decided to help him until some arrangements could be made about his future.

Toward the end of their first week together, the refugee proved to be a more valuable friend than any had imagined. Henri spotted a man who was a dead ringer for a German agent he'd seen in France.

Henri Brouvard said that the man was Hannes Schulz, an underling of the infamous Gestapo agent Baron Kurt von Karp. Schulz wasn't very important, but usually wherever he was, Baron von Karp was close. And Baron von Karp was dangerous. He'd proved it time and again in Europe.

While an investigation was initiated on the basis of Henri Brouvard's information, Captain Midnight was called to Washington to confer with Major Steele.

Major Steele had exciting and surprising news. The tides of war had been shifting. A board of strategists decided to expand the scope of the Secret Squadron's activities. "Now that you've caught up with the Secret Squadron's administration, it's an ideal time for you to help establish the

Secret Squadron's first *truly* overseas base. That is, a Squadron base on foreign soil, as opposed to the Pacific Headquarters on soil we control. The war in Europe is still capable of dealing us a few surprises, as the buzz bombs, for one, have demonstrated.

"We believe that there's an important job for the Secret Squadron in the European theater — in England, where there are many contacts to resistance groups from the continent," Steele said. Soon a fleet of transport planes would converge at Squadron Headquarters. Sufficient material and selected personnel would leave for England. Captain Midnight would receive his final orders from an important personage "in a most unusual manner."

Steele handed Captain Midnight a bulky package of sealed orders. "There is enough materiel at the Secret Squadron Headquarters to outfit several bases — but the enclosed listings will give the best proportion of equipment necessary to carry out your mission."

Captain Midnight was instructed to tell nobody about the forthcoming mission, save in the most general terms. He wasn't even to let anybody know that it involved establishing an overseas base until just before the mission was to be launched.

Captain Midnight returned to Bowling Field and, after grabbing a quick snack, clambered into his P-51 and took off for Grant City. The return trip was uneventful.

The following morning, Captain Midnight unsealed his packet of orders in the privacy of his office. Inside were sealed envelopes with orders for the arriving transports' navigation officers. An accompanying memorandum indicated that 35 transports would arrive, coming in five separate flights of seven aircraft apiece.

The Secret Squadron leader decided to hangar them in the underground area, which could hold twice their number. They would be gone over thoroughly by the Squadron's most skilled mechanics. Then they would be outfitted for the trip.

Captain Midnight called Ichabod Mudd to his office. He explained what he could: That a large number of aircraft were slated to go on a special mission. He told the Chief Mechanic to assemble his best crew. Mudd promised to get his top men for the job, even if he had to juggle schedules to do so.

After Ichabod Mudd left, Captain Midnight called in Agent SS-47, Todd Harrington. Agent SS-47 had been placed in charge of espionage investigations, and the Secret Squadron leader had an idea. "Harrington, in the next few days, several flights of cargo aircraft will be arriving at the Headquarters field," he said. "If anything will attract the interest of enemy agents, that will. Our security is tight, so they won't be able to get too close to the field." He walked over to a wall-mounted chart of the area surrounding

Squadron Headquarters. "Where do you feel they'd be most likely to go to observe the activities with binoculars or telescopes?"

Harrington joined him at the chart. "There are only two logical places, sir. One is here, at the Grant City municipal water tower, which is easily accessible to the public. The other is Devil Hill, there. Both provide about equally good vantage points."

Captain Midnight instructed Harrington to assemble two teams of agents, one for each area. Each team would conceal itself, in rotating watches, to see whether the arrival of the aircraft would result in anyone's undue interest. "We certainly can't disguise the arrival of so many airplanes, but we *can* use them as bait to trap any spies."

Several days later, the first flight of C-47s wheeled gracefully over Grant City and set down in the area reserved for the Squadron. Neither of Harrington's teams noticed anything unusual.

By the time the third flight came in, the team at Devil Hill noticed a few men loitering around a tourist area for extended periods of time. As the incoming flight of C-47s approached, one was seen watching the aircraft intently through some palm-sized, but powerful, binoculars. Another seemed to be taking notes.

The Squadron team, which was superlatively well concealed, was able to take telephoto pictures of the observers without being detected. The team didn't attempt to follow them. Since they'd been photographed, they could be picked up later.

Photographs shown to Chuck, Joyce, and Henri Brouvard resulted in the positive identification of one of the observers. It was Schulz. This clinched the idea that something sinister was going on.

Ordinarily, the Secret Squadron would have called in one of the more conventional law-enforcement agencies for coordination. However, though they gathered a great deal of circumstantial evidence, the Squadron wanted something concrete. Therefore, the Squadron decided to work alone for a while longer. And thus it was that SS-47's team uncovered an espionage headquarters.

A suspect was traced to a well known Grant City landmark, the Tower Building. He visited it frequently, and only after working hours. As a result, the side entrance used was staked out.

The Tower Building stakeout identified several "after hours" visitors, including Schulz. Infrared photographs of these visitors were taken and catalogued.

Copies of the photographs were forwarded by the Squadron to other intelligence agencies. One of the men photographed, a large, blond man with a patrician look, was identified as Baron von Karp by agents who'd seen him but hadn't been able to take a picture of him.

9. The War: Countermoves

The entire report landed on Captain Midnight's desk on the Monday morning preceding the week the European mission was scheduled to begin. He decided that something should be done, quickly.

Captain Midnight called in SS-47. He got a briefing on the physical layout of the Tower Building from Harrington. Midnight decided he'd have the place raided during the next get-together of the foreign agents.

The Secret Squadron obtained a warrant, and a team was formed for the raid. Since there were several entrances to the building, each was covered.

One problem troubled Captain Midnight. Without someone inside the building, it would be extremely difficult to determine where the suspects had gone after entering.

A Secret Squadron scientist came up with an answer. He presented Captain Midnight with a chemical that an operative could apply to the building's entranceway "after hours" before the time the suspects ordinarily arrived. When exposed to ultraviolet light, footprints of anyone walking over the chemical would be detectable. Under ordinary light, these footprints would be invisible.

At the appropriate hour, the Secret Squadron agents deployed themselves. In time, the suspects arrived, one by one. Each entered with his own key and moved out of sight. When it was deemed that all the foreign agents had arrived, the main Squadron force, led by Captain Midnight, moved in, guns drawn.

A technician came forward a bit awkwardly, handling a bulky device. Activating the device, the technician played the lamp along the floor; faint, glowing footprints sprang up. The train of footprints led down the hallway to a stairwell. There they led down to the cellar — and up to a blank wall.

It was immediately obvious that there was a secret panel in the wall. Ichabod Mudd solved the dilemma. He pointed out that the light switch for the basement area was hanging from a cord in the ceiling of the center of the room. "Now if I were gonna turn on this light, I'd have to stumble across half the basement in the dark to reach the cord. Now it seems to me that I wouldn't want to do that — unless the cord had another use." With that, he yanked it hard.

An entire section of the wall swung up, revealing a fair-sized room, quite empty. It had been quitted in extreme haste through a back panel that led to an underground draining area. Squadron agents, after taking care to make sure that there were neither traps nor ambushes, poured through the opening; but they took no captives.

Captain Midnight brought in the local police and showed them the hidden room. He was assured that it would never be used again.

When the forces returned to Squadron Headquarters, Joyce and Chuck, who hadn't participated in the raid, had good news. A childless couple had decided to act as foster parents for Henri Brouvard. The French youngster would be well taken care of in a Grant City suburb.

Captain Midnight turned over the responsibility of von Karp's espionage to more conventional authorities. "I'd have liked to have finished this myself," he told Agent Kelly, "but with this new assignment so close, all my resources will have to be devoted to that."

The following night, a courier from Washington hand-delivered sealed orders from Major Steele. "I don't know what's in 'em, sir," he said to Captain Midnight, "but the major said to tell you that these orders were only put in final form last night."

The Secret Squadron leader read them as soon as he was alone. Then he called in Kelly. He told SS-11 that departure would take place in 36 hours. Then he ordered that the word be passed to the flight crews.

"But where will you be going, sir?"

"Kelly," said Captain Midnight, "of all the members in this headquarters, you'll be the only one to know for now. We are going to England — to establish a Squadron base."

"England! But that's..." SS-11 began.

"That much closer to our ultimate foe," Captain Midnight finished. He added that while the Secret Squadron was doing much to help on the home front, it could add considerably to the full war effort. "We've faced the enemy in battle. We even have a base in the Pacific. But as far as dealing with the enemy in 'close combat,' we're going to the European theater."

Late in the afternoon of the following day, the great doors of the underground hangar swung open. One by one, the C-47 transports kicked over their engines, making a noise that could be heard for miles. One by one, the transports began to taxi; in one-minute intervals, they took off.

Along with the transports, there was one other aircraft, the last in line. It was Captain Midnight's twin-engine amphibian. Aboard it was the usual crew — Ichabod Mudd, Joyce Ryan, and Chuck Ramsay. The Secret Squadron leader decided that since they'd consistently worked so well as a team, there would be little point in breaking it up. Chuck was in the left-hand seat, and it was he who started the airplane's engines while Captain Midnight spent a last few minutes conferring with SS-11.

Just as the amphibian got the green light to taxi, Captain Midnight dashed to the plane and clambered aboard. "Taxi her out and take off, Chuck," he said. "You're in the pilot's seat." (In the radio show, he supposedly coached Chuck on takeoff technique; hardly necessary for a pilot of Chuck's proven ability. Actually, Chuck asked him where they were going, and Captain Midnight told him he should just follow the other aircraft.)

Some distance from Grant City, Baron Kurt von Karp watched the seemingly endless stream of airplanes rising and flying to the northeast. Ascertaining their direction of flight, he projected their course. He decided they were headed for an overseas destination — perhaps Iceland, but more probably England.

Although he'd barely managed to escape the raid, von Karp was able to get a quick look through the false wall's peephole. The proximity to the Secret Squadron Headquarters prompted the baron to peruse a file on the organization. Included was a photograph of Captain Midnight, purchased in early 1941 from Ivan Shark's organization. (This same photograph was what enabled Captain Kaga to recognize the Secret Squadron leader when he was fished from the water near X Island.) The Baron recognized the leader of the raid as Midnight.

The baron's forces could do little more in Grant City. In effect, their mission was destroyed, primarily through the leadership of Captain Midnight. Baron von Karp believed that somehow the Secret Squadron leader had targeted him; Captain Midnight was deemed a personal enemy.

The last aircraft were leaving the area when von Karp noticed that the final aircraft wasn't a transport. It was an amphibian. He recalled that for many operations, Captain Midnight tended to favor such aircraft.

An amphibian departing the Secret Squadron Headquarters wasn't in itself significant. One departing as part of a huge armada of transports was suggestive. It implied that a high official, most probably Captain Midnight (who was known to do a lot of field work), was involved. The amphibian would provide more flexibility on potential landing sites.

Von Karp wasn't unintelligent. If Captain Midnight, or some other high official, was involved with such a large force, it meant a major move by the Secret Squadron. Logically, it would mean the establishment of a new base — an *overseas* base. And that place would probably be in England, for the European continent was yet secure.

Baron von Karp took cold satisfaction from that deduction. His work in the United States was done — for the present. It would take him far too long to develop an equivalent organization at another sensitive area. Yet the information about the new move of the Secret Squadron was important. He could work effectively against them from France. He swore that he and Captain Midnight would meet again, but on *his* ground and on *his* terms.

Over the ocean, Captain Midnight at the controls, the amphibian broke formation from the transports. The C-47s, which had formed up into seven 5-aircraft formations (with an "extra" on the seventh), continued to wing their way toward refueling bases. The amphibian altered its course shortly before dawn. Ichabod Mudd was asleep, but both youngsters were awake.

Chuck pointed out that the amphibian was losing altitude. Captain

Midnight said, "You haven't been paying attention, Chuck. We're almost at our destination. Look ahead."

Chuck and Joyce both stared, nearly awed at what they saw. On the sea ahead of them was a massive fleet of ships in a large, circular formation. Captain Midnight said that they were to land in the center of the circle.

"Looping loops! Why?" said Chuck.

"I'll get my final briefing there," Midnight said.

Shortly thereafter, the Secret Squadron leader brought the amphibian to a perfect landing almost dead center of the circular formation. As the amphibian coasted — drifted — to a stop, a submarine broke the surface of the sea. And soon a rubber raft was launched to pick up Captain Midnight. He was brought aboard the U-boat, which shortly thereafter submerged to periscope depth.

Precisely what happened below the surface of the sea has never been detailed. In time, Captain Midnight was returned to the surface and then to his amphibian. He taxied the Squadron plane to the side of a carrier, where a line was lowered so that the airplane could be refueled. After its tanks were filled, Captain Midnight took off and headed for England, making another refueling stop along the way.

After the last refueling, the Secret Squadron leader pulled an envelope out of his pocket, commenting he'd received it when he was aboard the submarine. He opened it and showed its contents to Chuck.

It was a navigation chart of England. A specific field was highlighted, indicating where the amphibian was supposed to land. It wasn't the same field where the transports were going. With the chart was a special series of identification signs listed so those on the ground could recognize the Secret Squadron airplane.

The rest of the flight, and the landing, were uneventful.

The rollout barely completed, line personnel indicated the plane was to go to a remote spot on the tarmac. As Captain Midnight taxied his aircraft to the position, he could see that a small group of men seemed to be waiting for them to deplane.

The leader of this group was Sir Allen Brundage of British Intelligence. Sir Allen was one of the few men privy to the full story of what the Squadron intended to do. He was a key figure who had connections to elements of the resistance on the Continent. Further, he had access to many weapons developed both for resistance and espionage work. He also had contact with some key personnel involved in aeronautical research and development.

Introductions were made all around. Sir Allen observed that the Secret Squadron party seemed tired, saying that he understood the rigors of transatlantic flight, particularly in the current wartime conditions. He suggested that the Squadron party catch up on some rest prior to any substantive work. On behalf of the whole party, Captain Midnight thanked Sir Allen for his understanding.

On the following morning, after an obviously American breakfast of Spam and powdered eggs, the Squadron members were greeted again by Sir Allen. He'd arranged for a small bus to bring them to what would be their new base.

Located in the English countryside, not too far removed from the airfield, was a magnificent manor. Almost palatial, the house and lands had been placed at the disposal of the Secret Squadron for the duration. Sir Allen was a social acquaintance of the owner, a belted earl. The owner had extensive holdings in Africa, had other estates in England, and had an extreme dislike for the Germans. "Something that happened in Africa during the last war, you know," Sir Allen said. "When approached, he was delighted to make these lands available." Captain Midnight asked Sir Allen to convey the thanks of the Secret Squadron to the earl.

After a few days of settling in, Captain Midnight and Ichabod Mudd were taken to a special training facility by Sir Allen. Chuck and Joyce remained at the base to orient the newly arriving Squadron agents.

Captain Midnight and his Chief Mechanic were shown a variety of new equipment that could be used in unorthodox situations. Included were such items as plastic explosives, acid-delay fuses, miniature radio equipment, and miniature cameras. Mudd was encouraged to see if he could think up improvements to the gadgets, and to think up other, equivalently unorthodox gadgetry if he could.

A minor problem arose as agents arrived and settled in. In the United States, Secret Squadron members usually dressed in civilian clothes. Overseas, this seemed inappropriate, particularly because the Squadron was designated as a "limited armed force."

The final decision was that, as in the Pacific, the uniform would be insignia-less. The Secret Squadron would adopt a uniform almost identical to that worn by the U.S. Army Air Corps. In addition to no insignia, there would be no brass trimmings; belt buckles would be blackened rather than shiny brass. The uniform would be worn only during working hours; otherwise, civilian clothes would be worn.

The decision solved the immediate problem. Seen at a distance, the Squadron agents would blend into activities. They would appear to a casual observer to be just so many more Allied troops. However, events soon proved that it was just an interim solution.

Both the Allies and the Germans had been working on a new form of aircraft propulsion — a jet engine. Pioneered in England by A. A. Griffith, and more importantly by Fred Whittle (who was later knighted), jet turbine development had reached the point far enough so that aircraft had been designed for it. Two—the British Meteor and Vampire—were finished designs. The American XP-59 and XP-80 were still undergoing development. Whether these aircraft would see combat status before the end of the war was unclear; however, all thought that the Secret Squadron needed to have a few members familiarized with jets.

Officially, an XP-59 was exchanged for a Gloster Meteor; actually, a couple of American aircraft were shipped. One was brought to the secret airfield used by the Squadron; the "official" version was shipped to the British government. Various of the Squadron pilots, starting with Captain Midnight himself, were checked out in the plane.

During one of Chuck Ramsay's familiarization flights, something happened that gave the Squadron more exposure than anyone wanted. The day had dawned unusually clear, and after a weather briefing, Chuck took the jet aloft to increase his proficiency. But when he returned, an unexpected mist developed that effectively closed the field. The mist showed no signs of dissipating. Chuck radioed for advice.

Captain Midnight received the message personally. While Chuck orbited the field, the Secret Squadron leader hurriedly conferred with the airfield officers. Using an informal emergency code he worked out with his inner circle, he directed Chuck to land at any of several military airfields and wait to be picked up.

Chuck complied, found a military airstrip, and landed. He was promptly surrounded by British military police and arrested. When Chuck climbed from the still-classified aircraft, he'd no acceptable means of identifying himself to his captors (standing orders prohibited him from showing his Code-O-Graph, which was unknown to rank-and-file servicemen anyway).

It took the personal intervention of Sir Allen Brundage to get Chuck released. As they drove back towards the Squadron base, Sir Allen said, "I realize how important secrecy is to you chaps, but don't you think that this is going a bit far?"

Captain Midnight, who'd accompanied Sir Allen, said, "I've been thinking the same thing myself."

As a result, the Secret Squadron's presence was made known to security forces throughout Britain. Concurrently, the Squadron developed a form of identification that could be shown to outsiders, unlike the Code-O-Graph. Because of the nature of the Squadron, there were no marks of rank. Each member wore a cloth patch with the winged-clock symbol of the Secret Squadron. Those on flying status wore that patch over the left breast pocket, as with Air Corps and Navy wings. Those on ground duty wore it as a shoulder patch. Other than the patch, the uniforms remained plain and unadorned (these patches were used Squadron-wide, wherever uniforms were worn). Publication of the Secret Squadron's identifying characteristics made it almost certain that word of the Squadron's presence in England would reach unfriendly ears.

Baron von Karp, recently returned to Europe, received the news. It was satisfying to have his deductions verified. From his speculation and its verification, he was certain that Captain Midnight was among the Secret Squadron forces in England.

Captain Midnight was wondering about the Continent, particularly in regards to the area where the Squadron was most proficient — coping with anything unorthodox. Maybe that should be their role in Europe.

Sir Allen agreed. Moreover, he'd heard reports that suggested an opportunity well suited to the Squadron.

There seemed to be a great deal of German activity in an occupied mountain area. What was disquieting was that nobody could determine precisely what it was. One Resistance group, a semi-independent organization calling itself the Phantom Band, even made an aerial observation of the area. They could only determine that some sort of manufacturing was involved in whatever secret activity was going on.

Sir Allen pointed out that it seemed an ideal candidate for a Secret Squadron mission.

Captain Midnight agreed. He asked for details and contacts.

Sir Allen told him what he knew of the Phantom Band. The leader of the group was François Civeret. His second in command was an innkeeper, Hercule Berthold. They'd developed a highly effective means of spying on the Nazis, including an "air arm." Several old aircraft, with short landing and takeoff characteristics, had been secured and hidden. From time to time, a Phantom Band member who was a pilot would take one of the frail little things and fly it over German positions. Fortunately, by the time the Germans could get anything into the air, the Phantom Band's airplanes had landed and were hidden.

Captain Midnight chose his usual "headquarters" team of Ichabod Mudd, Joyce Ryan, and Chuck Ramsay to go with him. They'd worked so well as a unit, so many times, that it would be foolish to start from scratch with other agents. Midnight thought that after the field assignment, they could return to Squadron Headquarters. The British branch of the Squadron was operating to Captain Midnight's satisfaction.

Sir Allen supplied Captain Midnight with a few surprises when they were outfitted for the foray into continental Europe. In addition to the usual paraphernalia such as plastic explosives and time-delay fuse-detonators disguised as common items (in this case, fountain pens), Sir Allen issued several small electronic items he called "pocket locators."

The pocket locator was an ultra-miniature radio transceiver that incorporated extremely tiny components and operated at very low power. Its development was a highly classified joint venture between electronic laboratories in the United States and Great Britain. The resulting unit could literally fit into an agent's pocket — a remarkable achievement before the development of the transistor. (Unlike most World War II items, the pocket locator's design has never become fully declassified. It operated silently. Despite some deliberately misleading statements in the radio program's account of the device, it couldn't "work" long distances without an auxiliary electronic two-way booster.)

Sir Allen explained that the pocket locator was the result of a project that worked well experimentally. It was originally being developed for a field commander's communication system, but was deemed a little complex for ordinary military equipment. However, its unique numeric characteristics turned out to be an almost perfect complement to the Secret Squadron's Code-O-Graph. Once Sir Allen had been shown one of the initial (1941) units, he realized that the pocket locator might as well have been intentionally designed for the Squadron.

Both mechanical plans and electronic schematics for the pocket locator were presented to the Secret Squadron. These Captain Midnight had sent under high security to Squadron Headquarters, where Squadron technicians quickly worked out an efficient way to manufacture the units. (The Squadron's electronic experts, working with the Crypto Section, made modifications to the basic design that improved it for field work. The pocket locator became a staple for high-risk field assignments throughout the war and the peace beyond. In the 1950s, when the Code-O-Graph was replaced by a different enciphering approach, the pocket locator changed form. A dissimilar version, using highly sophisticated modulation techniques, also highly classified, was produced. Solid-state electronics, digital techniques, and communication satellites have vastly increased the effectiveness of the present-day pocket locator.)

Not all equipment came through British Intelligence or related organizations. The Secret Squadron also sent over equipment it had developed, including light-weight units to help ensure aircraft recognition (the MJC-10 airplane spotter; versions of this were also distributed to the General Reserve). Enough were supplied so that some could be distributed to selected Resistance members on the continent.

After the Squadron team was prepared, Civaret was contacted by radio, using extreme care. A tentative rendezvous schedule was set up: Depending upon the weather, a flight would be made to a semi-hidden field at coordinates specified by the Phantom Band. A "window" of three days was agreed upon for the operation.

9. The War: Countermoves

Since they were going into a battle area, the Squadron members' "limited armed force" status was activated by issuing identification cards. A form of "battle uniform" was devised. It consisted of Navy-blue slacks and shirt, black shoes and socks, a black cloth neckpiece (a cross between a neckerchief and an Ascot), and a black belt with black buckle. Flat, jet-black insignia were issued to the agents, with black hashmarks to Ichabod Mudd. Reinforced hollow heels in their shoes were used as before to conceal Code-O-Graphs. Technically, these changes made the Squadron members uniformed armed forces in case of capture.

Radio exchanges made Sir Allen aware that the Phantom Band was short on supplies; also, the radio the Resistance group was using seemed to be a bit unreliable. These items influenced the choice of aircraft Captain Midnight needed to get the team to Europe.

Besides the Squadron members, he decided to bring supplies to the Phantom Band, including two new, ruggedized radios to strengthen their effectiveness. This required a high-load-capacity aircraft.

After much thought, Captain Midnight chose a C-47, with a P-51 as the escort aircraft. The flight to France was uneventful, though the two aircraft practically had to hedge-hop after crossing the coast. The Squadron aircraft flew inland until they reached the rendezvous point, a valley near the small French town of St. Michel.

Dusk had come, and an agreed-upon signal was flashed from the ground. Chuck positioned the C-47 so that he had virtually the whole field for rollout and taxi. As soon as Chuck's aircraft was safely out of the way, Captain Midnight brought in the Mustang. The two aircraft were quickly covered with camouflage.

The Squadron members met the leaders of the Phantom Band, including Civaret, Berthold, and one "Captain" Demoviche (his guerilla rank), the only member of the group who could pilot an airplane.

The party cautiously made its way to the Resistance headquarters at St. Michel — a special underground meeting place constructed in secret next to the wine cellar of Berthold's restaurant. The cafe-inn was in many ways a perfect cover for Resistance activities; the few agents who came and went could mingle with the flow of normal customers.

The hideaway was surprisingly roomy. It was located behind a false wall containing a floor-to-ceiling wine rack. At a far corner was a short-wave radio transmitter and receiver.

Of the transmitter, Mudd said much later that, "it seemed like it would fall apart if you looked at it dirty." There were a few supplies and some very primitive sanitary arrangements for those who had to hide out. There was a fairly large table and chairs, around which the Squadron members and the Phantom Band arranged themselves.

Once Captain Midnight was assured that the meeting place was truly secure, he explained his role. The Secret Squadron was helping the Resistance movement. There were items from the transport that would make the job easier.

Civaret informed the Squadron members that the Phantom Band had managed to get one of their more daring members into a vital position. He was accepted as a collaborationist by the Germans. He'd become a form of guide for a high Gestapo officer who seemed to have a special interest in the activities. "The German soldiers, they are bad enough; but they are like many other soldiers. But this one, Baron von Karp…"

"Von Karp!" exclaimed Captain Midnight. Then, "Please excuse me. We tangled with him once before, and he is an extremely dangerous man. Please go on."

Civaret said that the Gestapo official had been in the area for some time. The Resistance member, Jaques Zoler, gained von Karp's confidence to the point where the baron gave him the rank of lieutenant in the secondary collaborationist force he was creating. To the Germans, Zoler seemed to be a sincere sympathizer with the Nazi movement, but in reality, he was sending back what information he could glean.

According to Zoler, three areas of activity were operating simultaneously. One was a stepped-up drive against the Resistance. Civaret had been identified, primarily through a true collaborator, a man referred to by most of the village as "the Toad." (This man was held in utter contempt by almost every one of the French locals; his German connections afforded him significant protection.) As a result, Civaret was on the run, spending most of his time in the cellar hideout. Only the arrival of Captain Midnight prompted him to emerge; the whole operation was so dangerous that had any of the Resistance been caught, he probably would have been discovered anyway. "So why not breathe the night air freely for a change and meet the great Captain Midnight at the same time?"

Captain Midnight tried to brush off the compliment. However, Civaret laughed. "Do not be modest, my friend. I was a soldier in the last war, and I heard of your exploits."

Zoler's reports indicated that the second area of activity was "along the coast." The reports were vague, because he only had scraps. Apparently, it had something to do with a hidden airfield and submarines. Zoler hadn't been able to obtain any greater details.

Compared to the third area of activity, though, the costal action data was comprehensive. All he could get was that it had something to do with rocket bombs, or aircraft, or something of that order. The only information he had was gleaned from chance remarks between the baron and a few of his visitors.

9. The War: Countermoves

After considering what he'd heard, Captain Midnight said that the information fit with other aspects of the war. He pointed out that while it wasn't common knowledge in the occupied countries, the war in the air was increasingly dominated by Allied forces.

Sabotage perpetrated by the Resistance might have impelled Baron von Karp to intensify activities against Civaret and his associates.

If the reports were correct, the new rocket or air device might be something the Germans were developing to tilt back the balance of air power. The short rocket fighter the Germans were beginning to deploy, the Me-163, gave indications of one dangerous trend.

Captain Midnight paused while he considered the interlocking problems. Then he asked whether Zoler knew the precise location of the rocket-related activities.

Civaret laughed bitterly. Unlike the German actions against the Resistance, which were local, the rocket-related activities were some distance away, in Germany. "As best we can find out, they seem to be in mountains where a castle owned by Baron von Karp is located," he said.

Captain Midnight said, "It's obvious that we need some more resources than those we've already brought. I'll have to explain the situation and see what can be done." He asked for writing materials and set about enciphering a message to the Secret Squadron's base in England.

After he'd finished, all turned in for the night. The Phantom Band sent the message.

At the proper time the next evening, the reply to Captain Midnight's message arrived (much more rapidly than was sent, since nobody cared whether the Germans triangulated a point outside of London — the Battle of Britain settled that point). Midnight set to decrypting it. Then he conferred with the Phantom Band.

The vague reports of a flying field and submarine installation concerned Allied Intelligence sufficiently that it was decided to send out a small raiding party of British commandos to work with the Resistance and Captain Midnight. As to the even vaguer reports of rocket activity, the intelligence community was searching for an expert to help them. As for helping the Resistance, certain additional resources would be made available.

Captain Midnight observed that the Resistance was already using one of the two new shortwave radio transmitters and receivers brought over by the Squadron team. The other set, plus the ample spare parts, would keep communications operational far more reliably than ever before. Berthold pointed out that one of the Resistance members, Pierre Simone, was a radio technician. He was convinced that when Simone saw the new equipment, he would be both amazed and delighted.

Demoviche mentioned that he was down to a single operational aircraft, which was more or less homebuilt. "It is more like a Breguet 14 than anything else," he said. With the materials shortage, the plane was barely operational, but as the French pilot pointed out, "One has to make do with what one has."

"That will be rectified quickly," Captain Midnight said. "I've arranged it so you will get an L-6, with plenty of spare parts." He then described the airplane, built by Interstate Aircraft, which was designed for short-field takeoffs and landings.

(In the radio show, the Phantom Band was supposed to have several pilots; Captain Midnight was supposed to have promised them more than *100* fighters. This was inserted to mislead enemy monitors, who knew that even presuming enough pilots were available, there was neither fuel to support that number of aircraft nor a place where so many airplanes could be concealed successfully. Like a later fictional incident, in which all the Secret Squadron members were captured by von Karp's forces, were put on mock trial, and were found "guilty of treason," such false clues were meant to confound: Monitoring agents would know that someone who is not a citizen of a country can't commit treason against it.)

Because Civaret was so wanted by von Karp's forces, it was decided to evacuate him to England, where he could help coordinate the efforts of various Resistance groups. Berthold was enthusiastic, pointing out that it was a great responsibility and a great mission.

As this was being discussed, the conversation was interrupted by a secret knock. A Frenchman entered the hidden area. It was Pierre Simone, the radio technician. Simone seemed distressed. He explained: He'd been apprehended by the Toad after curfew. The Toad's previous report of a similar apprehension had had Simone up before the Gestapo, and another would send him to a Nazi slave-labor camp — or to his death. In desperation, Simone sprang upon the Toad and killed him in the resulting struggle. He'd brought the corpse to the cafe.

After a hurried conference, it was decided that the body would be disposed of so that it would appear as if the Toad merely disappeared — or departed. That was all that could be done.

The disappearance of the Toad, along with some evidence of increased Resistance activities, was enough to anger Baron von Karp. Summoning Zoler, he drove to town to see what was going on for himself. He inspected the cafe, including the wine cellar; fortunately, he didn't discover the false wall. He returned to his camp, partially convinced that perhaps Zoler was right, and that the Toad hadn't been fully reliable. If such was the case, the baron mused, then some of the Toad's reports could have been fabrications.

Captain Midnight decided that events were moving too fast for his party to be pinned down inside a subbasement of a French cafe. The best

9. The War: Countermoves

thing would be to bring Civaret back to England after unloading the remaining supplies from the C-47. Then he could plan on tackling either the submarine facility or the one related to rocket activity.

Demoviche approached the Secret Squadron leader. He said, "Captain Midnight! That L-6 aeroplane, the one you are making available for me. You will need someone to fly it over from England. Is not that so?"

"Well, yes."

"Ah. Well, why can not that person be me?"

"Gee, sir, that sounds like a great idea," Chuck said.

Captain Midnight considered the proposal. "Hmm. How are you on cross-country work?"

Demoviche smiled. "Well, I am very good at following another aircraft."

Chuck chimed in. "What about engine-out procedures?"

The Frenchman chuckled. "With the aeroplane I have been flying, I am quite used to losing my engine and making forced landings." His proposal was accepted.

Before dawn, the two aircraft took off and headed for the Squadron base in England. Once they were well over the English Channel, they climbed for altitude, and reached the vicinity of the airfield around sunrise. They landed without incident.

Civaret was immediately "borrowed" by Sir Allen, who asked him to help develop some propaganda messages and to corroborate intelligence reports from the Continent. Captain Midnight went into a huddle with a Major Hackett, who would coordinate work between the Secret Squadron and the British Commandos. Demoviche had found the center of German activity, which seemed to involve some sort of airfield; this prevented him from spying it from his aircraft. He was able to provide only an approximation of its layout.

According to Demoviche's information, there was some sort of naval activity at the coastline, at a cove entranceway. One of the other sources indicated sighting a submarine. The cove entranceway was guarded by German soldiers who played a searchlight along the shoreline at night to spot possible intruders. By day they doubtless scanned the same area with high-powered binoculars. With careful timing, the searchlight could be circumvented by stealing along the shoreline.

About halfway up one side of the shore was a small cave that was hard to spot from the soldiers' perspective. By ducking into the cave, it would be possible to hide during the light's backsweep. According to the information, there was a rowboat in the cave that could be launched during the high tide.

Sir Allen and Captain Midnight conferred about the possible Commando action. If the German facility was as significant as the partial clues suggested, the raid would be important and could deny the enemy a significant resource. The only way to make certain, though, would be through a scouting mission; Captain Midnight decided to do it himself.

Sir Allen suggested that a successful raid against the installation should be followed as quickly as possible with a move against von Karp's castle. "It's a matter of trying to follow their thoughts, you see. They are methodological blighters, and after the first raid, their guard will be up. But I'd be ruddy surprised if they didn't think of a follow-up rather than a strike in a whole new direction."

Captain Midnight took Joyce Ryan with him on the scouting mission before the raid. When Major Hackett protested mildly about a young girl going into combat, Joyce giggled. The Secret Squadron leader pointed out that while acting as a tail-gunner in an Avenger, she was credited with shooting down four enemy aircraft, with a probable kill unconfirmed. "Besides," he said, "her vision is incredibly good, and she has more sensitive night vision than anybody else in the Secret Squadron, myself included. For the kind of work we're going to do, she's the best possible partner."

Secret Squadron agents SS-1 and SS-3 were set ashore up the coast from the German installation. They made it safely to the cove area.

Captain Midnight spotted a cave, and the two of them sprinted for it — just before the searchlight beam swung past. It wasn't the one with the boat.

Midnight pulled out field glasses and handed them to Joyce. She scanned the area. He took notes as she spied item after item of significance. When she wasn't certain about something, she asked for clarification; most of the time she didn't have to.

It became clear that the information pointed to the Germans establishing a major armed facility. The commando raid would do a lot of good, militarily.

Captain Midnight called a halt to her observations. He explained that they'd fallen behind their schedule. They had to get back soon, but unobserved.

Joyce spotted another cave. They stole over to it; there they found a rowboat. They decided that they might be able to regain their lost time by using it. Although it was an hour past high tide, they were able to launch the boat. Captain Midnight used the oars, while Joyce guided him in hushed tones.

There was one awful moment. When they were only 75 feet from shore, the searchlight swept right over them. The two froze, but the beam did not return. Captain Midnight speculated that after hours of playing the searchlight along the shore, the soldiers on duty had become careless or were half asleep.

9. The War: Countermoves

The two of them made it out to the raiding forces without further incident. After rendezvousing with Major Hackett's group, the Secret Squadron agents described what they'd observed. Joyce drew detailed sketches of her observations. These diagrams provided the commandos with sufficient information to formulate an effective attack plan.

The raid was successful. The commandos discovered that both an airfield and a submarine base were at the location. In quick, lightning moves, they drove back the German defenders. While the flying field was being put out of commission by the commandos, Ichabod Mudd, who had joined the effort, was able to seal the submarine penways. As he explained, "I had a little time on my hands. I found a good supply of explosives that just needed a primer, so I supplied one."

In military terms, the raid was effective. It denied the Germans resources, while easing pressures on the Resistance.

While the raid was being executed, Sir Allen had found just the person to help with the matter of von Karp's castle. Ris Jensen, a Norwegian scientist who until recently had been in a German slave-labor camp, had turned up. Dr. Jensen would be able to help; he'd been doing private rocket research in Norway before the war. So he was smuggled to St. Michel and ensconced in the Phantom Band's hideaway.

So Demoviche got his wish to follow an airplane back to St. Michel.

They landed safely, but to bad news. Zoler reported that von Karp had tried a ploy, which had failed. He had an aide, Hans Ebert, try to infiltrate the Underground by posing as an American — a downed member of the Secret Squadron! Had it not been for the previous presence of the Secret Squadron at St. Michel, it might have worked. The German, going under the name of Peter Quincy Daniels, was very convincing.

The township was in a serious position. Had it been collaborationist, the maneuver wouldn't have worked at all: The Toad, or someone of his ilk, would merely have turned "Daniels" over to von Karp's forces. However, to the townfolk, Ebert had been sufficiently convincing that he was introduced to members of the Phantom Band. This meant that reporting "Daniels" to the Germans would result in the capture or death of members of the Underground group and would put the whole town under suspicion.

Currently, Ebert was a prisoner of the Phantom Band, which was at a loss as to what to do with him. They thought that the British or Americans could wring some information out of him. Several days had passed. Zoler indicated that the baron was losing patience.

Baron von Karp was of the Gestapo, without troops of his own. However, he was able to intimidate the field commander, a General Klaus von Nord, into employing his troops upon occasion. According to Zoler, von Karp decided that if he hadn't heard from Ebert by the middle of the week,

B-24 "Liberator" bombers conducted raids in the European theater. A flight of these aircraft bombed the area near St. Michel, thwarting Baron von Karp's operation there. (Photograph: *National Air and Space Museum, Smithsonian Institution*, SI Neg. No. 83-16529.)

he'd use von Nord's troops. He would have them move against the town and take St. Michel apart, brick by brick if necessary, to find his agent.

Von Karp's move could jeopardize the whole Squadron operation. Somehow, it would have to be countered.

After a bit of thought, Captain Midnight spent time encrypting a message, which he sent to England. In a few hours, a message returned. It contained a plan, the result of consultation with American officers.

The war had progressed to the point where the Americans were making daylight raids. Both fighters and bombers were involved; such raids could go as far as Berlin. It was decided that during the raids, a group would be diverted to bomb the German emplacement near St. Michel. Since occasional forays from main bombing missions were not unknown, there was little likelihood that the Germans would link the action to von Karp's activities.

Captain Midnight sent a reply: In general, the basic plan was good, but he suggested adding a Secret Squadron member to the aircrew of the lead bomber. The flight could be updated by encrypted message should the Germans move. This modification was approved.

9. The War: Countermoves

Von Karp had the troops start to move on the town about half an hour before the bombers arrived. In one of those situations more suitable to fiction than fact, the troops had nearly reached St. Michel by the time the bombers were near.

After identifying the bombers with an MJC-10 Plane Spotter, Joyce was able to advise Captain Midnight what corrections were necessary to the bomb run.

With the precise information supplied by Captain Midnight, the bombardiers were able to bomb with extraordinary precision. They were able to "walk" the bombs to the very edge of St. Michel, yet not one building in the town suffered significant damage.

What happened to von Nord's troops was catastrophic. They were caught in an area of minimum cover, in rough terrain providing little protection. To say they were decimated would be an understatement.

The bombing run resolved much.

It appeared to the surviving Germans that the American bombers had been trying to attack St. Michel. Neither von Karp nor von Nord had any idea that the move on the town was known. Further, there was no military sense in bombing *fields* outside the town; therefore, it appeared that the bombs just fell short.

Just why the Americans would attack an obscure French village was unknown, but the Germans understood that armed forces don't attack friendly sites. The logical conclusion was that the village was certainly sympathetic to the Axis.

For von Karp, this resolved several things. One was his doubts about Zoler. His information about the town seemed more accurate, on the basis of the attack, than the baron had previously believed. Zoler had been saying as diplomatically as possible that Louis Erlette, the one the villagers called the Toad, might be supplying inaccurate information; an attack seemed to underscore this.

It also explained why Erlette may have departed: He was afraid of being found out. Von Karp supposed that in time he'd find out what Erlette was afraid he'd discover.

Additionally, the baron believed it resolved what must have happened to Ebert. The villagers might have become so enraged at the thought of an enemy agent among them that they executed him. Such was war.

Objectively, the bombing run destroyed whatever hold the baron had on von Nord. If von Karp ever tried to complain about lack of cooperation with the Gestapo, von Nord had grim statistics about what cooperation with the baron meant, in terms of both men and materials.

Finally, it took pressure off St. Michel. With the town judged to be friendly, the Germans turned their attention elsewhere.

In the wake of the raid, Captain Midnight conferred with Dr. Jensen. Prior to the war, the Norwegian had academic contacts in various rocket engineering societies in the United States, England, and Germany. Being financially comfortable, he did a great deal of independent development.

Captain Midnight said that he intended to investigate the rocket situation in person. He was planning to bring his team to the baron's castle, and said he understood that Dr. Jensen would be extremely valuable as an addition to the expedition.

Ris Jensen smiled. "I would be honored to join this venture," he said.

Demoviche was brought into the conference. The French pilot was certain he could navigate the Secret Squadron to an area close to von Karp's castle. The land was fairly desolate, and the closest place where an aircraft could land was a few hours away by foot.

Finally, everything was ready. Chuck Ramsay, Joyce Ryan, "Captain" Demoviche, Ichabod Mudd, and Dr. Ris Jensen boarded the C-47. Captain Midnight manned the P-51. The fighter took off first and orbited as slowly as it could while the transport became airborne.

The flight, though at near-treetop level, was uneventful, and they passed into Germany without incident. Demoviche, who was sitting in the right-hand seat, guided Chuck to the landing area he knew about from before the war. It was near a mountain region, and the surrounding forest area turned out to be unsettled. Despite a gusty crosswind, the airplanes landed without trouble. The whole party helped in pulling both airplanes to the edge of the clearing and covering them with camouflage netting from the transport.

The airplanes had to be left unguarded. It would have taken the whole party to defend them successfully in the event German troops found them.

Demoviche led the party. The forest was gloomy, but save for the momentary sight of a deer at one point, strangely absent of even animal life. Eventually, they reached a valley with a waterfall and river below the castle. The Frenchman said he'd learned that the lookouts and arms were concentrated on the side away from the waterfall; the rocks and the deluge were considered a natural defense.

Joyce borrowed Captain Midnight's binoculars and studied the castle intently. "Gee-manee," she said. "No wonder it isn't guarded! Captain Midnight, there's thirty feet of sheer rock below the castle, and some sort of fancy stonework that would prevent anybody from grappling."

Dr. Jensen, who hadn't said much to that point, spoke up. "Do pardon me, my friends, if I speak out of turn. But I do not believe that our position is as hopeless as you seem to think. You see, before the war, I had the hobby of studying the architecture of Medieval times. I would say that unless the baron is a scholar of those times, there is an unguarded way into it."

9. The War: Countermoves

Flabbergasted, Captain Midnight asked him to explain.

Jensen said that the castle once had a sinister reputation. During the Medieval-Renaissance period, the castle's inhabitants were notorious for causing some of their subjects to disappear. It transpired that in addition to the few dungeon cells one expects in any castle, this one contained a hidden dungeon. In this larger dungeon, their prisoners usually languished until death. One captive, thought to be dead, had been hurled out from a cave entrance. He'd been caught in a waterfall flow on his way down. After being carried downstream, he managed to make his way to the riverbank.

Dr. Jensen opined that fewer than 100 people knew about the Castle of Dread, and it was unlikely that Baron von Karp was one of them.

"If that's so, Dr. Jensen, then there should be some sort of access behind that waterfall," said Captain Midnight. "Let's go and find it."

Moving carefully, the party circled the edge of the clearing until they reached the riverbank next to the base of the waterfall. Dr. Jensen pointed out a slight rock ledge running behind the waterfall; the party picked its way over to it. At that location, Joyce spotted an opening in the cliff face.

Captain Midnight found it awkward to throw the rope-and-grapple behind the falls. After several tries, he succeeded. After a couple of false starts, he made it up to the cave mouth. The others followed.

The cave led back to where it had been altered to become a tunnel. The light had become so dim that Captain Midnight had Ichabod Mudd break out a flashlight. Then, leading the way, Midnight moved forward. In a few minutes, he'd brought the party to a large chamber. What they saw there made them stop short.

The chamber was populated with skeletons. There were skeletons on the floor, sprawled out or in heaps of bones. There were skeletons shackled to the walls. There were skeletons in iron body cages. It looked like a medieval notion of Hell.

Picking a trail between the remains, Captain Midnight led the party to what appeared to be a walled-over archway. Dr. Jensen opined that it was probably the back of a secret panel. "This would be at the rear of the regular dungeon area, probably out of sight of any prisoners they may have kept there," he said.

Dr. Jensen pushed and pulled on decorations in the "archway" frame. Suddenly, the blank area within the "archway" began to slide open. The Norwegian's speculation was correct.

Even as the Secret Squadron expedition was making its way through the tunnel, a fateful talk was taking place far above them in the offices of Baron von Karp. The baron was facing one who was as ruthless as he was. The other, Karl Schrecker, colloquially named "von Teufel," was taking his leave. "My staff car is waiting, von Karp. You still have time to join me."

The Gestapo man bristled. "Our recent setbacks will be rectified. And the Nazi heel will grind down upon the necks of the British, the Americans, and their allies."

Schrecker raised one eyebrow. "Ah ... yes. But if I am correct, it might take time. Therefore, I go to a refuge from which to prepare our counterblow. You *will* admit to the possibility of needing it?"

Scowling, von Karp grudgingly conceded, " I dare not take the chance."

Schrecker nodded. "Were it not such a long trip he has to take alone, and were it not for the fuel involved, I would travel with Lieutenant Tilling."

"Tilling is due to leave within the hour," von Karp said, glancing at a clock. "Would you care to stay and see him off?"

"I would like that, but I have my own schedule to keep." Schrecker straightened and gave the Nazi salute. "Heil Hitler!"

"Heil Hitler!"

Even as the staff car bearing Schrecker drove away from the castle, Captain Midnight's party traversed the dungeon area. They reached stairs leading from the dungeon. Although the dungeon was below the castle, the stairs led downward. As they studied it in the light from their electric torch, Ichabod Mudd pointed. "Cap'n, that there's a modern concealed panel. There's both a stairway and an elevator here." The panel was the elevator's door.

"Why do you suppose the stairs lead down, sir?" Chuck said.

"There must be another set of stairs behind a panel," Captain Midnight said. "Those would lead up to the castle. But this must be the one leading to what we're interested in."

Dr. Jensen agreed.

Captain Midnight decided to divide his party. He told Chuck, Joyce, and Demoviche to find places of concealment so that they could observe the stairway. "Should anything happen, try to contact me on the pocket locator," he said.

Dr. Jensen and Ichabod Mudd accompanied Captain Midnight as he moved to the stairs. He opted against the elevator, assuming there would be more freedom of movement by using the stairs. They descended carefully.

The stairway was unlit. Captain Midnight considered that a good sign. It implied that there was nobody downstairs. At the bottom, he had Ichabod Mudd check the door carefully.

Mudd spotted a simple contact switch. If the door had been opened, the switch would have probably activated an alarm. It took only a minute or two to bypass it.

They passed through the door, slowly and silently, and found themselves in a vast, cavernous area. In it they found what they'd been searching for. Along one side of the cavern, dwarfing them, were vatlike tanks of massive construction. But huge as these were, they formed a backdrop for something far more critical.

In the center of the cavern was the crystallization of all the vague stories they'd received reports on. It was an aircraft, but like nothing any of them had seen before. It was sleek, graceful, and beautiful; but it looked as deadly as a hooded cobra. The wings were somewhat swept back; it had no propeller. It looked like some sort of jet, but the tubes seemed too simple. Neither Captain Midnight nor Ichabod Mudd had seen anything like it.

After examining the engines as best he could with the flashlight, Dr. Jensen shook his head. "This is a radically new design, my friends," he said. "Whoever designed this was ... inspired." He stepped back and played his flashlight over the whole aircraft. "On the basis of the wing structure, this airplane has the potential for a very long range. Doubtless, this model is a prototype, but it looks quite able to fly."

"I don't get it, Cap'n," said Ichabod Mudd. "How could an airplane be test-flown from a mountain cavern?"

Captain Midnight said, "I think I know. The Allies have overwhelming air superiority. For something *this* radical, the Germans would have to develop it underground." He pointed at a ramp the aircraft was sitting on. "I'm sure that is some sort of built-in catapult to enable the plane to reach rotation speed when it leaves the cavern."

While they were examining the aircraft, Captain Midnight's pocket locator started flashing. Joyce was signaling that someone had entered the elevator. Acting quickly, he alerted Dr. Jensen and Mudd. All three retreated to the stairwell.

Leaving the door open a crack, they watched as the elevator door slid open. Then the lights came on.

Captain Midnight could see Baron von Karp and a younger man dressed in a pilot's outfit. The two talked for a short time, then gave each other the Nazi salute. The young man climbed into the aircraft and lowered the canopy. He appeared to start going through a checklist.

As the pilot finished, he made a gesture, presumably to von Karp, who was out of Captain Midnight's line of vision. Whatever the baron did, the lights dimmed and doors at the end of the cavern rolled back, letting daylight spill in. After a while, a loud, rocket-like roar started. The intensity increased.

Then, though the sound was almost unbearable, the Secret Squadron party could detect a subtle difference in it, and the aircraft started to move on its ramp. Accelerating rapidly, the plane shot away and out into the cloudless sky. It was out of sight before the doors closed. It took some time for the observers to regain their hearing.

After the doors closed, the lights extinguished. The elevator door opened, spilling light, and closed. Things became as they were before the baron had entered.

Captain Midnight waited a short time, then checked carefully to make sure that von Karp was gone. With the aircraft gone, they were able to see another, roughly three-quarters-completed, aircraft, plus some additional parts. The Squadron leader realized that they didn't have an unlimited amount of time. He instructed Ichabod Mudd to take a camera from a sealed carton and to shoot some pictures of the aircraft assemblies, using flashbulbs.

Once everything that could be recorded photographically had been, Captain Midnight had his team break out plastic explosives. Jensen placed charges at the propellant tanks. Captain Midnight placed charges at the partially assembled aircraft, in a way that both plane and the supporting tools would be destroyed. Mudd placed his near the elevator.

Setting the fuzes for half an hour, the three hotfooted it up the spiral staircase. They took steps two at a time — and ran straight into trouble.

Just as they burst out into the dungeon area, they heard a guttural oath. Von Karp had stopped at the dungeon area for some reason. Realizing that nobody was supposed to be in the secret area, the baron drew his Luger even before he saw who'd emerged.

Whipping out their automatics, they traded shots with von Karp. One bullet caused Mudd to grunt and stagger back; however, he recovered and said he was all right. After several more shots, Captain Midnight risked a ricochet shot and hit von Karp squarely in the chest. It was clear that the baron was out of the picture. Permanently.

Captain Midnight wasted little time. Holding the flashlight so that all could see enough to follow quickly, he set off at a fast lope. They traversed the chamber rapidly and, upon reaching the cave beyond, picked up the pace. They reached the cave opening slightly out of breath.

"There's no time to waste," the Secret Squadron leader said. "We'll have to risk a jump." With that, he dove out, intercepting the waterfall.

He was followed by the rest of the party, one by one. Fortunately, none was hurt. Soon they reached the river bank. Since it was still daylight, they had no trouble finding each other.

Chuck, panting, asked, "Why the rush, sir?"

Before Captain Midnight could answer, the several charges of plastic explosive went off as one. This was followed by an even larger explosion, which fractured a chunk of the mountaintop, reducing the castle, solidly as it was built, to rubble.

"That's why," Mudd said, somewhat redundantly. They later surmised that the larger explosion was a detonation of the aircraft propellants. Whether or not this was the case, it made their job of getting away easier.

As it happened, there were enough stories in circulation about research going on in von Karp's castle that nobody suspected that the explosions were the result of sabotage.

It was on the way back to England that Ichabod Mudd discovered that the "hit" he'd received from von Karp was directly in the metal-body of the camera he'd used to take pictures of the "rocket plane." The only documentary evidence that rocket planes existed had been destroyed.

"Perhaps for now," Captain Midnight said thoughtfully. "At least one airplane flew away to somewhere else. Maybe one of our boys saw it on radar. And there may be other such planes."

The soft-spoken Dr. Jensen said, "I take it you do not speak German, Captain Midnight?"

"No. Why do you ask?"

"I do, and I heard what Baron von Karp said to the pilot, Lieutenant Tilling. He said that the lieutenant was 'entrusted with the only completed aircraft of this new series.' Thus, wherever it is, the only existing rocket plane, or whatever it is, flies."

"I've got a hunch we'll be seeing it again," said Ichabod Mudd. And nobody felt like arguing with him.

10

The War: Resolution

Upon return to England, Captain Midnight satisfied himself that the Secret Squadron base there was fully established and running smoothly. In his absence, William Mittler, agent SS-2F16, had been acting base commander. The Secret Squadron leader issued a directive that removed "acting" from Mittler's title.

That done, Captain Midnight was able to take his personal team back to Squadron Headquarters outside Grant City. He was certain that he'd have a lot to catch up on since he started his field assignment.

One thing that still bothered Captain Midnight was the missing "rocket plane." It was an inspired and advanced design. It could become a more effective "super weapon" than the V-2 rockets. He promised himself that if he ever got a lead on the missing aircraft, he'd immediately issue himself a field assignment.

He told this to Barry Steele. The Intelligence major had to smile. "I might as well go along with it," he said. "You won't be worth a damn if you know about it and don't get a crack at it."

Meanwhile, the next chapter in the "rocket plane" saga began at a certain location in South America, at a large ranch owned by a very wealthy man with a German surname. However, a number of families with German surnames had lived in the country for more than a generation. Though sprawling, the ranch was isolated, with forest surrounding most of it.

It was several weeks before the ranch owner's return from a visit in Mexico. Nobody saw what dropped from the sky like some metallic bird of prey. An airplane, silvery, with swept-back wings and no propeller, set down almost silently.

Mostly on momentum, but punctuated by occasional short blasts from its unusual engines, the plane taxied close to a cliff face. As it approached, a section of the cliff swung open, and the aircraft taxied inside. The section then closed.

The owner found his way back to his ranch. After that, certain activities began.

Months passed. D-Day came and took its place in history. The Allied invasion was spreading on European soil. Paris had been liberated, and the Allies were moving into southern France. And some important men in Germany were beginning to agree with what Schrecker had said to von Karp. Time was not favoring them.

They decided to see how they could reverse the trend.

A plane approached the Secret Squadron field. It identified itself satisfactorily on a Squadron frequency. The aircraft entered the landing pattern on instructions from the tower. It touched down gently and cleared the runway. Once the plane had stopped and shut down, the pilot climbed out, bringing his courier pack with him.

One of the items in the pack was a heavy brown envelope designated to the personal attention of Captain Midnight. The envelope, along with several others, was conveyed to Captain Midnight's office. A clerk there deposited it in the "in" basket.

Captain Midnight reached his office about half an hour after his mail; he'd just completed a staff meeting. After seating himself and checking his schedule, he reached for his mail. The brown envelope was the third item he opened.

More than once, Major Barry Steele would accuse Captain Midnight of having "brilliant hunches." Whatever he had was working at full blast as he stared at the report he'd pulled from the heavy brown envelope.

It originated with a British officer, a Major Lancelot Childers, attached to Intelligence. He'd reported several suspicious items, all centering on a remote area of South America. For one, there was a marked increase in the purchase of aviation fuel in a remote region that was effectively unsettled. The consumption had picked up some months ago, quite out of proportion to the number of aircraft known to be in the area.

Also, industrial-sized loads of chemicals had been purchased by various buyers, and were diverted somewhere. Both American and British agents had tried to trace these shipments, but they weren't able to get a direct trail.

There may be no connection, the report pointed out, but a number of European art objects were rumored to have been brought to South America for sale to wealthy collectors. If something major was going on, it might need the funding that such sales would help raise.

While the report hadn't said much, Captain Midnight suspected that somehow there was a connection to the "rocket plane." There was nothing definite, but since the aircraft was of radical design, unless it landed in a remote place, it would have been noticed. And it hadn't been.

There was always the possibility that the airplane crashed after takeoff. But Captain Midnight didn't think so; his airman's instinct suggested that the aircraft's design was inspired and sound. Despite its rockets, or jets, or whatever, the aircraft had high-aspect-ratio wings, and therefore possessed some gliderlike characteristics, gentle sweepback or no. This meant that in addition to being able to fly fast and high, it probably could go far. But all the way to somewhere in South America? Conceivably.

Captain Midnight read through the report a second time. Something within him prompted him to investigate the matter personally. He decided to prime his "family" team of Chuck Ramsay, Joyce Ryan, and Ichabod Mudd about an impending mission. After alerting his staff, he would make special arrangements involving about two dozen of the Secret Squadron Headquarters' best pilots, just in case they might be needed.

In an underground chamber in South America, Schrecker cast a cold eye over an elaborate arrangement of pipes and tanks. Volume production of the propellants had begun. The first shipment to the Pacific way station was scheduled in less than three weeks. Soon, he and Tilling would go to the place in the Asian mountains where the counterstroke would be prepared.

Even with things progressing nicely, Schrecker was developing contingency plans.

Once Captain Midnight decided to issue himself a field assignment, he moved quickly. The command general staff was certainly able to handle things smoothly in his absence. He told Major Steele that through SS-11 he'd arranged for a special team to reinforce his efforts, if such should prove necessary.

Through channels, he arranged for a meeting with Major Childers in Central America. He made certain that Chuck Ramsay, Joyce Ryan, and he were thoroughly checked out in the twin-engine aircraft he chose for the mission: a slightly modified Lockheed A-29, which had some armament, including a rear gun turret, a useful load-carrying capacity, and a reasonable range. He chose to escort the Lockheed with a P-51.

The flight to the Central American rendezvous point was uneventful, but the meeting brought additional information. Major Childers brought with him a young RAF pilot whose excessively large front teeth gave a rather "rabbity" cast to his otherwise regular features. Childers introduced his companion as one Lieutenant Henry Austin, known to his friends as "Bugs" Austin ("Named me after that ruddy cartoon rabbit, don'cha know," Austin noted).

The RAF pilot was included in the meeting because of an experience he'd had that seemed to be related to some of what Childers reported.

Some weeks previously, the pilot had been directed to take a light civil airplane and fly through Argentina, stopping at airports along the way that were most likely to have a potential for suspicious use. He was to keep his eyes and ears open, particularly in the area where what slim leads had been uncovered suggested it might be of interest.

"Bugs" Austin did. He found nothing until he reached a certain airfield in a remote spot. It had surprisingly large and complete facilities. "I was told that it was an airfield started by someone trying to establish a commercial aerodrome, with a mail distribution or something of that sort. Didn't work, and it was abandoned, they said. But it seemed in ruddy good condition for something used only by occasional aeroplanes, don'cha know," Austin said. The RAF pilot made gentle inquiries without finding out too much.

He departed toward the Andes to look over the area. As he was overflying a section of land he described as "rather jungly looking," he spied some movement on a lake below him. It seemed to be a landing amphibian aircraft. He decided to investigate.

But something happened. He banked sharply, placing a greater load on the airplane. The aircraft began to behave ominously, Austin said, "as if it were preparing to come apart in the air." Which it proceeded to do.

The only thing that saved "Bugs" Austin was his parachute. He wore it habitually over unsettled country that had a lot of trees; he was at sufficient altitude to deploy it. What was left of the light plane smashed into the ground and was swallowed by the undergrowth.

Lieutenant Austin was no fool. There was no evident connection between the mysterious destruction of his aircraft and the activity below. He decided that he'd stand a better chance of survival if he acted very cautiously. When he landed, he very prudently concealed the 'chute.

"Bugs" Austin found the going a little difficult, since he was in unfamiliar territory. He worked his way in an approximately eastward direction. Eventually, he found a little farm.

The people there were good folk. Austin explained he'd been involved in an accident west of their farm. The farm folk, seeing his flying garb and knowing of pilots, asked him whether he'd encountered anyone after reaching the ground.

When he said he hadn't, he was informed that he was fortunate. In the jungle, there were scattered native tribes that answered to someone who called himself "The Scorpion," a bandit chief. The farm folk weren't certain why this Scorpion had the influence he had, but if the natives had spied Austin, they would surely have informed the outlaw. "There are those who say that The Scorpion is really the servant of a great landowner who has a ranch near the mountains. And they say that it is his job to keep strangers away from the ranch," the farmer had said.

To Childers, this was just too much. The isolation of the ranch, and the relatively hostile land surrounding it, gave the ranch a lot of natural protection. Why anyone would need to supplement such natural defenses with irregular guards seemed more than a little suspicious.

He'd just received the information. Even with the help of the friendly farmers, it had taken some time for "Bugs" Austin to make safe connections to reliable commercial transport. The young RAF pilot had made it to Major Childers only days ago.

Childers proposed that he and Austin join the Secret Squadron's expedition. "Certainly young Austin here knows the area better than any of the rest of us. And I dare say I could help you in the snooping-about department."

Captain Midnight did a little quick figuring. He decided it would neither strain his resources nor overload the A-29 if the two joined his party. Additionally, it would help maintain security to have extra friendly eyes helping them look after their equipment. He accepted the proposal.

"Bugs" Austin helped with the navigation on the last leg of the trip. He was able to locate the airport easily. Joyce brought the A-29 in smoothly; only after she cleared the active runway did Captain Midnight bring the Mustang down to pattern height. As he landed, he noticed the excellent condition of the runways. They were in far better shape than they should have been if the field was what it had been represented to be. No *abandoned* attempt to boost air commerce should be so good — unless someone was paying a great deal to maintain the field. To do that made no economic sense.

Captain Midnight was relieved to have Major Childers and Lieutenant Austin in the party, since they both spoke fluent Spanish. Not only could the two British officers translate, but they could also follow up leads on their own.

Through Childers, Captain Midnight negotiated rental of a large, deserted hangar located some distance from other facilities. The A-29 and P-51 were moved into it. Midnight had Ichabod Mudd alter the locks so that even the airport manager couldn't enter the hangar without permission. Finally, he had everyone check the building carefully to make sure there were no concealed means of access.

Mudd decided to add a few burglar alarms, just to be on the safe side. By the time he was through, the building was quite secure.

Captain Midnight decided to make the airport a temporary operations center. The altered hangar could double as a temporary quarters. There were few facilities for tourists in the neighborhood, anyway. There were marginal sanitary facilities attached to the Hangar. Ichabod Mudd said he could spruce them up, and that he and "Bugs" Austin could throw together a workable shower stall "with sufficient privacy for Miss Joyce." Austin ventured that he should be able to buy healthy fresh food from the local farmers, "perhaps picking up a bit of gossip in the process."

Since the Secret Squadron members weren't in a war zone, they wore civilian clothes. Joyce wore slacks, as she did on all field assignments; that wasn't unusual clothing for air travelers who were more than pure *turistas*. A P-51 in the possession of someone wearing "civvies" was sufficiently unusual that Captain Midnight didn't bother having the Secret Squadron symbol on its sides blanked out.

While escorting the A-29 to the field, Captain Midnight had studied the terrain carefully. He decided that for a little sniffing around by air, neither of the aircraft he'd brought would be efficient. The A-29 would be cumbersome. The P-51 would be too fast. So he delegated Austin and Mudd to find and purchase a two- or four-place civil aircraft to be used for a bit of local work. He was confident that the Secret Squadron's Chief Mechanic could detect any serious flaw in a prospective airplane before any deal was made.

After a couple of days, Austin and Mudd had unearthed a Piper Cub, Model J-3, for which they had to pay a high price (fortunately, the Secret Squadron's mission was well-heeled financially). After bringing it to the hangar, Ichabod Mudd went over the little yellow airplane with a thoroughness that bordered on ruthlessness, and pronounced it airworthy. The rest of the day, all the pilots in the party took turns flying it to get the feel of a slow, light plane. At least that was their excuse. Captain Midnight arranged to go up the following morning with Austin to investigate the area near where he'd had his accident.

The following morning, the little Piper Cub took off early. The Secret Squadron leader was the Pilot-In-Command, with "Bugs" Austin as his co-pilot and guide.

Captain Midnight let the Cub reach a reasonable height, then asked Austin to fly to the area where his airplane had come to grief. Soon they were heading toward an area where the jungle began to thicken.

As they were flying toward the region of interest, a flash of light caught Captain Midnight's eye. He assumed control of the Cub and began circling back.

Soon both of them saw it clearly: the wreckage of an airplane. They could make out that it was the remains of a large, twin-engine aircraft.

Both men were armed, and Captain Midnight thought the wreckage was worth investigating. He headed straight for a clearing that was more than ample for the little airplane's needs.

After landing, Captain Midnight secured the plane so that only he or Austin could fly it (Ichabod Mudd had rigged a quick-disconnect pair of wires to the magnetos; while not elegant, it served its purpose). The two men approached the wreckage as cautiously as they could.

They found the dead body of a German airman in the co-pilot's seat. Captain Midnight carefully moved its head and said, "He's just recently been killed. A pathologist I knew told me that *rigor mortis* starts in after about four hours, and usually starts around the head. This is a very fresh crash."

The two started to explore the wreckage. They were stunned to find that the airplane carried a cargo of fine art — jewels and a few paintings — and several ingots of gold. From the looks of it, the cargo represented several million dollars' worth of loot.

"This ties in with something Major Childers reported," Captain Midnight said. He reached among the pieces and picked up a jeweled brooch. "There isn't much we can carry in the Cub, but maybe he can make something out of this."

The two of them left the wreckage and retraced their steps as cautiously as they had when approaching the crash site. As they neared the clearing, they discovered two Germans had reached the Cub first.

One of the two was trying to work on the engine while the other stood nearby, nervously scanning the edge of the clearing. Captain Midnight understood at once what had happened. The Germans were the crash survivors. Perhaps they even heard the Cub's engine. While the abandoned wreckage was being examined by Austin and Captain Midnight, the Germans had searched for transportation. Only Captain Midnight's precaution and Ichabod Mudd's "disabler" kept the two Allied agents from being stranded in the jungle.

The Germans didn't appear to be armed, so Midnight and Austin worked themselves to a position that would frustrate any attempt at a quick getaway. Then they rushed the Cub.

Although the Germans started to run, one shot from Captain Midnight's automatic and they froze. Midnight addressed them in English, but they didn't seem to understand. Austin tried Spanish. The senior of the two responded to that in a halting fashion. The RAF pilot told them to move toward the center of the clearing, away from the Cub.

The two sullenly complied. After they were made to sit on the ground, which would hamper them from making sudden moves, Captain Midnight had Austin interrogate them. Their prisoners were Kraus and Fritz Hautmann.

They claimed they knew little of their mission, but that they were to fly some cargo to a location where they would meet someone calling himself The Scorpion. He would help them reach their final goal.

Abruptly, the situation altered sharply. On the far side of the clearing appeared a band of Indians, beyond the range of their automatics. The natives were fierce looking, and they were accompanied by a man who was dressed in civilized clothes instead of the native breechcloths. He was apparently leading the tribe.

The leader called to them in Spanish. Both Austin and Kraus yelled back simultaneously. Kraus was silenced by a gesture from Captain Midnight, who was covering him with his .45. But the damage had been done, and the next call from the leader was more hostile in tone.

The Secret Squadron leader told Austin to cover the two prisoners, and then instructed the Germans to walk slowly toward the group of natives without looking back. As the two complied, Captain Midnight quickly restored the Cub's disconnect wires, then ordered Austin into the plane. As he clambered aboard, he said, "Those Indians won't hold back once they realize we're not covering the Germans."

The engine kicked over, and the Indians broke into a run for it, but they hadn't closed enough distance by the time the Cub started to taxi toward the far end of the field. Captain Midnight performed part of his run-up as they were moving, a technique normally reserved for floatplanes.

The takeoff was routine, though when they returned to the airfield, Ichabod Mudd found a couple of blowgun darts stuck into the Cub's fabric. Evidently, a couple of natives got within their range and must have thought that it wouldn't hurt to try to down the yellow bird their way.

(In the radio drama, the action was more protracted. In it, Chuck, Joyce, and Major Childers found the wreckage. The whole Squadron party was supposedly set upon the natives, and was saved by an old friend of Captain Midnight's who "just happened" to see their plight in the jungle. When Midnight heard about the drama, he pointed out that the radio show was usually fairly close to his actual adventures, and speculated that the script writers felt the real events were a bit too tame.)

While Captain Midnight and "Bugs" Austin were away, a trimotored airplane, which Ichabod Mudd said looked like "a flying pig," landed at the airfield. An older, stiff-backed man with a military bearing deplaned. He had close-cropped blond hair and, despite his civilian clothes, looked so much the professional military man that Chuck Ramsay observed that he probably "fell asleep 'at attention.'"

This personage was followed by his pilot, whose grim efficiency contrasted with the casual atmosphere of the more unsettled regions of South America.

10. The War: Resolution

Chuck went to the primitive office in their "base" hangar and checked some recognition charts. The strange-looking aircraft was a Junkers Ju 52/3m, an aircraft used as a jack-of-all-trades by the Axis. However, it was a large airplane for just two men.

Major Childers, whose curiosity was also aroused, wandered casually over to a worker at the field and exchanged small talk. In the midst of it, he asked, as if in an offhand manner, who was visiting.

He was told that the man was a very powerful rancher who lived close to the mountains. His named was *Señor* Schrecker, and he was even richer than most ranch owners.

Joyce watched what was going on, but she wasn't a lip reader. Even if she had been, she couldn't understand Spanish. All she could report was that the two were in a meeting with the airport manager, *Señor* Prado. Schrecker and Prado seemed to come to some sort of agreement, and the meeting broke up.

The Junkers was just departing the traffic pattern as the Piper Cub returned. Captain Midnight taxied over to the Squadron hangar and, after going through his shutdown procedure, climbed out and asked Chuck to round up everybody so that they could compare notes.

With all the airplanes safely hangared, the meeting got under way. It took some time for the various stories to be told in detail.

The evidence dovetailed nicely. German airmen were looking for a local bandit, yet they brought with them items of such monetary value that no local bandit could handle it. The supposed bandit, though, was supposed to be under control of a powerful rancher who lived west of where "Bugs" Austin went down. There suddenly appeared a mysterious personage who displayed a military bearing worthy of the German General Staff. He arrived in a Junkers Ju 52, a workhorse of the German air arm. That person was reportedly a very wealthy and powerful rancher whose ranch was to the west. A very good case could be made linking Schrecker to Nazi-related activities.

There was no shortage of aviation fuel at the airport, which tied in with Major Childers' initial report about the unusual characteristics of the place. The following morning, Captain Midnight departed early in the P-51, having fueled it to the brim.

As he departed, "Bugs" Austin stared after the receding airplane with something approaching deep respect. "Extraordinary," he said to Chuck Ramsay. "Yesterday was the first time I ever flew with that gentleman, don'cha know, and I have never seen a light plane handled so superbly. Today he takes off in that ruddy Mustang with as much finesse as I've ever seen."

Chuck nodded. "And if he took up the A-29 tomorrow, you'd swear it was the only plane he'd been flying for the past 20 years. I gave up trying to figure out how he adapts so instantly. I'd bet that if he could find that rocket plane, he'd be able to fly it with less than an hour's training."

Hearing this, "Bugs" Austin and Major Childers began to discern that Captain Midnight had more than just a professional stake in the mission.

A few minutes past noon, Captain Midnight returned, setting the Mustang down with as much finesse as he did with the Cub. Leaving Ichabod Mudd to postflight and hangar the P-51, he retired to an inner work area. He started the laborious process of enciphering a long message.

A few hours later, a radio operator named Zoell handed a sheet of paper to one Peter Hortmann, a cryptologist who had arrived at Schrecker's ranch a little more than a month previously. The paper was covered with a string of numbers. The code expert was gratified at the message's length: The longer the message, the easier it would be to crack.

(Normally, this would be the case. But at one meeting in Washington, D.C., Captain Midnight had discussed cryptography with one of the United States' greatest experts and was told of this weakness. A partial solution was worked out: For a very long message, he would start with one key, and within the message, this key would be changed, changing the encipherment. The Secret Squadron leader used this method rarely; but at this time, he thought the effort worthwhile.)

Schrecker held a meeting with some of those he'd brought to the ranch. He had a map illustrating the situation on the European battlefront. Things did not look good. The gamble based on the Battle of the Bulge was failing: Troops under Patton and Hodges had moved the front back to Germany, and the Russian troops were beginning such a gigantic offensive that all available forces had to be transferred to the Eastern Front. The number of operational aircraft available to Germany was estimated at fewer than 1,000.

Schrecker pointed out that the European theater of the war seemed to favor the Allies. "Some of us predicted this months ago, which of course is why you are here. We have been developing wonderful new weapons, but there has not been enough time to place them into action in a meaningful way."

"But Count ..." began one of the staff members.

"Silence!" Schrecker snapped. "Here I am neither Count von Schrecker nor General von Schrecker, and never forget that.

"I suppose you were going to object that our new aircraft would make the difference? It would, had we the time. You see, we have but one of this wonderful aircraft. One! We cannot afford to use this aircraft in battle until we can darken the skies with them!

"No, Mueller, there is no paradox. We have been busy here, but not manufacturing airplanes. We have been manufacturing *fuel*. There has been prepared for us a great facility in Asia, but we have to get the aircraft there.

10. The War: Resolution

We know how to make the propellants, and all these months we have been manufacturing enough of it so that the airplane can reach its destination. Then, if it takes three years, airplanes will be manufactured at such a rate that we will sweep the skies of anything sent to oppose us. We will regain all we have lost, and we will make our enemies pay!"

Hortmann, the code expert, grunted and then said, "But already they are suspicious of us. The Americans at the airfield show that."

Schrecker smiled thinly. "The Americans will be taken care of."

That day, "Bugs" Austin noticed that there were a couple of new line boys at the airport. One, named Pedro, approached the RAF pilot. The line boy said he had but recently been employed at the airport though he had a few duties, he had enough spare time that he could help out at the Squadron's hangar. "I am a good mechanic," Pedro said. "For many years, I worked with the airlines, Señor."

Austin said that he would tell the others, particularly the Chief Mechanic, who might be looking for help. Later, he told Childers, Joyce, and Chuck about the matter. They all wondered how Captain Midnight would react when he returned.

The Secret Squadron leader and Ichabod Mudd were aloft in the Piper Cub. They were retracing a route that Captain Midnight had flown *from* on the previous day in the Mustang, although at a much slower speed. In time, they reached their destination.

Beneath them there suddenly appeared a fairly large clearing. As Captain Midnight positioned the Cub to start his landing sequence, he asked, "Notice anything unusual about this, Ikky?"

"No, Cap'n. Should I?"

"I'd hope not. Joyce might have spotted it, though." The Cub was on final now, and touched down to a very soft landing. And Ichabod Mudd stared in amazement at what he saw.

From the ground level, he saw camouflage nets that concealed a number of airplanes and some tents. He could see that there were at least a dozen airplanes. Two were the ubiquitous C-47s, and to Mudd's slight surprise, several Chance-Vought F4U Corsairs ("Loaned to us courtesy of the Navy Department," Midnight explained).

The Secret Squadron leader taxied the Cub under one of the camouflage nets and shut it down. Then he introduced Ichabod Mudd to the men stationed at the hidden field. They were all Secret Squadron agents, and they'd established a base where neither The Scorpion nor *Señor* Schrecker's men would be likely to discover it. Yet they were close enough to reach the airport in a hurry if they were needed.

"This is tricky business, Ikky," said Captain Midnight. "When we move, we'll have to do so fast. And it's a good strategy not to show all your cards to the other side. I don't even discuss this camp back at the airfield, in case someone could overhear us."

After spending time with the Squadron agents, Captain Midnight and Ichabod Mudd left. The Secret Squadron leader decided it would be better to fly back to the airport along a different route, so he circled the Cub to the southwest. It was on that leg that they saw the other airplane.

Captain Midnight was the first to see it; he pointed it out to Mudd. It was approaching from roughly east of them, and was about 500 feet lower than they were. Once it came close enough, Midnight recognized it. Despite the civilian paint job, it was definitely an Arado AR 196. He tried to project the line of flight. It seemed to be heading into the general area where the young RAF pilot had his accident.

After he returned to the airfield, Captain Midnight heard of Pedro's offer. "He's doubtless a plant," Captain Midnight said. "But perhaps we can use him to get information. Let's give him a job that keeps him out of the hangar, and keep an eye on him."

So it was arranged. Pedro was told that while most of the work was done by the American party, there were some things he could do. Primarily, when any of the aircraft were outside, he was to make sure that the planes' fuel tanks were topped off. Additionally, he could keep the area neat. Pedro accepted the job quickly.

It became a revolving duty among all the Squadron members to keep an eye on Pedro without his becoming aware of it. The only exception to this was Captain Midnight, whose presence as the party's leader made it next to impossible to be unobtrusive.

One afternoon the Piper Cub was left outside deliberately. Joyce, who was on duty at the time, noticed that Pedro was poking around the engine cowling—a fairly strange place to check the Cub for gasoline. Joyce had concealed herself well, so when Pedro suddenly glanced around to see whether he was being observed, he didn't see anyone. Satisfied he was alone, he reached inside a pocket and brought out something that Joyce couldn't see well enough to identify. Pedro worked quickly, then returned whatever he had to his pocket. Then he checked the Cub for gasoline. His duties done, he wandered off.

Joyce passed the word to Ichabod Mudd. Later he inspected the airplane almost microscopically.

Mudd reported his findings to the group. It appeared that Pedro had placed a sufficient amount of slow-acting acid on the engine-mount bolts so that the engine would separate from the airplane in flight. The results would be seen as a very regrettable—and fatal—accident.

At this point, "Bugs" Austin turned white. "Why, the same thing could have been done to my wing struts! Perhaps *that* is why the wings separated!"

10. The War: Resolution

Joyce, however, was so infuriated at what had been done to "such a nice little airplane" that Captain Midnight said that if it survived the mission, he would give it to her as a gift. (He did, too. Having plenty of his own money, he bought the Cub from the Secret Squadron by paying what it had cost. If Joyce hadn't spoken up, the Cub would have been considered expendable and probably abandoned.) Ichabod Mudd removed the acid and replaced the engine-mount bolts. He made sure that the Cub was completely airworthy; but he also made sure that the bolts he used looked the same as the ones Pedro had doctored.

Chuck came up with an idea. He suggested that they contrive to have the A-29 where Pedro could get at it, and give him some opportunity to sabotage it. If he did something that could be countered without his knowing it, and if he could be somehow tricked into being in the airplane when it took off, then it would be easy to get the truth out of him.

Joyce suggested they tell Pedro that they wanted the aircraft washed the following day. That would mean he'd know that it would be outside by the time he got to work, or shortly after that. And it would give him an opportunity to work all around the Lockheed, maximizing his opportunity to attempt some sort of sabotage.

Pedro cooperated beautifully. When he came to work the next day, he brought an innocent looking lunch box.

Chuck, who was on "Pedro watch," wasn't surprised when, around lunchtime, Pedro entered the A-29 with the lunch box and departed without it. The young Squadron agent quickly found Captain Midnight and Ichabod Mudd and told them what had happened.

Midnight and Mudd stole carefully to the aircraft and were able to enter unseen. Mudd found it very quickly. The innocent-appearing lunch box was opened carefully. It revealed a devilish little device known as an "altitude sensitive" bomb. As long as it stayed above a preset altitude, all would be well. But once the aircraft descended back through that altitude, the bomb would detonate.

Mudd disarmed it. Once he'd rendered the device impotent, he repackaged it so that his handiwork wouldn't be detected unless inspected closely. Then he returned the lunch box where he had found it and positioned it the way Pablo had left it.

Concealing themselves within the aircraft, they waited for Chuck. The young agent had been coached on what to do if Midnight and Mudd didn't return to the hangar. Chuck brought Pedro to the plane, using gestures and body language.

The young Squadron agent gestured to "Bugs" Austin, who came over to the aircraft. After speaking briefly with Chuck, Austin spoke to Pedro. Austin opened the door of the A-29 and called for Pedro to come inside.

He was told to go aft, having been made to understand that he was to help unload some equipment stored in the rear. As the lineman moved aft, Chuck carefully and quietly closed and latched the door.

The first indication Pedro had that anything was wrong was when he heard a voice up forward yell, "Clear left!" This was followed by the roar of an engine, then a "Clear right!" By the time he could collect his thoughts, the A-29 was rolling. Somehow the door he'd passed through had become jammed.

By the time he managed to get back into the main compartment area, the A-29's runup had been completed, and the aircraft was entering its takeoff roll. Although Pedro tried frantically to leave the airplane, it soon was high in the sky. He was almost hysterical with fear.

Chuck's idea worked. Faced with what he thought was certain death, Pedro talked, through Austin. He told Austin plenty: that he was a hireling of *Señor* Schrecker; that more than once he'd tried to sabotage their aircraft, though seemingly without success; and that various airplanes regularly landed on or near Schrecker's ranch.

(The radio-program recounting was more dramatic. The altitude-sensitive bomb was supposed to be a time bomb [altitude-sensitive bombs weren't yet public knowledge], and that disposal of the bomb supposedly crippled *both* engines of the airplane, forcing a dead-stick landing on Schrecker's ranch. Any explosion that damaged both engines of an A-29 would almost certainly have been fatal to anyone in the airplane. The producers of the program doubtless believed a deadstick landing would be more exciting.)

To the world at large (including the airport manager), Pedro just disappeared. Actually, Captain Midnight flew the A-29 to the secret base and turned his prisoner over to the Squadron agents there. To the manager, what happened was simple: He saw Pedro get on the airplane, but he never climbed off.

The airport manager decided to play a careful game. True, Schrecker had poured a lot of money into the upkeep of the airport. Yet Prado had also done Schrecker many favors, including letting Pedro pass himself off as an airport employee. Prado felt that if he allied himself too closely with Schrecker, it might have serious consequences if Captain Midnight's forces prevailed. Yet he dare not do nothing. So Prado just relayed the information to Schrecker.

Given reversed positions, Schrecker would have thought nothing of disposing of someone like Pedro. However, he felt he'd better make some sort of countermove. So he called the local chief of police, who owed him several favors, and issued instructions.

The next day, Chuck and Joyce had gone to one of the nearby villages

10. The War: Resolution

to pick up some food. Before they were able to reach the market area, they found themselves surrounded by police. They couldn't understand what the policemen were saying, but sensed they were being placed under arrest. There was nothing they could do about it.

They were brought into the presence of a Colonel Gonsales, the local police chief. He could speak fluent English, and informed the youngsters that they were being held in the investigation of a mysterious death the other day. Someone was killed by an object falling from the sky, and at a time when the two of them had been seen flying the Piper Cub. He would give no more details.

A couple of hours later, the Squadron agents were brought back before Gonsales. They were told that "the great *Señor* Schrecker" had interceded in their behalf. Some of his men would be arriving soon to escort them safely back to the airport.

Both young Squadron agents immediately smelled a trap, but there was little they could do. And soon after that, a pair of men arrived and said in English that they were there to pick up the youngsters.

As the two of them were being escorted toward a waiting car, both Chuck and Joyce made an effort to get rid of their Code-O-Graphs. They were certain Schrecker knew who Captain Midnight was by that time (they were correct), but they didn't want to compromise the Secret Squadron cipher or verify their identities.

Both succeeded, but neither needed to have bothered. A second car pulled up. Inside it were Captain Midnight and Major Childers. The two men "escorting" Joyce and Chuck started to reach for their guns but found themselves facing two already-drawn automatics. Captain Midnight questioned the youngsters while Childers covered the Schrecker men.

Once he heard the story, Captain Midnight told the men, through Childers, to leave and not to return. After they had driven off, the youngsters went to retrieve their Code-O-Graphs, but Joyce couldn't find hers.

Captain Midnight had to assume that the device could not be found, and decided to have the replacement issued. He then joined Childers in straightening out the incident with the police chief. Given the changing political situation in Argentina, the chief decided to remain completely neutral in the future.

When they returned to the airfield, Captain Midnight called Ichabod Mudd and told him that a new Code-O-Graph was to be issued. "You know, Ikky," he said, "I'm beginning to think that a cipher field agent's use should be changed periodically, just on general principles. So, with my instructions to issue the new Code-O-Graph, I'm ordering that it be dated. Will that cause a significant delay in altering the dies?"

Mudd shook his head. "No, Cap'n. The design change will be easy."

"Good." Thus, the first message to go out in the new "Armageddon" cipher was an order for the design alteration.

Ironically, a day later Chuck and Joyce retraced their steps and found Joyce's Code-O-Graph, which had fallen, freakishly, into a crack between two stones. In fact, the cipher had *not* been compromised; and the temporary cipher was more vulnerable to being cracked.

(In the radio show, Schrecker's agents had succeeded in getting Joyce's Code-O-Graph, which would have gone to Hortmann. The cryptanalyst *did* succeed in breaking the emergency cipher, just as the new Code-O-Graphs were distributed to field agents.)

Captain Midnight decided it was time to move against Schrecker. But he was a United States government agent in a foreign country and would have to work through diplomatic channels. Worse, diplomatic channel procedures might warn Schrecker, but, unlike the Mexican adventure, the operation would be too big *not* to work through the government.

(During the diplomatic activity, the radio drama interpolated several fictional incidents, including Schrecker supposedly visiting a hidden submarine base on the coast. This imaginary base was presented as having been discovered and sabotaged by Captain Midnight's party. Actually, the Nazis were in no position at that phase of the war to support such a base. The story was a fictionalized account of a Squadron raid made months previously in Europe.)

Finally, all the paperwork was cleared, and Captain Midnight was granted permission to "investigate" the Schrecker ranch. He investigated in force, calling the fighters from his secret base to join him. He flew the P-51.

Midnight was met by a bunch of German aircraft, mostly Arados. With the fighters at Midnight's disposal, the German planes were totally outclassed. The Squadron leader wondered why they bothered at all. Then it became clear: They were sent up as diversions.

A section of the cliff below them fell away, and a silvery aircraft like no other rolled out. It gathered speed, lifted, and started to climb rapidly. And although Captain Midnight pushed his Mustang to the limit, he was quickly outdistanced.

Midnight tuned to an emergency frequency. He instructed monitors to try to trace the flight of the "rocket plane," which was still climbing and heading west. As he was speaking, he saw a flash out of the corner of his eye. Turning his head, he saw a vast column of smoke rising from the side of the cliff.

Breaking off from his futile chase of the "rocket plane," he returned to the area of the ranch, and landed. What German planes had been sent up were either destroyed or had fled once the "rocket plane" became airborne.

10. The War: Resolution

On the ground, there was very little mopping up to do. Schrecker, as fanatic as Baron von Karp, had mined his ranch and the cave facility. His Nazi companions died at his hands to prevent them from becoming information sources to the Allies.

The only piece of intelligence anyone was able to obtain was that Schrecker and the pilot, Lieutenant Tilling, were taking the aircraft to a facility "in Asia." This, SS-11 pointed out, narrowed the search down to only the planet's largest continent.

Captain Midnight returned to Grant City in the P-51, while the others returned at a more leisurely pace. Joyce had already been told that the Piper Cub was hers, but it was impractical to have her fly the little aircraft all the way back from Argentina. Midnight had her fly it to a field where it could be disassembled and shipped back. With the Secret Squadron leader's assent, Ichabod Mudd flew with her to help in the disassembly. Chuck flew the A-29 to the field; once the Cub was ready for shipment, the three of them returned in the A-29.

The Code-O-Graph issued just before the beginning of 1945 was the first dated unit. It possessed an added feature — a magnifier in the rotor. This unit also used a different message key setting scheme which became the dominant method for Code-O-Graphs for the next few years. (Photograph: *Stephen Kallis, Jr.*)

As soon as Mudd returned, Captain Midnight had the Chief Mechanic meet with the cryptological staff to rough out the design for a new Code-O-Graph. They had come up with a feature beyond its cipher scales in the latest version — a built-in magnifier. The feature was to be tried in the field, but Captain Midnight suggested that there might be other features of equivalent utility to consider for future Code-O-Graphs.

Although he assumed his administrative duties, Captain Midnight made it crystal clear that he didn't consider his self-imposed field assignment closed. It was merely on hiatus until he could get a concrete lead on the "rocket plane."

Intelligence on the leading-edge aircraft began arriving soon. It had been spied leaving an island in the Pacific by a Navy ship's officer of the deck. Its rate of climb was spectacular; he estimated it could easily outclimb a P-38. A similar report came from another ship, further out in the Pacific, from a location astonishingly close to some American-held islands.

Captain Midnight plotted the paths reported on navigation charts and came to an interesting discovery, which he pointed out to his "inner circle." He said, "The rocket plane is flying great-circle routes. Extending the last of these would place the landing site as somewhere around here." He pointed.

"Looping loops!" said Chuck. "Tibet."

Captain Midnight nodded. "A pretty logical choice, since China lies north of the flight path. Both India and Indo-China would be inappropriate places to set up a covert facility."

"But gee-manee," said Joyce. "Tibet's a pretty big place."

"That's true," Captain Midnight said. "I suspect we'll get more clues as we investigate."

The intelligence was enough for Captain Midnight to take to the field once more. He chose a Boeing B-17 Flying Fortress for his investigation. The normal B-17 crew varied between six and ten members; he augmented his team of Chuck, Joyce, and Ichabod Mudd with three Squadron agents: Ward Prentiss, SS-141; Michael Bivens, SS-222; and Louis Neumayer, SS-423. All were qualified pilots. They spelled Captain Midnight, Chuck, and Joyce in flight duties. Ichabod Mudd considered his own duties for long-distance flights as getting in a lot of sleeping, and indicated that he didn't need anyone to spell him on that.

Rather than slogging across the Pacific, the Squadron plane flew across the Atlantic, down to Africa, and then eastwards. It encountered no problems en route.

The Secret Squadron's B-17 touched down at an Allied field near Tibet. Captain Midnight sought out the base commander, Colonel Andre. He explained his mission. The colonel said he'd be glad to give any assistance he could, but he hadn't the slightest idea of how he could help.

"Perhaps some of your pilots or aircrew members saw something unusual, such as catching a glimpse of the aircraft we're looking for. If not, possibly anything out of the ordinary could give us a clue."

The colonel scratched his chin. "Things are pretty routine here. Our missions are logistical, for the most part. About the only thing we'd call 'out of the ordinary' is that a couple of our pilots, Captains Bill Hawkes and Wallace Young, never returned from a mission and are presumed lost."

Since it was the closest thing to a lead, Captain Midnight asked if the colonel would show him the route they flew. Colonel Andre smiled, pointing out that for all practical purposes, the logistical pilots all flew a fixed route. It took little time to trace it out.

What interested Captain Midnight was the time the flight in question took place. Based on the flight performance the Secret Squadron leader had determined for the "rocket plane," and projecting its flight path, it would have been over Tibet during the time the two pilots' flight would have them there, too. Captain Midnight had a hunch that the pilots' disappearance was linked to the arrival of the aircraft he sought.

All the Squadron members except Ichabod Mudd were bone-weary, Captain Midnight included. He decided that things could wait until the next day, when everybody had a chance to rest up. Then they'd all have clear heads.

The next morning, Captain Midnight held a meeting in a small briefing room. He explained what he'd found out and what he could derive from it. He drew his projection of the "rocket plane's" great circle route, plus the established route of the plane flown by Hawkes and Young. They intersected at a point over a fairly remote section of Tibet.

"If flight paths were like railroad tracks, I'd say we'd have pinpointed the location within a mile of the encounter — if there actually was one. Of course, it isn't quite that simple. However, I'll be willing to bet that if there *was* an encounter, we'll find the missing airmen in the shaded area, here, if they're still alive." Captain Midnight pointed at a lightly filled-in trapezoidal area on the chart overlay.

There were several spare observation aircraft and plenty of fuel, so Colonel Andre was willing to loan a couple of planes to the Secret Squadron agents. Captain Midnight and Ichabod Mudd took one plane; Chuck and Joyce, the other. The remaining three agents had orders to monitor the radio in case something happened.

The Squadron leader's plan was simple. The two observer craft were to fly to the plotted intersection of the two flight paths. Then they would separate, flying equivalent and complementary search patterns.

Joyce spotted the survivors. Her keen eyesight picked up a tiny sparkle of light. She had Chuck circle while she took a closer look. What she'd first seen was sunlight reflecting off a scrap of metal one of the men was holding. As they circled, she became certain they were men, and not snow formations. Chuck flew lower and Joyce became more excited. They were apparently Americans, soiled and bearded. She relayed the information to Captain Midnight.

Chuck dropped lower, and studied the ground. "I ought to be able to land here," he said. He turned the words into action.

Joyce was a little unsure about the tactic, but as the airmen ran over to the plane, she had to agree that it wasn't a bad thing to have done. She was amused when the two stopped and stared at the black-clad Americans who climbed down from the airplane. The downed fliers hadn't expected to see a young woman out there.

They identified themselves as Hawkes and Young. Outside of a certain scruffiness brought about by being forced to live off the land for a while, they seemed to be in reasonable shape. Both were curious about the youngsters who found them, but before any serious conversation could get started, they heard the drone of another airplane overhead.

It was Captain Midnight. He radioed that he'd return to the field, drop off Mudd, and get Prentiss to fly back in another observation plane so that both men could be evacuated.

Knowing that Captain Midnight would want to be involved in any discussion of what the men had seen, Chuck and Joyce spoke to them of other things. They talked of news from the States, explained about the Secret Squadron's general overseas mission (without touching upon the present business), and generally kept the men at ease until the other two planes came to evacuate them.

Hawkes and Young had been returning to base when they encountered the "rocket plane." They said it flew around them as if they were dead still in the sky. One burst of machine guns and they were out of it.

Young said, "When we hit the silk, he didn't come back to finish us off. That isn't like the Japs."

"We believe the pilot was a German," Captain Midnight said.

"Oh. Well, after gunning us, the whatchamacallit started letting down, and headed for a low range of mountains. We lost sight of it after then, but we tried to see where it had gone."

"And did you find out?"

"Yes." Young pointed on a navigation chart. "Right here. It's almost like a mesa, but there's no landing field. But it didn't look like it was in trouble, and we didn't hear a crash."

Captain Midnight smiled. "It's an old pattern. We've run into it often. It's got to be an underground base." He thought for a few moments. "I'll have to study the terrain."

Fortunately, the air base was well provisioned. The next day, Captain Midnight was able to obtain an aerial camera, which he had Mudd mount in the B-17. Then he flew over the region. He instructed Mudd to trip the camera's shutter at specific times. After several passes, he returned to the field.

Captain Midnight processed the film himself. Then he made prints. When they'd dried, he mounted two seemingly identical prints on a piece of stiff cardboard. He studied them intently, using a rather strange-looking lens device.

10. The War: Resolution

"This is a stereo comparator," Captain Midnight said to Chuck. "It's used to view pictures of the same target taken at slight different points. Aerial photographs of this sort, when viewed with the comparator, will merge into a single picture with greatly exaggerated depth. Have a look."

Chuck Ramsay peered through the lenses. "Looping loops! The whole scene seems ... kinda ... to jump out at me."

"True enough," said Captain Midnight. "But you don't have a trained eye for these things yet. See that flat area? It looks like a natural plateau to the naked eye, but here in the viewer it's shown to be artificially flat."

"Sure. I can see that. The way everything jumps out at you, any little bump would look like a hill, sir."

"That's exactly right, Chuck. Now look at the left end of that rectangular area. What do you make of it?"

Chuck unconsciously caught his lower lip between his teeth. "I'd say that it looks sort of ... regular, too."

"Yes," said Captain Midnight approvingly. "That's another of those swing-away cliff faces. I suspect it was open when the rocket plane landed."

"Then that's where we have to go."

Captain Midnight said, "From what we've learned from the Germans we captured at Schrecker's ranch, this is the place where they plan to manufacture a fleet of rocket planes. If you look here, and here, on the print, you'll see the guard areas. The camouflage netting stands out sharply in a stereo view."

After studying every detail of the target site, Captain Midnight came to a reluctant conclusion. The only possible way to infiltrate that stronghold would be from above. By parachute. And it would be a rough go.

He spelled out the problem to the other Secret Squadron agents. All of them volunteered to make the jump. Captain Midnight said, "Wait a minute. There are several things we've got to do before I can worry about that phase of the mission. We have to figure out how to put that base out of commission, and how to get away with a whole skin."

At that point, Ichabod Mudd spoke up. "You know, Cap'n, from what you told us, I may be onto an idea. Could you give me a few hours to think about it?"

"Certainly." Captain Midnight added, "I'd welcome ideas from all of you. But why don't you do what Mudd plans to? 'Think about it' for a few hours. The next time we get together, we can compare notes."

The meeting resumed the following morning. In addition to all the Squadron members, as a courtesy, Colonel Andre was invited to sit in. Captain Midnight outlined the problem once more, and asked if anybody had any thoughts, suggestions, or comments.

Ichabod Mudd was first. "You know, Cap'n, if I recall correctly about

Baron von Karp's castle, they had to manufacture special fuel for that rocket plane."

"Yes, that's right. It was also the case at Schrecker's ranch."

Mudd nodded. "And they're probably doing the same thing here. And maybe, if they're going to make a lot of such planes, they're going to need lots of that special fuel. A whale of a lot, Cap'n, just sitting at that base."

"I'm beginning to see," said Captain Midnight with a slight smile. "Please go on."

"Now it seems to me that we might be able to use that fuel to our advantage," Mudd said thoughtfully. "A few of us with some plastic explosives and some good detonators would be all that was necessary to take care of that base. We did pretty good at Baron von Karp's castle that way."

"Fine," said Captain Midnight. "But how do we get away?"

"I ... er ... haven't figured out that part yet."

Joyce Ryan said, excitedly, "But I have! It depends on the size of your raiding party. I guess you don't expect it to be very large?"

"As Mudd said," Captain Midnight pointed out, "a few of us would be all that we'd need. In fact, too large a party would work to our disadvantage."

"Well then," Joyce countered, "we should be able to work some method of picking up the party by landing on that artificial plateau. We could land a C-47 to evacuate any of us who manage to infiltrate the place. Of course, we couldn't *land* any infiltrators there, since it would alert everybody at the base. But if we landed and kept the engines running, a few could jump aboard and get away."

Chuck nodded enthusiastically, but Colonel Andre said, "What about defenses?"

"We can't be absolutely sure," said Captain Midnight. Using a pointer and an enlarged print of the aerial picture, he continued, "I believe that this point here and that point there conceal weapons. There may be others. Those two could be put out of commission by a raiding party, but others would have to be taken out in other ways."

"Fighter support?" said Prentiss.

Nodding, Captain Midnight said, "That's one possibility. If we could keep any other gunners pinned down long enough, it would work."

Colonel Andre objected that the timing between the raiding team and pickup squad would have to be very close, probably too precise to be practical. This started a discussion in which everybody evaluated all aspects of the plan, from infiltration to escape to detonation of the fuel.

The final plan, while not perfect (and acknowledged to be extremely dangerous), was agreed to be "the best shot" at cracking the base. Destruction of the base was top priority, but it was agreed that if an opportunity to get plans or blueprints of the "rocket plane" presented itself, the documents would be taken.

Ichabod Mudd spent the better part of the morning working on a couple of devices. He also unloaded several packs of plastic explosive from the B-17.

Captain Midnight chose the final team: He, Ichabod Mudd, and Chuck Ramsay would attempt the infiltration because the three of them had so much experience working as a team. That little edge might mean the difference between success and failure. Young and Neumayer would pilot one C-47, to be used as a parachute ship. Prentiss, Bivens, and Joyce would act as the crew of the pickup aircraft. After overflying the target area, Young and Neumayer would return to base. Neumayer, as a Squadron pilot, had been checked out in several fighters. After returning to base, he would man one of the base fighters. He would return to the area of action, along with the best fighter pilot attached to Andre's command, Captain Daniel Gordon. They would orbit the area to support any escape attempt.

Joyce objected vehemently to her assignment, complaining that she'd been left out of the main action. Captain Midnight mollified her, somewhat, by explaining, "We need someone who can coordinate our escape. You'll have to monitor the radio in the C-47 to pick us up. Most important, your eyesight is the sharpest in the party. We'll try to give a visual signal, but it will be very faint. We're depending on you to help us get away."

Everybody tried to rest and catch as much sleep as they could. The mission was scheduled for early morning, well before dawn. Captain Midnight would attempt to time his mission to be completed shortly before dawn, when the half-light would help the C-47 land.

Fortunately, the sky was reasonably clear. There was a waning, but still three-quarters-full, moon. There was no difficulty in taking off in the drop plane. It slowly climbed to its service ceiling, which, at just under 22,000 feet, was beneath the peaks of many of the mountains. All aboard were on oxygen.

In time, they reached the drop zone. Captain Midnight, Ichabod Mudd, and Chuck Ramsay jumped. The plan was "delayed deployment," meaning that they would drop a great distance before opening their parachutes.

At a signal from Captain Midnight, they pulled their ripcords. The parachutes were darkened so that they would be almost invisible against the night sky. At the top of each parachute, surrounding the central hole, was a white ring, so that whoever was above could track the progress of the lowest parachute.

In the faint light, Captain Midnight steered himself toward the top of the false cliff face. He hit the level above, rolling. Ichabod Mudd and Chuck dropped behind him, almost as silently. The three of them gathered their parachutes, collapsed them, and pinned them under several rocks.

In their uniforms, and with their faces darkened, the three were nearly invisible in the darkness. After shucking their parachute harnesses, they rearranged their packs. Captain Midnight led them silently toward what looked like an outcropping of rock. They were able to discern, even in the faint light, that the "outcropping" was artificial.

It became clear that the "outcropping" was indeed a guard point. Before they reached it, though, they discovered a trapdoor arrangement some distance away from it. From what the Squadron members could see, the trapdoor was in the guard point's blind spot. This meant that they had a chance of sneaking inside without being detected.

Not having to tangle with any troops on watch meant that they wouldn't have to worry about any alarms being raised; even if they'd taken them all out, the guards' relief might have shown up before the Squadron members could complete their mission. But it meant that armed soldiers would be positioned to bar their escape. It was a calculated risk.

There was a possibility that the trapdoor had an alarm mechanism, but it was unlikely that those developing the base would consider someone trying to break in by that route. However, if it was guarded or had an alarm, the three of them would be caught in a certainly deadly crossfire.

Captain Midnight had to risk it. With utmost care, he lifted the trapdoor. Luck seemed to be with them, for no light emerged. (This might have been a precaution against aerial observation.) The Secret Squadron leader unclipped a gunmetal blue pencil flashlight and lowered it past the opening. He put his thumb over the bulb so that only a dim, reddish glow would appear when he turned it on.

Although it was difficult to make out, the faint light revealed the ghostly form of a ladder. A quick, whispered exchange, and the party entered the opening, led by Captain Midnight. Ichabod Mudd brought up the rear, closing the trapdoor behind him.

The three of them climbed down for some time. At last, Captain Midnight felt his foot strike a floor, and he whispered the information to Chuck and Mudd.

The three gathered at the base of the ladder, still in total darkness. Captain Midnight flicked on his pencil flash again, masking its bulb with the webbing of this thumb to produce a reddish glow (red light does the least to upset a person's night vision, once adapted to darkness). In the dim light, they could see a door.

Midnight and Mudd unsheathed knives with blades treated in metal bluing. These had been designed for throwing as well as for hand combat.

10. The War: Resolution

Virtually invisible in dim light, they could be used quickly and silently. It would have been almost suicidal to use guns.

They eased the door open carefully. The corridor was dimly lit. Captain Midnight commented that perhaps the underground lighting was controlled to match the day and night cycles. If so, it would help them, since most facility personnel would be asleep.

And so it proved. Despite various fictional accounts of professional agents with no nerves in their bodies, the nerves of the Secret Squadron members were quite taut as they crept along the darkened corridors.

Twice they were nearly discovered. Once they heard the soft, unintelligible conversation of two people walking down a corridor that intersected the one they were on. The Squadron members flattened themselves against the wall, knives ready to strike. But it wasn't necessary: The two talkers were so engrossed in what they were saying that they passed through the intersection without glancing down the corridor where Captain Midnight's party was.

A little later, the trio just avoided being discovered by Schrecker himself. While they were searching a corridor, the three heard a doorknob rattle, and ducked behind a case. Schrecker stepped through a nearby door and closed it behind him. Fortunately, he didn't look in their direction, but all three were able to see his profile clearly. He turned away from them and walked down the corridor until he reached an intersection, which he headed down.

Captain Midnight had never seen Schrecker. He and "Bugs" Austin were away from the airfield in Argentina, in the Piper Cub, when the count had landed to meet with the airport manager, Prado. Both Chuck Ramsay and Ichabod Mudd had seen Schrecker, though, and as soon as they felt they were safe, identified him to Captain Midnight.

The Secret Squadron leader realized that Schrecker wouldn't be visiting an unimportant area at that hour. He examined the door carefully, checking the crack at the bottom to see if any light was coming from the other side. There was none.

The door was unlocked. Moving quickly, the three stepped through and eased the door closed behind them. Realizing that turning on any room lights might possibly reveal their presence, Captain Midnight used his flashlight again. The thin white beam of the penlight swept the room, which was exceedingly large. Along one side were many huge tanks which resembled the much smaller tanks at the launching area of the von Karp castle. They'd found a large supply of "rocket plane" fuel.

"We've hit the jackpot," Captain Midnight said. "From what we've seen in Germany and Argentina, I'd say we could level this base with what's here."

Chuck commented that it seemed highly dangerous for such a great amount of high-explosive fuel to be located where it was. Ichabod Mudd pointed out that there didn't seem to be many alternatives available to the base personnel. They really couldn't store the stuff outside. He added that the tanks seemed to be highly armored, unlike those at von Karp's castle. It would take an explosion the magnitude of the plastic explosives he'd brought to rupture them. "And at that, I may have to jigger up the explosive charges a little," Mudd said.

The three approached one of the tanks; both Mudd and Chuck took out their own flashlights. Ichabod Mudd inspected the tank quickly, then said, "Yeah, Cap'n, this is what we want. That valving there's the type used in high-flammable situations. The gage there tells that the tank's near full."

He asked Chuck and Captain Midnight to hold their lights so that he could set the charge. Mudd opened a rucksack and removed a sizable lump of plastic explosive, which he kneaded carefully. "The tank there's pretty thick, and even a wad of this stuff'll need a bit of help. I'm going to mold this into a shaped charge and place it back here, where it'll be stuck to the seam. And I'll place *two* fuze-detonators here. One's a chemical timed device, and t'other's my special gizmo." Then Mudd repeated the equivalent operation on four of the other tanks, activating the timer-fuse in each case.

Captain Midnight asked how much time each timer fuse was set for. "Three hours, Cap'n. I figure that if my gizmo doesn't work, they'll do the job. In three hours we'll be out of here and safe," he said. His unspoken words, understood by all, were, "or we'll have been discovered and killed." The positions of the explosives and fuzes were such that a casual inspection wouldn't reveal them.

With the work completed, the three traversed the chamber and paused, extinguishing their flashlights. "I guess the next thing is to get out of here," Ichabod Mudd said.

"Yes," agreed Captain Midnight. "We should try to find a way to the plateau surface. The pickup plane can't land anywhere else. I'd hate to have to go back to where we started and then try to climb down that fake cliff face."

"Do you have any idea how to reach the plateau, sir?" asked Chuck Ramsay. "I feel like we're lost in a great big maze."

Captain Midnight nodded in the darkness, even though nobody saw it. "I believe I do, Chuck. Pipes from the back of several of these tanks lead into the wall behind them. Ikky's objection about extended lengths of pipe as weak points is still valid. I suspect that on the other side of that wall is the hidden hangar. That would make it the next door down."

With due caution, Captain Midnight eased the door open a crack and checked the hall. It was deserted, so the three slipped out of the fuel area

10. The War: Resolution

and headed toward the door beyond which, the Secret Squadron leader deduced, the "rocket" aircraft was housed.

Although the door was well down the corridor, the trio reached it without incident. A quick check revealed no light from the other side of the door; nor was it locked. Captain Midnight decided that because of the external defenses, the base was considered so secure that no interior area was locked.

The three slipped through the door and closed it carefully behind them. They found themselves on an unlit catwalk one flight above where the "rocket plane" was located. The room wasn't unlit, but the lights, which seem to have been dimmed for the night period, were suspended below the area of the catwalk. Little light spilled upward.

All three strained to hear any sound that might indicate the presence of others, but they heard nothing. Since lack of such sounds couldn't guarantee that they were alone, they moved with extreme care.

Midnight motioned the others to follow him. He stole down the catwalk toward a blank wall, which was obviously the rear side of the artificial cliff face. Toward the front, they could see a steep, ladder-like set of metal steps, similar to those found aboard naval vessels. They led to the floor of the hangar chamber.

As the Squadron members worked their way forward, they studied the scene below them. There was one "rocket plane" there, doubtless the one flown from Germany via South America. Unlike the area under the von Karp castle, the "rocket plane" wasn't surrounded by partially assembled aircraft. Midnight later surmised that the base was still building the "rocket plane's" manufacturing tools.

At the top of the stairs, they scanned the area below them for signs that they weren't alone. They didn't find any. When they reached the floor, they moved toward the "rocket plane."

In the dim light, it looked even more impressive than it had in Germany. Ichabod Mudd took a good look at the jets or rockets and said that they didn't seem to make sense. (Much later, on the basis of what he remembered about the engines, Mudd was the first to speculate about them being a ramjet variant. The design was alien to anything he was familiar with, and there wasn't enough time for him to study it in detail.)

The nature of the mission precluded too much snooping around, particularly since the time fuses had been activated. All three spread out quickly to see whether they could find any plans of the plane; they didn't uncover any. But Chuck Ramsay did discover the release lever for the hangar door — the artificial cliff face.

More important, he found the nearby exit door to let personnel out to the plateau. He called softly to the others and they came to the exit.

Looking at his watch, Captain Midnight said, "We've been extremely lucky so far. Let's not press that luck. We'll go outside and call in the pickup plane."

Captain Midnight cautioned both Chuck and Mudd to stay flat against the cliff face after going through the door. "The observation posts shouldn't be able to see us if we stay against the 'cliff.' Because of their positions, that should be a blind spot for them."

Mudd examined the door to make sure it had no alarm circuit. It appeared to have none. The door was opened very gingerly, and the three slipped through quickly. Since the area behind them had some light, they paused, hearts in their throats, waiting to see whether the sudden splash of light would attract the attention of any guards.

There was no reaction. Captain Midnight surmised that the guards were scanning the skies, or were half asleep. There was also the possibility that they might think anyone opening the access door from the hangar would be facility personnel and wouldn't need to be challenged.

The three of them worked to the center of the "cliff" face. At a signal from Captain Midnight, Chuck reached into his pack and withdrew a walkie-talkie. A special, miniaturized unit developed by the Secret Squadron, it had sufficient power to reach the orbiting C-47. Chuck activated it and pressed the transmitting button. "Okay, Joyce, we're ready," he said.

Joyce acknowledged by pressing the "transmit" button of her unit twice, producing a pair of soft clicks in the walkie-talkie's speaker. She realized that keeping vocal responses to a minimum made it less likely that anybody would be alerted.

There was nothing for the three of them to do but wait. They squatted down and stared at the brightening pre-sunrise dawn. Just as the sun was rising, Captain Midnight and Chuck almost simultaneously spotted a brief flash of reflected sunlight from the wings of an aircraft. As it approached, the sound of its engines became discernable.

Glancing at his watch, Captain Midnight reached over and took the walkie-talkie from Chuck. "Neumayer and Gordon. Plan your passes in five minutes," he said softly. He was answered by two pairs of clicks.

Midnight timed well. The guards in the watchposts above them had seen many airplanes fly by, some even quite close to the plateau. However, since it was a concealed base, making any moves against them wasn't considered. To passing flight crews, it had been reasoned, the area appeared completely deserted. If they opened fire on any, they'd give their position away. And it wasn't until nearly five minutes after the C-47 was first spotted that it became clear to them that it was on a final approach.

A burst of excited chatter broke above where the Secret Squadron party

10. The War: Resolution

A militarized version of the DC-3, the C-47 was used throughout the war. Among other things, the C-47 was used to rescue the Secret Squadron agents who infiltrated the base in Tibet where "rocket planes" were to be assembled. (Photograph: *National Air and Space Museum, Smithsonian Institution.*)

waited. The guards, speaking in an Oriental language, apparently were unsure what to do and held their fire as the plane neared.

Just as the C-47 touched down and began its rollout, the guardposts opened fire, though they hadn't gauged their range. As their fire was closing in, the fighters struck.

Neumayer and Gordon dove down from a higher altitude and struck the two "outcroppings," firing at the gun flashes. One was silenced; the other tried to fire at the departing fighters. The guards must have activated an alarm; a klaxon horn started hooting.

The C-47 came close to the "cliff" but swerved in a controlled ground loop so that it could turn and face "out" for takeoff. As it completed the maneuver, the door opened and Joyce beckoned. Captain Midnight, Ichabod Mudd, and Chuck Ramsay sprinted for the airplane and clambered aboard, stray bullets smacking into the ground near them.

Captain Midnight was the last one to climb aboard. He called, "Prentiss, get us out of here." The C-47's throttles were advanced, and as the plane began its takeoff roll, several things happened at once.

The fighters returned. As they began their second pass, the whole false face of the "cliff" began to swing up. Uniformed men raised rifles and shot at the departing C-47, though they fell flat as the fighters continued their pass.

The Douglas lumbered into the air before it reached the end of the plateau, though in the rarefied air of Tibet, it had practically no rate of climb. As it withdrew from the plateau, it began to climb slowly.

Ichabod Mudd reached into his pack and withdrew something that looked like a walkie-talkie. He requested that Prentiss inform him when they were about five miles away from the Axis facility, and then to turn the C-47 to a course parallel to the "cliff" face.

Shortly, this was accomplished. From the ports they could see the base they just left, the still-open "cliff" face revealing the interior of the "hangar room" as a miniature horizontal line. "Let's see if my little gizmo works," he said, holding his odd-shaped device in front of a window. He depressed a key.

An eye-searing flash obliterated the view of the base, followed by some rising debris and volumes of smoke. About a half minute later, a dull, rumbling *crack!* was heard. The explosion was muted by the range and masked by the noise of the Pratt & Whitney engines.

"Gee-manee!" said Joyce, concurrently with Chuck's "Looping Loops!"

Ichabod Mudd explained that he'd developed a radio-controlled detonator. It responded only to a unique signal Mudd was able to transmit with his jury-rigged transmitter. He confessed, "I wasn't completely sure I could get it to work, Cap'n. That's why I backed it up with chemically timed fuzes." From the violence of the explosion, Captain Midnight guessed that there was probably another fuel cache beyond those "mined" with plastic explosives. In fact, the whole top of the mountain was effectively leveled.

Captain Midnight shook his head in wonder. "I guess that there'll be no chance of finding any clues to the rocket plane in that," he said. A column of smoke continued to climb as the airplane swung onto a course that would take them back to base.

(The radio drama made major variations to the actual story, in part because what performance characteristics had been observed on the "rocket plane" were vague, providing the writers with dramatic license. In the radio program, Chuck and Joyce were shot down near the hidden base. They were said to have met the downed Hawkes and Young. The program had Schrecker aware of their presence. Supposedly on radio advice from Captain Midnight, they surrendered to the "German nobleman." In the meantime, Captain Midnight was supposed to have led a rescue party that included a "local priest" and 20 Chinese mountain men. American prisoners supposedly managed to break out of their cells. All joined forces near the "rocket plane." Captain

10. The War: Resolution

Midnight was supposed to have flown everybody out just as the base was destroyed. The base was supposedly built on a volcano, which conveniently erupted during the fighting, obliterating the base and killing its personnel. The script writers were possibly recalling the adventure of the Phantom City. Even if the "rocket plane" had survived, it wasn't a transport; it was a two-place fighter-class aircraft. Even if it *had* been capable of carrying all these people, skilled as Captain Midnight was, there is no realistic way he could have successfully flown an airplane he'd never been in [and based on a foreign technology], with a completely uncertain weight-and-balance situation. Perhaps the idea the base was built on a volcano was based on reports of the violence and extent of the explosions Ichabod Mudd had touched off.)

The affair was the last significant foreign assignment for Captain Midnight's team during the war. The Squadron party stopped at Hawaii, where Midnight conferred with military commanders to get some perspective on the war. The Pacific War had settled into a conventional course, and there were no indications that the Japanese were developing any super-weapons (suicide pilots in aircraft and torpedoes certainly didn't qualify as "super-weapons"; on the contrary, they portended desperation).

After a few days of rest in Hawaii, the Secret Squadron team continued to the West Coast, where Captain Midnight took a couple of days to inspect a regional Secret Squadron base. Then he and the others returned to Grant City.

With the war in Europe over, and the war in the Pacific moving in the direction of victory, the Secret Squadron found itself having to do less unorthodox work. Far from having work grind to a halt, however, the Squadron remained busy, but more of the work it was doing was parallel to and in coordination with conventional law-enforcement agencies. The Squadron base in England didn't disband, but its operations were changed to a pure support function. Squadron personnel at the Pacific island base, still technically in a theater of war, stayed in an action-ready state; but few thought that they would be called on for any "special" work.

Captain Midnight could sense a change taking place within the Squadron. It bothered him. Where would the Secret Squadron fit in the coming peace?

Captain Midnight was proud of the organization he headed. He was proud of the caliber of the people it had attracted, the way it had grown, and what it had grown into. Yet its future was uncertain.

Troubled, Captain Midnight decided to confer with Major Barry Steele. The Secret Squadron had been issued one of the early models of what later was to be called the P-80 Shooting Star, a Lockheed design. Midnight had been checked out in it, and he decided it would be an appropriate vehicle for his Washington trip.

Captain Midnight didn't feel exactly out of place in the new airplane as he cut through the sky. The new jet was an aircraft he felt perfectly at home in, but like the "rocket plane" at von Karp's castle and Tibet, it represented a new extension in aviation — and in some ways, a significant transition. It would fight well, but not the way it was done throughout most of the war in propeller-driven fighters. He smiled as he reflected briefly on his first action in what had been called "the war to end all wars" and what differences there were between his Nieuport and the P-51 he favored. Perhaps an extension was inevitable.

The Secret Squadron leader refueled at a military field with the proper facilities and then headed for Bowling Field, which he reached after dark. His jet was taken to a high-security hangar. There he met Major Barry Steele, his administrative superior and old friend.

Major Steele brought him to a secure area away from the field, and the two began to talk. They didn't talk about the reason Captain Midnight came to Washington; that would arrive in its own good time. Rather, they started talking about inconsequential things, as people who have traveled different paths for years often do when meeting again. This was the first time in far too long that Captain Midnight could treat the intelligence officer as a friend rather than as a member in the chain of command; the pressure of the war had finally eased to that extent.

Finally, conversation turned to the Secret Squadron's early days. That led Captain Midnight to voice his concerns. "It's not that America couldn't get along without the Secret Squadron," he said. "America got along without it until 1940. But it has been developed into something *good*. So good that it would be a shame to throw it away.

"The Secret Squadron has developed a team spirit that's unequaled anywhere in the United States, but already I'm starting to see it erode. For the first time, I feel helpless."

His old friend nodded. "I understand. You couldn't have known, of course, but there have been some high-level meetings in Washington addressing the same question. You and I both know that the Secret Squadron was born out of a need that seems to be disappearing — although whether it really is has been open to argument. At any rate, the war will be over soon, perhaps sooner than many think.

"But one thing that has been made very clear to us is that this war, unlike others, isn't going to end cleanly. Your own experience with Count von Schrecker makes that point: He was enough of a realist to see the collapse of the German forces long before many of his countrymen. Yet he and a number of fanatics were willing to spend years building a weapon that they believed would win back for them what they'd lost. We'll always have to be on guard against like groups.

10. The War: Resolution

"Oh, I know," the major went on, when it appeared as if Captain Midnight was going to object. "Surely, that doesn't require an organization as large and complex as the Secret Squadron. But there are other considerations. Devices developed in this conflict will find their way into civilian hands after the war. For aerial navigation, say, radar will be a good thing. But the criminal class may try to use some of the new explosives and the rifle attachments — that sort of thing — to help them commit crimes. There will be dislocations and some confusion as the wartime economy tries to adjust to peace. And the Secret Squadron can help here."

Captain Midnight looked interested and was sitting a bit straighter. "How?" he said.

Barry Steele leaned forward. "There will be some areas where a whole new class of criminal will be born — one who has been trained in the latest weapons and who will try to use that knowledge in criminal activities. The Secret Squadron can complement the function of, er, conventional law enforcement agencies." The major smiled for a moment.

"Also, there has been and will continue to be a class of criminal that has been and will continue to be beyond the power of standard agencies. Remember Ivan Shark?"

"*Shark!*" Captain Midnight said. "Has he...?"

"As far as we know, he's still inactive," Major Steele said. "But we don't know much. An international criminal of his stature will always be a potential source of danger. There will always have to be an organization like the Secret Squadron, which is chartered to operate both within and outside the United States, to oppose such international criminals."

"Then you're saying that the Secret Squadron has a place in the postwar world?"

Major Steele nodded. "I know it has. In fact, I even have directives to that effect. You can let that be known throughout the organization."

Captain Midnight stared at his friend thoughtfully. "You're saying you know the war will be over soon? I've heard that it might take occupying forces years — maybe until 1947 — to clean out the last vestige of the Japs on their home islands."

"Even as a friend, I can say only so much," Major Steele said carefully. "You might say that in one sense, the war ended in mid-July. But that is all I will say."

"I don't understand," said the Secret Squadron leader. "The war ended earlier this month?"

"You weren't supposed to understand," said Major Steele quietly. "You'll know soon enough, and you'll have to trust me on that.

"But let me add this: You've been working at a high-fever pitch for close to five years now. You deserve a little relaxation. Spread the word about the new missions for the Secret Squadron after the war ends. Then take a vacation." The major's eyes strayed to a calendar. "I'd say you owe yourself a good month's rest.

"Your general staff's operating at peak again, and each one of *them* has had a month's leave. So leave the Secret Squadron in their capable hands until the beginning of September."

Captain Midnight agreed to this, and eventually the reunion broke up. The Secret Squadron leader found temporary quarters and rested.

Early the next morning, he clambered into his jet and took off. The rest and his previous night's conversation with Major Steele had renewed him. The major was right: He needed to relax. So did Chuck, Joyce, and Ikky.

As he guided the jet almost semiconsciously through the sky, he thought of a real vacation for the first time. Yes, it would do him a world of good. Ma Donovan still had some property at Black Gulch, and it would make a great retreat for a little rest. He'd check with Ma Donovan after he landed. He was certain that his "family team" would like the idea a lot.

Eventually, Captain Midnight requisitioned one of the Squadron's C-47s for his vacation. Captain Midnight, Chuck, and Joyce took turns piloting the Douglas aircraft; Ichabod Mudd, out of habit, snoozed. In time, Captain Midnight landed the airplane on a field that was part of Ma Donovan's property.

After the four had secured the airplane, they started across the open field. Then, almost as one, they stopped, struck with the peace and tranquility of the place. Though the land hadn't been "worked" for a few years, it had a flavor of the West. Its timeless quality struck them all.

Joyce had never seen the ranch, but both Captain Midnight and Chuck had been there before. They'd once helped the citizens of Black Gulch, a year before the Secret Squadron was formed, when Captain Midnight was still mostly known as Red Albright, and when the only menaces were criminals. To both Midnight and Chuck, it was virtually as if no time had passed since they'd last been there. Yet each also felt as if he'd lived almost a full lifetime since those more innocent days.

Chuck shook off the mood first. He walked to Joyce and began to tell her about the ranch. He started to recount some of the early adventures he and Captain Midnight shared. The two strolled off, with Chuck pointing out various features of the ranch and the land surrounding it.

Ichabod Mudd, who'd first met Captain Midnight in Black Gulch, and who'd become his mechanic for the first time there, glanced at the ground. He said, "You know, Cap'n, it's funny to go through all we've gone through and then come back to a place that hasn't changed at all."

Captain Midnight stood lost in thought for a few moments. Then he said, "I guess we had to go through all that so that this *wouldn't* change, Ikky. And that, I guess, made going through it worthwhile."

Then he and his mechanic began to walk toward the ranch house, where he and those who comprised his "family" would find rest and, not too many days later, would hear tidings of peace.

Appendix 1:
Secret Squadron Equipment

Since the Secret Squadron was formed as a quasi-military organization, much of its equipment wasn't unique. Thus, the standard items, such as aircraft, vehicles, laboratory equipment, and the like, were no different than those supplied to the regular armed forces. Such items need no particular discussion. However, there were several items unique to the Secret Squadron.

The best known piece of special equipment was the Code-O-Graph. As has been noted, the Code-O-Graph in its earliest form was what is technically known as a *cipher disk.** A cipher disk has two concentric circular scales that can be repositioned with respect to each other. One scale has the *cipher alphabet;* the other, a plain alphabet or numerical scale. The cipher alphabet is scrambled in one way or another.

Cipher disks have a long and colorful history, dating back to the 1400s, when Leon Battista Alberta described one in detail. Many cipher disks are employed using *simple substitution*— where a single letter or number is used to represent the enciphered letter. This method was rarely used by Squadron members employing the Code-O-Graph. Instead, it was used in combination with other ciphering techniques, because straightforward simple-substitution ciphers fall easy prey to statistical analysis. When situations

---

*A replica of the original (1941) Code-O-Graph is available from Klutz, Inc., 455 Portage Avenue, San Pedro, CA 94306. For jewelry, "Captain Midnight" is a trademark of Klutz, Inc.

forced its use as a simple-substitution device, abbreviations were used and vowels were avoided to lessen the chance of success by analytical techniques.

From its beginnings as an identification device in 1941 and 1942, the Code-O-Graph became multifunctional. Additional features included a magnifier (1945), a signaling mirror (1946), and a signaling whistle (1947). The 1948 model had a mirror and a compartment. The 1949 model replaced the concentric scales with two toothed gears (each with a scale on it) and a pair of windows for a letter-number combination to be presented. The gears could be reset using a clutch mechanism.

The 1949 model was the last "classical" version. It was compact, worked accurately, and proved so easily concealable that it wasn't compromised. After 1949, the Secret Squadron decided that the Code-O-Graph would no longer be the primary means of identification. A Secret Squadron identification card, similar to the "ID cards" used by the Armed Forces, was issued.

While the 1949 model was retained, the complementary ciphering scheme was altered.

In 1955 the Secret Squadron changed the form and enciphering method of the Code-O-Graph. For several years it was modeled after the U.S. Army's M-94 device, which used multiple disks with scrambled alphabets to encipher messages. More recently, an electronic version was developed which, for security reasons, cannot be detailed.

After 1944, the instrument most closely connected with the Code-O-Graph was the Pocket Locator. Still classified, only a little can be said about it; however, some things can be noted. The original Pocket Locator was, frankly, a marginal device, relying on ultraminiature vacuum tubes and miniature batteries. It had very limited range without a repeater/amplifier and transceiver/converter. The advent of transistors and etched-circuit production techniques made the second version of the Pocket Locator much more effective. The current version is presumed to employ microprocessors, satellite communications, and some form of firmware, but Secret Squadron officials will not comment on the matter.

Two Secret Squadron items that can be discussed in more depth made their debut in World War II. One, the popularly called "Magic Blackout Light-Ups," was adapted for existing war conditions. Its official designator was "MJC Blackout-Light PS" (for Military-operation-related Joint-distribution C-class Blackout-Light Phosphorescent Specialty item; "Joint distribution" meant that it was available both to active agents and members of the General Reserve, and "C-class" meant it was made of paper or cardboard). The official terminology was quickly corrupted to the more familiar name.

During World War II, many countries had a great concern about possible bomb attacks, particularly at night. This led to the "blackout" procedure in which all lights in a city or town were extinguished as soon as air-raid sirens were sounded. This decreased visibility, and this made it more difficult for overflying aircraft to find targets. The phosphorescent paper Dr. Barbados developed during his search for Juvarium was what became the "Light-Ups." They were relatively inexpensive to produce, but enabled people to find their way under blackout conditions.

The other World War II item that can be detailed was designated the MJC-10 Plane Spotter. Although both active agents and General Reserve members of the Secret Squadron used the item, the latter used it more than the former because, being paper based, the Plane Spotter was relatively delicate. General Reserve members used it primarily to augment Civilian Defense activities.

The device consisted of a short cardboard tube, 6 inches in length and slightly over 1.25 inches in diameter. One side of the tube served as an "eyepiece"; this consisted of a cardboard disk with a one-eighth-inch hole in its center. The other end was open, but was designed to accept cardboard slides inserted into a slit 5.625 inches from the "eyepiece" end.

One of these slides was used for "sight clarification" and the determination of aircraft range. The side had two holes and was otherwise opaque. One hole, one-eighth inch in diameter, was labeled "5000 feet"; the other, half that diameter, was labeled "16,000 feet."

To find the range (called "altitude") of an aircraft, one would fit the wingspan in the appropriate hole. If the wingspan *just* filled the hole, the airplane was assumed to be the number of feet distant associated with that hole (e.g., an aircraft whose wingspan just fills the larger of the two holes would be assumed to be 5,000 feet away). Analysis reveals that the smaller hole in the MJC-10 slide corresponds to an aircraft at 10,000 feet with a wingspan of slightly over 110 feet.

A second type of slide came with the MJC-10. This slide type featured a pair of aircraft identification silhouettes on translucent paper, and a central "10,000 foot" hole. Four completed slides of this sort came with the unit, plus additional silhouettes on translucent paper so that the Squadron members could make more. The supplied slides were of the British Manchester and Spitfire, the American P-43 and B-17, the German Focke-Wulf 200C and 189, and the Japanese Mitsubishi Type 97 and Zero. A list of aircraft wingspans is listed below (those supplied with the MJC-10 Plane Spotter are italicized).

Comparative Aircraft Wingspans

Manchester	90 feet
Spitfire	32–40 feet

Comparative Aircraft Wingspans (continued)

B-17	104 feet
P-43	36 feet
Zero	39 feet
Mitsubishi Type 97 (or Ki-21)	74 feet
Focke-Wulf 200C	108 feet
Focke-Wulf 189	60 feet
B-24D Liberator	110 feet
Lockheed P-38	52 feet
Grumman TBF-1 Avenger	54 feet
P-51 Mustang	37 feet
Arado 196	40 feet
Hurricane	40 feet
Hienkel He 177	103 feet
Messerschmitt Me 109	32 feet
Messerschmitt Me 163B	31 feet
B-29	141 feet
Piper Cub J-3	35 feet
P-47	41 feet
Douglas DC-3/C-47/R4D	95 feet
Lockheed C-5A	223 feet

In the listing we can see that the World War II aircraft that most nearly match the "ideal" aircraft are the larger ones — the bombers. A Lockheed P-38 just filling the 10,000-foot hole, for example, would actually be about 4700 feet away. Designing the spotter as a ranging device for bombers was quite proper, since, compared to the fighters, the bombers were both slow and high. Also, from the beginning of the war, bombers caused more concern. It is interesting to note that someone today using an MJC-10 to estimate the altitude of a C-5A and locating it at 10,000 feet would be off by 10,250 feet.

As noted in the instructions that came with the MJC-10, the Plane Spotter's range finder could only help the observer determine the *distance* of the airplane, not its altitude above the ground. Only if the aircraft were directly overhead would altitude and range coincide. This is illustrated below.

Aircraft Altitude for Constant Range of 10,000 Feet

Angle Above Ground (degrees)	Altitude
0	0 ft.
10	1,736 ft.

20	3,420 ft.
30	5,000 ft.
40	6,428 ft.
45	7,071 ft.
50	7,660 ft.
60	8,660 ft.
70	9,397 ft.
80	9,848 ft.
90	10,000 ft.

From this listing it can be seen that there is a less-than-600-foot margin between range and altitude. Secret Squadron agents were advised to attempt altitude reckonings only when the aircraft were nearly overhead.

A third function of the Airplane Spotter was a speed scale. This was fairly unsuccessful, since it required observation at a fixed altitude and fixed viewing position. Few people could maintain steady enough hands to hold the unit still, without tracking. However, two out of three isn't a bad average.

A couple of Secret Squadron rings are worth mentioning briefly. Shortly before the war, the Squadron issued a "siren ring" to be used for agents to signal each other. The unit had a small siren built into the ring. Blowing through it produced a high-pitched sound that could carry for some distance. However, to use the ring effectively required the agent to remove it. Outside of its use in the tunnels under Hong Kong, it wasn't used very often in field conditions, and was abandoned within a year.

The Mystic Aztec Sun God ring was an item issued in 1946. It was developed as a reminder of a mission in Mexico. It had a brass base and what appeared to be a square ruby stone. The "stone" was actually hollow and could be slid so that the compartment could be used to conceal small messages on thin paper or microfilm. It was decorative; however, a production problem caused many rings' stones to be easily loosened, resulting in some losses. It was retired from active use after a few months, but many General Reserve members used them as jewelry.

Appendix 2:
Captain Midnight in the Media

The Secret Squadron, which actually started out as a *secret* organization, became extremely well known, and stories relating to Captain Midnight (and hence the Secret Squadron) abounded for a while. Those closest to reality were the radio dramas. As Captain Midnight has pointed out himself, they were fairly close to what really happened. Where there were deviations, they were either for security reasons or because having once started a radio drama, the actors had to do *something* during those times when the Squadron agents were actually waiting for something to happen. (Ichabod Mudd once suggested that "a great subject for a program would be a dramatization of the way I beat Chuck at gin." The writers never took the hint.)

The radio show took an odd turn: In the 1949–1950 season, it took a half-hour "complete story" format that had little to do with the real Squadron. The Secret Squadron, trying to assume a lower profile consistent with its mission at the time, didn't object to the shows *per se,* but the shows were quite juvenile (as were the leads: Captain Midnight was portrayed as less intelligent, and both Chuck and Joyce seemed to lose about six years of age). The show lasted one season, then disappeared.

Later on, a television show aired, supposedly based on Captain Midnight's adventures. In it, Captain Midnight was a wealthy private individual who formed a *private* crime-fighting organization identified as the Secret Squadron. In deference to the sensitivity to the letters "SS" generated by

World War II, the supposed designator for the Squadron became "SQ," with Captain Midnight's identifier now ostensibly "SQ-1." Ichabod Mudd was played as pure comic relief. A new, totally fictional character, "Tut," was introduced. Described as a "science wizard," Tut showcased many supposed scientific developments. One of Tut's inventions, for instance, was a lens that could focus emanations from radioactive materials. The "science" on the show was usually highly fanciful and technically inaccurate.

The star of the television show bore little resemblance to the real Captain Midnight. Also, the Squadron activities were effectively undefined. By this time, the show was so clearly fantasy that the Squadron paid it no attention.

A few recordings of the old radio drama exist of the Secret Squadron years; these are available from dealers of such memorabilia. Some of these shows, complete with commercials, were released in the 1970s on LP record disks. When asked about various portrayals, Captain Midnight said, "If anyone wants to have some idea of what we really were doing, the radio tapes will give a pretty good idea, even the fictionalized ones. The telecasts are very far removed from reality."

Beyond the broadcast media, the most prevalent depiction of Captain Midnight was in comic books, published primarily by Fawcett. The Fawcett treatment virtually dissociated Captain Midnight from the Secret Squadron (he'd agreed to the comic book to "help boost morale for the war effort").

Fawcett had already established a character called Spy Smasher, an aviator who possessed some strange gadgets and fought supervillains. To Captain Midnight's chagrin, his comic-book persona was modeled after the Spy Smasher character, with a few twists.

The Captain Midnight of the comic books had a rather garish uniform: a purplish aviator's helmet, skin-tight red uniform with shiny black boots, and "gliderchute." This last item was a web stretching from wrist to ankle, somewhat like a flying squirrel's apparatus. How the comic-book character activated and deactivated it was never explained; as depicted, it seemed to be retractable somehow.

The gliderchute was supposed to enable Captain Midnight to bail out of an airplane and "glide" to the ground without benefit of a parachute. A Squadron member once pointed out a depiction of the gliderchute in action to Midnight, jocularly inquiring when this would be standard equipment for field agents. The Secret Squadron leader said, "Great guns! Once, when I was barnstorming, I saw some poor fool try a gadget like that. He ended up a mess. I certainly hope nobody takes *that* suggestion seriously!"

The comic-book version of Captain Midnight (correctly identified in his "civilian" identity as Captain Albright) was supposed to be an inventor. Therefore, the writers gave him some "scientific" gadgets, primarily something called a "doom beam." This was apparently some form of heat ray that projected a clock-face-at-twelve image on the target as it was heated.

A short-lived newspaper comic strip appeared. It was much closer to the radio show than the comic book's fantasy.

A movie serial was also released. As with the comic book, Captain Midnight was supposed to be a loner rather than the head of an agency. He was, again, correctly identified as Captain Albright, who was loosely connected with Military Intelligence. As was common in such serials, "Captain Midnight" was a secret identity. When Albright was "being" Captain Midnight, he actually wore a mask. Joyce was transformed into an inventor's daughter. As was often the case in such serials, she did little more than get into trouble and scream while others strove to rescue her. Chuck and Ichabod Mudd were associates who worked at Captain Albright's ranch. Ivan Shark was portrayed as a master of disguises. His gang was responsible for aerial bombings of aircraft factories, though why they did so was left vague. Fury's role was diminished; the movie version wasn't half as ruthless as she was in real life — or as portrayed on radio. The movie-villain Ivan Shark had gadgets at his various hideouts that would have brought slow and painful death to victims. The actual Shark was more efficient. He wouldn't have wasted time building such elaborate ways to do away with people when bullets, knives, and poisons were easily available and cheap. As with the comic book, Captain Midnight had no control over the serial's content.

This serial, produced by Columbia Pictures, was released to VHS videocassette in 1995. Among collectors of movie serials, this serial was known of for years but was considered "lost" until its release.

Appendix 3:
A Quick Overview of Cryptology

There are many excellent books on cryptology (the study of codes and ciphers) and cryptanalysis (the "cracking" of such messages). What follows here is merely the peak of the iceberg's tip, but it may provide an overview of an interesting subject.

The purpose of codes and ciphers is to send a message, usually so that it can't be understood by those it's not intended for. A *code* is a group of symbols that represents a message: SOS is a nonsecret code that means "I am in trouble and require help." Some "commercial codes" weren't used for secrecy but rather to save charges during the telegraphic era, when a charge for each word was imposed (e.g., in the *Bentley's Complete Phrase Code* book, two five-letter groups were combined to create a ten-letter word: IDFAH means "very important"; EKNUR means "development(s)"; UZIPY means "uncovered"; KULIK means "in New Zealand"; therefore, the message "very important development uncovered in New Zealand" could be compressed to IDFAHEKNUR UZIPYKULIK, which was treated as only two words by the telegraph company). Although their primary purpose was to save transmission costs, they did provide a little privacy.

A *cipher* is a character-by-character substitution of letters by other letters or numbers. One very simple cipher, for example, would have each letter represented by its equivalent numerical place in the alphabet:

A B C D E F G H I J K L M N O P Q R S T U V W X Y Z
1 2 3 4 5 6 7 8 9 10 11 12 13 14 15 16 17 18 19 20 21 22 23 24 25 26

Under this scheme, the word "code" would be 3-15-4-5. This method is called "simple substitution," meaning that everywhere in the message, the letter "e," for instance, would always be represented by a 5.

If the letters were scrambled, then the numbers wouldn't show the position of the letters. For instance:

A G H T V Q S E P Y J I F L X K D C W R B O N Z M U
1 2 3 4 5 6 7 8 9 10 11 12 13 14 15 16 17 18 19 20 21 22 23 24 25 26

Here, "code" would be 18-22-16-8. The scrambled letters are called the *cipher alphabet*. The particular cipher alphabet shown is the one used on the 1946 Code-O-Graph. By mounting the letters and number on a pair of dials, it becomes possible to reposition the numbers in relation to the letters. For instance:

A G H T V Q S E P Y J I F L X K D C W R B O N Z M U
9 10 11 12 13 14 15 16 17 18 19 20 21 22 23 24 25 26 1 2 3 4 5 6 7 8

"Code" here becomes 26-4-25-16. To make sure the letters were correctly aligned, a "code setting" was broadcast. In 1946 this was done by giving a single letter-number combination (e.g., "code setting S-15"). It usually was preferred to choose a letter not used in the actual message.

One can add a "progressive" component to such a cipher. For instance, suppose every number after the first had a "3" added to its number and the previous addition (i.e., a four-number message would add "0" to the first number, "3" to the second, "6" to the third, and "9" to the fourth). Because the highest possible number in the number-letter correspondence is 26 (because there are only 26 letters), any number that goes higher must have 26 subtracted from it. Applying this sequence to the message above, we get the following:

(26 + 0) = 26; (4 + 3) = 7; (25 + 6) = 31 and (31 − 26) = 5; and (16 + 9) = 25. The resulting message is therefore 25-7-5-25. If deciphered using the "S-15" setting, the result would be "cmnc."

There are other ciphering schemes, including those that interchange letters by some scheme, or others that tie the message characters to some complex mathematical relationship. To cover all of them adequately would require a full text.

Superenciphering methods, where a cipher is itself enciphered by some scheme, could also be used. Most Squadron field messages were superenciphered.

Occasionally, a message was enciphered with the Code-O-Graph used as a superenciphering device. This was done very rarely, because superenciphering with simple substitution ciphers doesn't increase security from cryptanalysis.

Sometimes circumstances dictated that a message had to be sent in simple substitution. In such cases, means were taken to minimize the likelihood of successful statistical analysis. This was done by the elimination of vowels, abbreviations, and the like. For instance, CDGRFLSTCHNGCFR would be understood by every Secret Squadron member as "Code-O-Graph lost. Change cipher." The brevity of the message, and its lack of vowels, would make analysis difficult.

Cryptanalysis is "cracking" a code or cipher. This is done through a variety of means. One is through *letter frequency*, because in text, some letters show up more frequently than others. Another is by *word patterns*.

Suppose we have a message like 12-9-24-16 7-16 4-8-12 12-4 12-11-16 3-9-22-22 19-9-7-16. The grouping of individual characters (letters) is a hint: In English, two-letter words have at least one vowel. Therefore, the numbers 7, 16, 12, and 4 are all likely candidates to be vowels. So do three-letter groupings, so 11 could be added to the list. 16 appears four times in the short message, as does 12. 9 appears three times; 22, 4, and 7 appear two times; all the others appear once.

In order of maximum appearance, the most frequent letters in the English language are: E T A O N I S H R L D C U P F M W Y B G V K Q X J Z. If we look at our numbers, either 12 or 16 looks like a good candidate for E, with the other being a good candidate for T. Suppose 12=E. Then the message would likely be: "E-9-24-T 7-T 4-8-E E-4 E-11-T 3-9-22-22 19-9-7-T."

There are few two-letter English words that begin with E. So, supposing that 12=T and 16=E, the message would read "T-9-24-E 7-E 4-8-T T-4 T-11-E 3-9-22-22 19-9-7-E."

There are not too many two-letter words ending in E; and 11 looks like a good candidate for H, making "T-11-E" become "THE," one of the most common words in the language. 7 could then be B, M, or W; but "BE" or "WE" are unlikely in the last word (as in 19-9-W-E), suggesting an M. So far, the message becomes "T-A-24-E M-E 4-8-T T-4 T-H-E 3-9-22-22 19-9-M-E." Since each two-letter word contains a vowel, 4 is most likely an O, making T-4 into T-O, and resulting in "T-9-24-E M-E O-8-T T-O T-H-E 3-9-22-22 19-9-M-E." If 9 is a vowel (since it appears three times), it may be the next vowel in line after E (i.e., A). The message then becomes "T-A-24-E M-E O-8-T T-O T-H-E 3- A-22-22 19-A-M-E." Trial and error substitution (plus a little common sense) ought to provide the rest of the message, which was enciphered using the 1946 Code-O-Graph's S-15 setting.

Usually, messages aren't sent in word groups but are sent in groups of letters or numbers, usually five or six characters long. Word length and division, as we have seen above, helps in analysis. By removing word lengths, the cryptanalyst's job becomes more difficult.

Serious cryptanalysis goes far beyond the elementary example shown, but the basic principle is the same: finding clues that will provide a relationship between enciphered messages and plain language.

Cryptanalysis of the highest level German and Japanese ciphers during World War II significantly affected the outcome of the war.

Appendix 4: The Radio Show

Radio drama is something of a lost entertainment medium. Yet, paradoxically, anyone with an audio cassette player can experience it today. There are tapes of many old radio shows available, some in bookstores and record shops, others through specialty dealers.

Among available show tapes are a few of the *Captain Midnight* adventures sponsored by Ovaltine. There are many more tapes of the Skelly Oil series. The earlier Skelly Oil programs were pre-Secret Squadron, involving Albright's individual adventures.

In the Skelly Oil sponsored episodes, Captain Midnight was played by Bill Bouchy. The shows were transcribed on huge records, which were played at 78 RPM speed. These recordings were distributed to the various individual stations carrying the show. These adventures were spiced with a lot of technically accurate information on flying, such as how to perform a takeoff from a short field, and the proper technique for performing an inside loop.

The Ovaltine-sponsored *Captain Midnight* show started with the tolling of a tower clock, over which one could hear the sound of a diving airplane and an announcer calling out "Captain Midnight" in a drawn out fashion. Ed Prentiss played the title character during the 15-minute episodes, and anyone listening to tapes of the show today recognize his voice as the authentic sound of Captain Midnight. The noncanonical half-hour version had Paul Barnes playing Captain Midnight. Various people played the other characters. Boris Alpon played Ivan Shark magnificently; Earl George played Gardo. Marilou Neumayer played Joyce Ryan the longest, though Angeline Orr also played the part. Chuck Ramsay was played first by Bill Rose, then by Jack Bevins, and finally by Johnny Coons. Fury Shark was played by Rene Rodier and Sharon Grainger. The announcers were Pierre André and Tom Moore.

From the Skelly Oil days, the show offered premiums. This was common to radio shows of the period: Premiums not only helped encourage brand loyalty among listeners, but, more important to the shows, the premiums enabled the producers to determine statistically how many were listening (a 1940s method of determining ratings that was less expensive than the Hooper Rating Service used by the evening shows).

Skelly Oil premiums included membership cards in the "Captain Midnight Flight Patrol," several photographs of the characters, a *Trick and Riddle Book*, "Weather Forecasting" Flight Wings, a brass membership "spinner" token, and an airline map of the United States. The Flight Patrol was rather like a fan club. Ovaltine premiums included the Code-O-Graphs (and manuals) which made listeners members of the Secret Squadron (General Reserve). The Magic Blackout Light-Ups were one premium (mine still glow well, better than 50 years after they were made). The MJC-10 Plane Detector was another (though except for occasional "warbird" air shows, there's nothing to rangefind on these days). There were many others, including pocket telescopes, initial printing rings, and secret compartment rings.

On a personal note, I "joined" the Secret Squadron in late 1945, sending in an Ovaltine label with my name and address printed on its back to "Captain Midnight, Chicago, Illinois." In time, a brown envelope arrived containing a 1946 Code-O-Graph and a beautifully printed handbook. I continued this practice for the remainder of the show's run, maintaining my "membership" throughout. The Code-O-Graphs were not just for Squadron identification, though.

Usually twice a week, at the end of the show, the announcer would say some variant of, "Stand by ... for a Secret Squadron signal session." Then he would indicate what the "code setting" should be, and would recite a message that was generally between two and five words long. Messages would give a hint of the following day's action, at least partially resolving the predicament (e.g., BAIL OUT ABOVE OCEAN or OUTWIT VON KARP) or introducing a new story element (e.g., MYSTERIOUS STRANGER). Thus, someone with a Code-O-Graph would consider him- or herself an insider.

One premium unlike the others available to *Captain Midnight* listeners from Ovaltine was the Shake-Up Mug. This was an orange plastic mug with a blue plastic top. Into it, listeners were instructed to pour milk, cracked ice, and the appropriate amount of Ovaltine. Then, by snapping on the blue lid, the Shake-Up Mug turned into a cocktail-shaker-like device, mixing up a "rich, foamy drink" using the new chocolate-flavored Ovaltine. It was "like having your own soda fountain," the announcer pointed out. Once the drink had been mixed, the user could remove the top and have an 8-ounce glass to drink it from. As has been observed, it is the ultimate premium: One buys the product to get the premium — so you can use more of the product.

The Shake-Up Mug had one interesting feature. On its side there was a bas-relief portrait of Captain Midnight. He is shown wearing a leather flying helmet and goggles; he appears to be in his mid to late 40s.

Appendix 5: Rocket Planes

Before the end of World War II, there was an increased interest in rockets and jets. In the United States prior to the war, "rockets" and "rocket ships" were things people didn't take very seriously. They were the stuff of comic strips; *Buck Rogers* and *Flash Gordon* featured interplanetary travel in the Sunday funnies. But the idea that there could be people serious about rockets was generally scoffed at before the war.

During the war, though, people discovered that *some* people took rockets and jets seriously. The first the public really heard about rockets was when the German "vengeance" weapons (the V-1 robot bomb and the V-2 ballistic missile) started pounding England. There was sufficient confusion that some people referred to the airplane-like, pulse-jet bombs as "V-1 rockets" for years after the war.

In one sense, the breakthrough device was the V-2 rocket. Here was a device that lobbed a respectable payload more than 200 miles from the launch site. What made that possible (in those days) was the development of *liquid propellant* rockets.

The advantage of liquid propellants was that the amount of energy available in liquid propellants was far greater than in the solid-propellant rockets of the time period (in the late 1950s, developments in solid-fuel rocket technology changed all that). With liquid propellants, two components are needed: a *fuel* and an *oxidizer*. In the case of the V-2 rocket, for example, the fuel was alcohol and the oxidizer was liquid oxygen.

Because it carries its own oxidizer, a liquid-fuel rocket is independent of an outside environment. A rocket engine can work in air, in space, or even under water; by contrast, a jet engine can't. A jet engine and a rocket engine both propel a vehicle by the same basic mechanism, "reaction." The expulsion of gases under high pressure in a direction opposite that of the flight causes a thrust in the desired direction. The difference is that while a rocket carries its own oxidizer, a jet has to use the oxygen of the surrounding air.

Liquid oxygen is the best *practical* oxidizer for rockets, having a high concentration of oxidizer per unit volume (theoretically, the best is liquid fluorine, which would produce higher thrust; however, the combustion products are both corrosive and toxic). However, liquefied gases need to be stored at extremely low (cryogenic) temperatures. Oxidizers for missiles can be cryogenic, since the launch of such rockets is completely under the control of the military command and can be scheduled hours to weeks ahead of time; fighter aircraft don't have that luxury.

An aircraft used as a fighter has to be able to be "ready." Its pilot must be able to "scramble" with it; that is, when required, the plane has to be able to take off in minutes. This means that it's impractical to use cryogenic oxidizers. Liquefied gases would boil off over time and would have to be renewed constantly.

The Messerschmitt Me 163B ("Komet") fighter used highly concentrated hydrogen peroxide as the oxidizer. The normal medicinal peroxide available is generally about twelve percent peroxide in water; the peroxide used in the Me 163B was over 90 percent. This is extremely hazardous: The concentration was so high that when one pilot was immersed in it during an accident, he was literally dissolved alive.

However dangerous this oxidizer was, it had one virtue: It could be stored at normal temperatures. Other noncryogenic oxidizers include nitric acid and nitrogen tetroxide.

As the war was coming to a close in Europe, the German rocket-plane design evolved. The Junkers Ju-263 added improvements to the Me-163 design. In addition to the standard rocket engine, there was an auxiliary combustion chamber to cruise more economically.

Although the rocket planes had some performance characteristics that Allied flight crews found astonishing, such as a maximum speed of nearly 550 miles per hour and a climb to 30,000 feet in 2.6 minutes, for the Me-163B, it was restricted by design to limited action. It had only a limited amount of fuel and spent most of its time as a glider when airborne.

With all this background, a little speculation on the "rocket plane" developed at Baron von Karp's castle is possible. We can discuss things about the aircraft, but not why it was developed independently.

The one thing that's abundantly clear is that its powerplants were not (or at least not primarily) rockets. Rockets of the period were capable of producing tremendous thrust (and acceleration), but this could be sustained for only a short time. The "rocket plane" was known to have an extended range, presumably all the way from Germany to Argentina.

Captain Midnight and Ichabod Mudd both observed that the aircraft had a wide wingspan, implying that it could glide. Probably the aircraft was designed to be "flown wings wet," meaning that the entire interior of each wing had been converted into a propellant tank.

Some liquid propellants are *hypergolic*, meaning that when the fuel and oxidizer come together, the combination spontaneously combusts. For an aircraft that had to respond quickly, hypergolic propellants would be a decided plus.

A *ramjet* is an engine for jet propulsion that has few parts; the basic "moving part" of the engine is the air flowing through it. When air flows through at a sufficient speed, fuel is injected and ignited, and it will provide thrust to drive the airplane forward as long as the critical speed is maintained.

A variation is the *rocket ramjet*, sometimes known as the *rocket ram*. This kind of engine features a rocket engine within a ramjet tube. The rocket can be used to initiate propulsion to the vehicle; when sufficient speed is achieved, additional fuel can be added so that the ramjet effect kicks in. Thus, the aircraft could make use of external oxygen, and the rocket aspect could be throttled back, thus conserving oxidizer.

If the speculations of Captain Midnight and Ichabod Mudd are correct, a rocket ramjet design would go a long way toward explaining the way the aircraft was able to travel for extended distances. Regrettably, not one reliable image or detailed sketch of the "rocket plane" is known to exist. Unless some hitherto undiscovered notes from Professor Lenge, the "rocket plane's" designer, are ever uncovered, we'll never know for certain and can only speculate.

Index

Numbers in *italics* refer to photographs.

Aerial Instrument Company 40–47, 50
aerial photography 9, 10, 64, 65, 136, 137, 171, 224, 225
Ah Ting 162–168
air mail, experimental 16
altitude-sensitive bomb 217, 218
Andre, Col. Jock P. 222–223, 226, 227
Arado AR 196 floatplane 216, 220
"Armageddon" signal 105, 106, 220
Austin, Lt. Henry ("Bugs") 208–218
AZON guided bomb 69

B-2 Stealth Bomber 122
B-17 ("Flying Fortress") 141, 152, *154*, 155–160, 222
B-24 ("Liberator") *196*
Barbados, Dr. Joachim 123–124, 126–132, 134–139
Barkley, Cdr. Eliot 83–84
barnstorming 14
Barracuda, The 74–75, 79–80, 81, 82–90, 100–102, 105, 108–110, 115–118, 120–122
Base 7, Secret Squadron 28, 45–46, 91
Battle of Britain 21, 191
Battle of Midway 146
Berthold, Hercule 187, 189–192
biological weapons 9–10
Bivens, Michael 222, 227
"Black Fleet" 18

Black Gulch 238
blackouts 130
bombs, radio-directed 64–65, 68–69
bombsight, secret 42–48, 50–51
Borgmann, Hans 36, 44–45, 53, 62
Bosmouth, Mrs. F. W. 101–102, 104, 110–111, 116, 119–120; *see also* Rotan, Carla
Bostwick, Capt. E. Merritt 55
Boudreau, Capt. Pierre 161–163, 172
Bowling Field 66, 68, 91, 123, 138, 179, 236
British Intelligence 56, 60, 70, 82–84, 134, 188
Brouvard, Henri 178, 180, 182
Brouvard, Maurice 178
Brubaker, Ralph 48
Brundage, Sir Allen 184–189, 193–194, 195
Burgess Field 40, 41, 43, 45, 49
Burley, Capt. Peter 113–119, 121–122
"Buzz Bomb" *see* V-1

C-47 180, 182–183, 189, 193, 198, 215, 226–227, 232–234, *233*, 238
Carstairs, Jack 101, 111, 116, 121
Castle of Dread 199
Chamber of Skeletons 199, 202
chemical laboratory, portable 128–129

Chihuahua, Mexico 92
Childers, Maj. Lancelot 206–209, 211–215, 219
Cho Yuk (Pirate Chief) 85–87
Chu, Gen. 162, 167, 172, 176
cipher disks 49, 93, 106
ciphers, emergency 28, 33, 46–48, 49, 93, 105, 123, 220
Civaret, François 187–193
Cocos 125–127, 134–136
Code Books 28, 46
Code-O-Graph 49, *49*, 93, 98, 103, 105–108, 123, 145, *145*, 186, 188–189, 218–222, *221*, 241–242, 250–252, 254
Conway, Jack 41–42
counterfeit money 97–98
counterspies, U.S. 27
Crane, Maj. Charles 47, 50
Crimson Feather Society 127–129, 135, 138
Cross, Lt. Mark 142, 149–150
Cryptanalysis/Cryptanalysts 46, 47, 48, 214, 220, 251–252
Crypto Group/Section, Secret Squadron 93, 123, 188, 221
cryptology 49, 110

D-Day 206
DC-3 42, *43*; *see also* C-47
Daniels, Peter Quincy 195
Demoviche, Capt. Charles 189, 191–193, 195, 198–200
"dollar a year" men 29
Donovan, Elaine ("Ma") 35–38, 40, 238
Donovan, Patsy 35, 37
Donovan, Steve 33, 35, 40, 45
Dungeon, Medieval 199–203

Ebert, Hans 195, 197
electronic eavesdropping device ("bug") 60–61, 65
England, Secret Squadron Base in 179, 182–183, 185, 191, 193
Erlette, Louis *see* "the Toad"
Escadrille Americane 10
Espada, Enrique 95–96, 98

F4U ("Corsair") 215
Fan, Lt. 162
Fang (Shark servant) 17–18, 24, 44, 52, 60, 71
Flossie 119, 121–122

Flying Bombs 64, 68–69
Flying Laboratory 42–43, 50–51
Flying Wing 99–110, 112–113, 118–122, *120*
Franz, Capt. Otto 100, 108–109, 120, 122
Fu Manchu, Dr. 73

Gardo (Shark lieutenant) 17, 24–25, 40, 48
gem, solar *see* Solar Gem, Incan
General Reserve, Secret Squadron 49, 188
Gleason, John 47, 50–51
Gloster Meteor 186
Gonsales, Col. Ernesto 219
Goto, Col. Okami 74, 78, 83, 85–89
Grant City 74, 78, 83, 85–89
Griffith, A. A. 185

Hackett, Maj. Jeremy 193–195
Hall, Jerome 56, 59–60, 62, 64, 70
Harrington, Todd 179–181
Hautmann, Fritz 211–212
Hawkes, Capt. William 222–224, 234
Hidden Valley 161–163, 172–177
Himakito, Rear Admiral Ito 146, 148–160, 166, 173, 176
Hiro G2H1 170, 177
Holbrook, Hollis 63, 65–66
Holmes, Sherlock 9
Hortmann, Peter 214–215, 220

Ichi, Lt. Taru 148
infrared viewer, experimental 97
Ishii, Capt. Okabi 76, 78

Jenkins, Eric 44
Jensen, Dr. Ris 195, 198–203
jet-propelled aircraft 186, 236, 238
"Jones," Mr. 25, 61, 67, 92, 138
Junkers Ju 52 213
Junkers K-37 77
Juvarium 128, 129, 130, 135, 136, 138

K-14 (military base) 140
Kaga, Capt. Ituro 155, 156–157
Kawasaki Type 88 82
Kelly, Agent Lyle William (SS-11) 23, 25, 28, 33, 50–51, 55–58, 60–61, 65–66, 71, 95, 105, 110, 182, 207, 221

L-6 ("Grasshopper") 192–193
Lambert, Pilot 42–46, 50, 63–65
Langley Bi-Motor 94–96

Lee, Lt. 169, 172–177
Lend-Lease Act 61
Lenge, Prof. Hermann 258
Lockheed A-29 ("Hudson") 207, 209–210, 213, 217–218, 221
Lockheed 14 Transport 124–126, 135, 136–137
Luke, Lt. Frank 13
Lutro ("Incan Priest") 133–136, 138

McCaffrey, Cdr. Bruce 70–71
McDonnell, Col. Hugh 141–142
MacDonough, Cdr. Craig 142, 150, 153–155, 157–158
Madison, Bill 112–118
"Manuel" (Philippine Underground) 144–148
Marshall, Lawrence 42–43, 45, 47
ME-163 ("Komet") 191
microfilm 50, 52, 81–84, 88, 90
Mitsubishi Ki-2 77, 82
Mitsubishi Ki-21 ("Sally") 173–176
Mittler, William 205
MJC Blackout-Light PS 242–243
MJC-10 Plane Detector 188, 243–245
Mong (Pirate lieutenant) 86–87
Moriarty, Prof. James 73
motion picture stunt flying 15, 17
Mudd, Ichabod 15, 17, 19, 45, 47, 50, 54–57, 59–60, 64, 68–70, 75–79, 81–82, 85, 87–88, 98, 104–108, 110, 112, 114–119, 121, 123–124, 127–128, 130–133, 136, 140–142, 151, 156–160, 163–165, 169–172, 176–177, 179, 181–182, 185, 187, 189, 195, 198–203, 207, 209–212, 214–217, 219, 221–234, 238–239

N1M Flying Wing ("Jeep") 99
Nakajima B5N ("Kate") 153–154, 160
Nakajima Ki-27 137
Neumayer, Louis 222, 227, 232–233
Nieuport XVII*bis* 8, 9–10, 14
night vision, maintaining 228

Onti (sun god) 132–134
"Operator 23" (Shark spy) 62–64
OSS 27
Ovaltine 3, 253–255

P-38 ("Lightning") 222
P-39 ("Airacobra") 142–144, 147

P-43 ("Lancer") 136–137
P-51 ("Mustang") 123, 138, 140, 179, 189, 198, 207, 209–210, 213–214, 220–221
P-80 ("Shooting Star") 235
Panama Canal 56, 58, 62, 73
parachute jumps 50, 60, 69, 75, 80, 208, 225, 227–228
Paris, liberation of 206
Patch, Secret Squadron Identifying 186–187
Patton, Gen. George 214
Pearl Harbor 83–84, 90, 145
"Pedro" (Schrecker spy) 215–218
Peters, Harold 98
Phantom Band 187–193, 195
Phantom City 126, 129–133, 136–138
Piper Cub (J3) 210–213, 215–217, 219, 221
Pocket Locator 187–188, 200–201
Prado, Agosto 213, 218
Prentiss, Ed 4, 253
Prentiss, Ward 222, 226–227, 233–234
Preston, Maj. Davis 142, 152, 155–156
Puerto Rican Secret Squadron base 61, 63–64, 68–69
Purple Star (Japanese group) 135–138

quick-disconnect anti-theft arrangement 211–212

radar-coupled antiaircraft guns 139, 153, 155
radio navigation "beams" 149, 152
Ramjet 231, 258
Ramsay, Chuck 13, 14 *ff*
Ramsay, Mary 14–15
Ramsay, Sean 13–15
Randall, Spike 170–172, 177
Resistance, French 187
Roberts, Bill ("Red") 15, 18, 124, 135
"Rocket Plane" 191, 201, 203, 205–207, 214, 221–231, 234–235, 256–258
Rocket Societies 198
Rogart, Hannes 62, 65
Roosevelt, Pres. Franklin Delano 23
Rotan, Carla 100–105, 108–111, 115–117, 120–121
Russell, Clyde 63
Russell, Ted 100, 102, 110, 122
Ryan, Joyce 36 *ff*

St. Michel, town of 185, 195–198
Samuels, Prof. Irving 94–98

Schrecker, Count Karl 199–200, 206, 207, 213–215, 218, 219–221, 226, 229, 234, 236
Scorpion, The 209, 212, 215
Seabees, U.S. Navy 141–142
Secret Dragon Society 161–163, 169
Secret Service 27, 54
Secret Squadron 22 *ff*
Secret Squadron Code Book 28, 46
Shark, Fury 18, 31–32, 36–39, 44, 50, 52–53, 58–63, 65, 71
Shark, Ivan 7, 9–11, 17–18, 21, 23–26, 31–33, 36–37, 39–40, 43, 48, 50, 53, 56–58, 60–62, 65, 69–73, 79, 120, 134, 136, 237
Si Fan (organization) 73
Silver Mine, Secret Squadron 29
Simone, Pierre 191–192
Skelly Oil 2–3, 254
Slater Farm 21, 25, 32, 67
Smithsonian Institution 16
"Smoke Screen," binary chemical 139–140, 149–154, 157
Solar Gem, Incan 131–133
"SS" designator, origin 23
Steele, Major Barry 16, 21–22, 40–43, 47–48, 53, 60–61, 66, 74, 78–84, 87, 88, 123–124, 140, 160, 178–179, 182, 205–207, 235–238
stereo comparator 225
Submarines 53, 58–60, 61, 62, 68, 70, 71, 142, 150, 153, 157, 160
Sun, Maj. 81–82
superencipherment 48, 50, 250

Taggert, Cleveland 127–128, 130, 135–137
tail skid, aircraft 110
TBF-1 ("Avenger") 140–142, *143*, 149–151, 155–156, 158–160
tent hangar 76–77
tiger pilots 84
Tilling, Lt. E. T. A. 200, 203, 207, 221
Toad, The 190, 192, 195, 197

triangulation, radiodirectional 27, 46, 56, 105, 107, 108–109, 191
trilobites 95

U-boats *see* Submarines
Uniform, Secret Squadron 93, 101, 144, 185–186, 189

V-1 ("Buzz Bomb") 174, *175*, 177, 179, 256
V-2 rocket (ballistic missile) 205, 256
Valdiva, Col. Ernesto 125–128, 130, 132–134, 136–137
Velez, Pablo 94–98
von Falz, Rolf 166, 171, 173, 176–177
von Grift, Magnus 126, 134, 136
von Karp, Baron Kurt 178, 180, 182–183, 187, 190–191, 192, 195–197, 199–203
von Nord, Gen. Klaus 195, 197
"von Teufel" 199

"whisper galleries" 132
Whittle, Sir Fred 185
Wilkins, Dr. Xaviar 139–141, 142, 145, 149–150, 152
winged-clock symbol 99, 101, 186, 189
wolf pilots 100, 103, 109, 121–122

X Island 140–142, 144, 148–158, 160
XP-59 jet aircraft 186
XP-80 jet aircraft 186; *see also* P-80

Y-14 compound 152, 157
Y-24 compound 150, 152, 157
YB-49 Flying Wing 122
Yamamoto, Adm. Isoruko 146
Yoshita, Capt. Okabe 135–137, 138
Young, Capt. Wallace 222–224, 227, 234

Zero (Mitsubishi A6M) 144, 147–153, 155–156, 160, 169
Zoler, Jaques 190–192, 195–197

www.ingramcontent.com/pod-product-compliance
Ingram Content Group UK Ltd.
Pitfield, Milton Keynes, MK11 3LW, UK
UKHW041932140426
5217IPUK00014B/445